State Aid and Tax Law

International Tax Conferences of the University of Luxembourg

---

VOLUME 3

General Editor

Alexander Rust

ATOZ Chair for International and European Taxation
University of Luxembourg

State Aid and Tax Law

Editors

Alexander Rust
Claire Micheau

Wolters Kluwer
Law & Business

Published by:
Kluwer Law International
PO Box 316
2400 AH Alphen aan den Rijn
The Netherlands
Website: www.kluwerlaw.com

Sold and distributed in North, Central and South America by:
Aspen Publishers, Inc.
7201 McKinney Circle
Frederick, MD 21704
United States of America
Email: customer.service@aspenpublishers.com

Sold and distributed in all other countries by:
Turpin Distribution Services Ltd
Stratton Business Park
Pegasus Drive, Biggleswade
Bedfordshire SG18 8TQ
United Kingdom
Email: kluwerlaw@turpin-distribution.com

Printed on acid-free paper.

ISBN 978-90-411-4557-4

Printed and Bound by CPI Group (UK) Ltd, Croydon, CR0 4YY.

List of Editors and Contributors

Margarida Afonso, European Commission, Legal Service, Brussels, Belgium.

Gauthier Charles de la Brousse, European Commission, Case-handler at DG Competition, Brussels, Belgium.

Humbert Drabbe, European Commission, Director at DG Competition, Brussels, Belgium.

Frank Engelen, Prof. Dr., Leiden University and partner at PwC in the Netherlands.

Joachim Englisch, Prof. Dr., University of Münster, Germany.

Anna Gunn, PhD student at the University of Leiden, State Aid Working Group at PwC, Rotterdam, Netherlands.

Tracy A. Kaye, Professor of Law, Seton Hall University School of Law. B.S., University of Illinois; M.S.T., DePaul University; J.D., Georgetown University Law Center.

Raymond H.C. Luja, Prof. Dr., Maastricht University and Director of the Maastricht Center for Taxation; Of counsel to Loyens & Loeff N.V., Amsterdam, Netherlands

Claire Micheau, Dr.,LL.M., European Commission, Case-handler at DG Competition, Brussels, Belgium.

Anne Muller, ATOZ, Luxembourg, Luxembourg.

Keith O'Donnell, Managing partner, ATOZ, Luxembourg, Luxembourg.

Pierpaolo Rossi-Maccanico, Esq., LL.M. (NYU), European Commission, Legal Service, Brussels, Belgium.

Alexander Rust, Prof. Dr., LL.M. (NYU), University of Luxembourg, Luxembourg.

Edoardo Traversa, Prof. Dr., Catholic University of Louvain, Belgium.

Summary of Contents

Table of Contents

Foreword

On November 17, 2011, a much noticed "Conference on State Aid and Tax Law" took place in the frame of the International Tax Law series of the University of Luxembourg. This conference, which brought together experts from academia and professional practice, was very successfully organized by Alexander Rust and Claire Micheau. The written version of the contributions made on this occasion is contained in the present volume. They provide a very informative and fairly comprehensive in-depth view of the current state of discussion, under various relevant points of view. Thus, this mere foreword has little to add.

The aforementioned conference took place only two days after the judgment of the Court of Justice in joint cases C-106/09 and C-107/09 (*Gibraltar* case) had been delivered. In the keynote speech I had the honor to give at that conference, I at first touched upon the delicate part of a judge asked to speak on issues of judicial review. I then made some short statements on tax law related elements of the State aid notion under Article 107(1) TFEU as well as about some specific problems of recovery of indirect aid measures in the field of tax law. Now, given the thorough character of the contributions contained in the present book, I do not deem appropriate to give a full account of that keynote speech in the present foreword.

Nonetheless, even in view of the following contributions, a few particular aspects of most recent case law may seem to deserve additional attention.

As to the question of *selectivity* of an advantage conferred by a measure in the field of tax law, the General Court's judgment of March 7, 2012 in Case T-210/02 RENV, *British Aggregates Association v. Commission*, has first resumed step by step the methodology to be followed for such an assessment, as recognized by the ECJ jurisprudence (see paragraphs 45–49), and then equally step by step applied this methodology to the facts of the case (see paragraphs 51–92). In doing so, the General Court has made it utterly clear and undeniable, that, in reality, the central questions of whether there exists or not an advantage and whether or not an advantage is justified are nothing else but a *specific variant and manifestation of the general principle of equal treatment* and consequently of the general requirement of objectivity. Indeed, the steps to be followed in order to assess the selective character of a tax advantage are virtually equivalent to those for ascertaining that a legal act is violating the principle of equality:

it is necessary to, *first*, identify the pertinent general system of legal rules (i.e., the "nature and general scheme of the tax system" / the "common or 'normal' regime applicable in the Member State concerned") and its extrinsic and intrinsic objectives, *second*, establish the existence of an effectively differentiating/unequal treatment in comparison between persons or legal entities who, in the light of the objective(s) assigned to the general system, are in a comparable legal and factual situation (i.e., the existence of an "advantage" granted by the tax measure at issue), and, *third*, ascertain whether this differentiating measure concerned is not objectively justified in the light of the objective(s) assigned to the general system (i.e., whether the tax measure is "selective").

In this respect, even if the effects of a measure to be examined are of course of decisive importance for its State aid character under Article 107(1) TFEU, it must be clearly recalled and emphasized that the *object and purpose* of the measure are extremely important criteria for the comparability and justification of any differentiation as to the relevant factual effects (see, in this respect, also the contribution by F. Engelen & A. Gunn, Chapter 9 "Towards a Theoretical Assessment Framework", at section §9.04[C][7]).

The ECJ seems to have followed the very same three-step-logic described above in its judgment of June 21, 2012, Case C-452/10 P, *BNP PARISBAS and BNL/ Commission*. In this judgment, the ECJ has set aside a judgment of the General Court because it had failed to examine the relevant tax realignment scheme in its entirety (see paragraph 104f). The ECJ then very consistently, in the frame of the third step of analysis mentioned above, re-examined itself whether the tax measure in question, which differentiated between undertakings, arose from the nature or general scheme of the system of which it formed part. It reached the conclusion that the tax scheme at issue, which conferred a tax advantage on companies to which assets had been transferred under a specific national law, did not appear to be justified by the inherent logic of the Italian tax system (see paragraph 137).

However, this rigorously methodological approach seems to be different from the one the ECJ chose in its judgment of November 15, 2011, in joint Cases C-106/09 and C-107/09, *Commission and Spain v. Gibraltar and U.K.* In that judgment, the ECJ seems to have followed another methodological approach as to the definition of the relevant overall national taxation system (see paragraphs 85–109). With regard to this judgment, new questions might arise: To what extent are there limits set by EU State Aid law to originality and imagination as to the creation and shaping of a new general taxation system? Is it illegal to create a tax system simply because it does not fit with the taxation systems hitherto known and described in traditional public finance manuals? Does the ECJ's judgment in the *Gibraltar* case have the consequence to set in a significant manner a limit to any possible competition between taxation systems of different Member States? The ECJ did not pronounce itself on the question of regional selectivity. One therefore might ask oneself, as did the CFI in its judgment of December 18, 2008 in Cases T-211/04 and T-215/04, *Gibraltar v. Commission* (at paragraph 106), whether in a federally structured Member State, like Belgium or Germany, any system of communicating financial vessels between the Central State and autonomous regions would necessarily exclude regional tax legislation.

Concerning the method of ascertaining the possible existence of fiscal State aid, mention can also be made of the ECJ judgment of June 5, 2012 in Case C-124/10 P, *Commission v. EDF*. In this judgment, the ECJ examined for the first time the applicability of the *private investor test* to fiscal measures and in doing so it fully upheld a General Court judgment under appeal. It stated that in view of the objectives underlying Article 87(1) EC and the private investor test, an economic advantage must—even where it has been granted through fiscal means—be assessed *inter alia* in the light of the private investor test, if, on conclusion of the global assessment that may be required, it appears that, notwithstanding the fact that the means used were instruments of State power, the Member State concerned conferred that advantage in its capacity as shareholder of the undertaking belonging to it (see paragraph 92). Thus, the fiscal nature of the process used by a Member State to grant an economic advantage upon an undertaking belonging to him through fiscal measures does not automatically rule out the applicability of the private investor test (see paragraph 108).

With the recent EU case law, much seems to be in a state of flux, and we experience a colorful variety of perspectives for possible future developments. As a matter of fact, looking at the recent evolution of case law in State aid matters may sometimes leave the impression of looking into a kaleidoscope: with every move, the same basic elements get into a new flamboyant and sometimes unexpected composition. But isn't this exciting?

Josef Azizi

President of chamber at the General Court of the European Union (Luxembourg) and Honorary Professor at the Faculty of Law of the University of Vienna (Austria). All views expresseed are personal.

Acknowledgements

In the fall of 2010, the ATOZ Chair for European and International Taxation of the University of Luxembourg, in an ongoing effort to keep practicing tax attorneys and advisors, judges, scholars, students, agents of national administrations and EU institutions, apprised of the latest information in tax law, launched a new series of conferences and publications intended to bring to the reader a timely and current look at some of the most pressing tax issues of the day. Each volume in the series is the culmination of the presentations given by leading experts at a conference arranged by the ATOZ Chair at the University of Luxembourg on the particular topic. This volume, *State Aid and Tax Law*, is the third in the series.

The editors gratefully acknowledge the support of the European Commission in connection with this series: several of its staff members participated in the conference both as lecturers and discussion participants before making their insights available as relevant and comprehensive chapters in this book. Their in-depth contributions, which put the accent on the European perspective, have significantly enriched the intellectual debate and the substance of this book. Equally, the editors earnestly thank ATOZ, the tax advisory firm, for its ongoing sponsorship of the ATOZ Chair, and in particular Keith O'Donnell, its managing partner, who in addition participated in the conference and wrote a contribution to this volume. The editors also owe a considerable debt of gratitude to Dr. Azizi, President of chamber at the General Court of the European Union, who gave the keynote speech during the conference and is the author of the foreword of this volume. His relevant insight, his interest for this topic and his intellectual support has provided scholarly and valuable inspiration for the completion of this work.

The editors would like to express their sincere gratitude to each of the individual authors for not only making interesting presentations at the conference but also quickly converting those presentations into the very readable chapters contained herein.

Finally, many thanks must also go to our publisher, Kluwer and especially Lijntje Zandee, for their assistance in assuring the swift and timely publication of this book, as well as to Katarina Köszeghy and Suzanne Larsen for their assistance in arranging the conference and editing the chapters contained herein.

Alexander Rust
Claire Micheau

CHAPTER 1

Introduction

Alexander Rust

§1.01 THE CONCEPT OF STATE AID IN THE FIELD OF TAXATION

The founding fathers of the Treaty establishing the European Economic Community regarded free competition as so important that they felt bound to prohibit State aid in the original text.[1] From that point on, within what is now the European Union, enterprises were to be established, goods to be sold, and services to be provided without competitive distortions.

Within the European Union,[2] two Treaty provisions ensure free competition without distortions arising from the Member States' actions: Article 107 TFEU[3] prohibits State aid except in certain limited circumstances set forth therein and Article 108 TFEU gives the Commission, as a neutral institution, the power to enforce the Article 107 TFEU prohibition.

Article 107(1) TFEU provides that State aid is incompatible with the internal market. Article 107(2) TFEU allows, under certain conditions enumerated therein, the Member States to grant State aid, the inclusion of such conditions representing an acknowledgement by the Member States that, on rare occasions, the social or economic benefits obtained by granting State aid can outweigh the harm done to the internal market from the competitive distortion. However, to monitor the Member States' compliance with the requirements of Article 107(2), the Commission was given the

1. See Arts. 92 et seq. of the Treaty establishing the European Economic Community.
2. The State aid provisions also apply within the European Economic Area. See Arts. 61 et seq. EEA Agreement.
3. Specifically, Art. 107(1) TFEU states: "Save as otherwise provided in the Treaties, any aid granted by a Member State or through State resources in any form whatsoever which distorts or threatens to distort competition by favouring certain undertakings or the production of certain goods shall, in so far as it affects trade between Member States, be incompatible with the internal market."

task of verifying whether such prerequisites are fulfilled.[4] Further, Article 107(3) TFEU gives discretionary power to the Commission to permit State aid if the particular measure is intended to achieve one of the specific objectives enumerated in that paragraph.

To ensure compliance with the Treaty prohibitions, Member States are obliged to notify the Commission of all new State aid before implementing such proposed aid. The Commission is granted the discretion to determine whether the proposed aid is or is not compatible with the internal market. If the required advance notice is not given, any aid to be provided by a Member State is automatically illegal (regardless of whether or not such aid would have been found compatible with the internal market had it been properly notified to the Commission) and cannot be implemented.[5] The Commission is further obliged to constantly examine whether existing systems of aid constitute prohibited State aid.[6]

At first, the State aid provisions were applied to prevent Member States from giving direct subsidies to their own enterprises. However, the Treaty notion of State aid is substantially broader than that of a simple government subsidy; rather, it embraces positive benefits as well as those measures which, regardless of their form, reduce the amount which would otherwise be due to a Member State and those which, without falling within the strict definition of the word "subsidy," are of a similar character and have the same effect.[7] For example, renouncing tax revenue is, arguably, just a more direct means of giving aid than a classic subsidy (where money is first received into a Member State's coffers in the form of tax revenue and then given to the subsidy's beneficiary). A reduction of tax revenue otherwise due to a Member State has the same effect as a subsidy: it consumes a Member State's resources.

Thus, as early as the 1970s, the Court of Justice of the European Union (formerly known as the European Court of Justice and hereafter referred to as the ECJ) confirmed that the Treaty's State aid prohibitions apply to selective advantages granted through the Member States' respective tax codes.[8] In that regard, the ECJ made clear that it is irrelevant to the State aid prohibitions what method a Member State uses to grant a benefit; rather, it is the effect of a particular State measure which is decisive. Thereafter, toward the end of the 1990s, the Commission became much more active in investigating tax provisions which appeared to grant prohibited selective advantages to enterprises.

4. Kühling in Streinz, EUV/AEUV (2nd edn, München, Beck, 2012), Art. 107 AEUV para. 6.
5. Art. 108(3) TFEU provides: "The Commission shall be informed, in sufficient time to enable it to submit its comments, of any plans to grant or alter aid. If it considers that any such plan is not compatible with the internal market having regard to Article 107, it shall without delay initiate the procedure provided for in paragraph 2. The Member State concerned shall not put its proposed measures into effect until this procedure has resulted in a final decision."
6. See Art. 108(1) TFEU: "The Commission shall, in cooperation with Member States, keep under constant review all systems of aid existing in those States".
7. See e.g., ECJ, *Adria-Wien*, Case No. C-143/99 [2001] ECR I-8265 para. 38.
8. ECJ, *Italy v. Commission*, Case No. 173/73 [1974] ECR 709.

§1.02 OVERVIEW OF THE CONTENTS

Each chapter of this book analyzes a different aspect of the State aid prohibitions as they relate to tax matters.

Chapter 2, by Tracy Kaye, illustrates the sometimes disastrous consequences for an economic union when State aid is not adequately controlled. In that regard, Kaye discusses the experience of the United States, whose Constitution does not contain an explicit provision prohibiting State aid.

Although some argue that the so-called "dormant" commerce clause[9] prevents the individual States from introducing discriminatory State aid, the US Supreme Court has yet to resolve the issue. It is difficult, if not impossible, for State taxpayers to gain the appropriate standing—that is, the legal right to start a judicial proceeding—to challenge the discriminatory effect of a particular tax incentive or other aid offered by an individual State. With no plaintiff having the requisite standing, the US Supreme Court can never hear the merits of a case alleging such discriminatory action by a particular State.

In the absence of an explicit prohibition against State aid or a definitive ruling thereon by the US Supreme Court, virtually every State in the US offers some type of tax incentive to persuade businesses to locate, maintain, or expand their operations within that State. The need to compete with other States leads to a "race to the bottom": more and more tax incentives are granted, thereby reducing the States' tax revenues without a commensurate increase in overall investment. Inevitably, the tax incentive competition between the States becomes a zero-sum game; it simply moves economic activities from one State to another, with a "win" by one State resulting in an offsetting "loss" in another State. As Kaye shows, tax incentives granted are often not even capable of forcing businesses to invest in areas with high unemployment.[10]

Kaye acknowledges that, as it is not realistic to expect the US Congress to intervene in the near future to prohibit the individual States from giving such detrimental tax incentives and it is unlikely that the US Supreme Court will have an opportunity to address the issue, individual States would be well advised to, at a minimum, increase transparency when granting such tax incentives and thereafter carefully monitor the recipient's results to ensure that the goals envisioned by such tax incentives are actually met (e.g., States should include clawback provisions in all incentives, in the event the recipients fail to fulfill their obligations or if the promised benefits to the State fail to materialize).

Pierpaolo Rossi-Maccanico, in Chapter 3, first sets out the EU definition of State aid and then describes the procedure for notifying the Commission of State aid, comparing and contrasting the current notification procedure to an advance ruling procedure. In that regard, the Treaty requires that before introducing a tax incentive,

9. The "dormant" commerce clause, which purportedly limits the ability of individual States to take actions that would negatively impact commerce between the States, is said to be implicit in the explicit grant of authority to the US Federal Government to regulate interstate commerce (see, US Cons., Art. I, sec. 8, cl. 3).
10. The fight against high unemployment is regarded as a legitimate objective which may make State aid compatible with the internal market. See, e.g., Art. 107(3)(a) TFEU.

the Member State asks the Commission for its opinion about whether the incentive is compatible with the State aid provisions. Once the Commission authorizes the implementation of the tax incentive, the Member State may implement the measure, certain in the knowledge that the incentive has been determined to be in line with the State aid provisions. Moreover, taxpayers can rely on the Commission's decision: once a particular measure is authorized by the Commission, a taxpayer is assured he can make use of it without suffering the risk that he could be required to thereafter disgorge the aid. The notification procedure is, therefore, highly advantageous for the taxpayer.

However, as demonstrated later by O'Donnell and Muller in their Chapter 11, the legal certainty offered by the notification procedure is patchy, at best. For example, no notification procedure is available for existing aid, such as existing beneficial tax provisions. Thus, a taxpayer may have relied for years on an advantageous provision in force, but which finally comes under the Commission's scrutiny and is then declared incompatible with the internal market. The same uncertainty exists with respect to almost any new advantageous tax provision; it may later be determined to constitute State aid. Member States only notify the Commission if they already believe a measure constitutes aid; if a Member State does not so believe, it will not notify the Commission, but will simply implement the measure. It is only later, when other constituents come to believe that the already-implemented measure constitutes State aid, that the Commission will become aware of the measure. At that point, those taxpayers who have relied on it risk having to repay all the benefits they have received. Those authors suggest that such a result lacks legal certainty for the taxpayer, and it would substantially increase legal certainty if the Treaty would be amended to allow a process similar to advanced rulings which would permit both Member States and taxpayers to obtain the Commission's advance confirmation that a particular measure does not constitute incompatible State aid.

Chapter 3 also deals with the relationship between the Code of Conduct[11] and the State aid provisions. Both pursue the same objective—reducing competitive distortions within the internal market.[12] However, just because a tax measure is classified as "harmful" under the Code of Conduct does not mean, automatically, that the measure constitutes State aid. Inversely, not all measures which qualify as State aid are necessarily "harmful" under the Code of Conduct. The Commission has already stated that the geographical scope of the Code of Conduct is broader than the scope of the State aid rules as the Code of Conduct also applies to the dependent and associated territories.[13] However, the geographical scope of the State aid rules is also relatively wide: according to Article 52 TEU, and Articles 349 and 355(3) TFEU, the State aid provisions apply to all European territories to the extent the relevant Member State is responsible for a particular territory's external relations. Moreover, State aid rules also

11. Council Conclusions December 1, 1997, 98/C 2/01.
12. See EC Commission Report of February 9, 2004 on the implementation of the Commission notice on the application of the State aid rules to measures relating to direct business taxation C(2004)434 para. 64.
13. EC Commission Report of February 9, 2004 on the implementation of the Commission notice on the application of the State aid rules to measures relating to direct business taxation C(2004)434 para. 64

apply, pursuant to Article 355(1) TFEU, to many territories outside Europe. In addition, State aid rules are also contained in each of the EEA Agreement and the EC-Switzerland Free Trade Agreement.[14]

Both the State aid rules and the Code of Conduct classify a measure as harmful if it is selective. On the one hand, Article 107(1) TFEU uses selectivity as part of its definition of State aid; on the other hand, the Code of Conduct applies to measures which "provide for a significantly lower effective level of taxation than those levels which generally apply in the Member State in question." In addition to the selectivity criterion, to classify a measure as "harmful" under the Code of Conduct, the following must be taken into consideration: (1) whether the advantages are (a) accorded only to non-residents or with respect to transactions carried out with non-residents, (b) ring-fenced from the domestic market so that they do not affect the national tax base, or (c) granted even without any real economic activity or substantial economic presence within the Member State concerned; (2) whether the rules for profit determination with respect to activities within a multinational group of companies depart from internationally accepted principles; and (3) whether the tax measures lack transparency. As a rule of thumb, harmful measures under the Code of Conduct are selective measures favoring non-resident taxpayers or transactions with non-resident whereas State aid provisions prohibit all selective measures irrespective of whether or not such measures are intended to attract foreigners or transactions with foreigners. In that regard, the State aid prohibitions are substantially broader than the Code of Conduct.[15]

Distortions of competition can also arise as a consequence of beneficial general (i.e., non-selective) tax measures. Whereas distortions within a Member State can be remedied by the State aid rules or the Code of Conduct, distortions as a consequence of the different tax systems of the Member States can only be addressed by harmonization. Articles 116 and 117 TFEU permit the European Parliament and the Council to issue directives to eliminate distortions arising from general measures; however, this procedure has not yet been used in the area of taxation.[16]

Chapter 4, by Margarida Afonso, addresses recovery of illegal State aid. If the Commission finds that aid granted by a Member State is not compatible with the internal market, the Member State is obliged to abolish it or, perhaps, restructure it so that it is compatible. In addition, the Commission is obliged to ensure the Member State recoups the incompatible aid.[17] This makes perfect sense: The State aid prohibitions

14. Arts. 61 et seq. EEA Agreement are nearly identical to Arts. 107 et seq. TFEU. The State aid rules in the EEA Agreement are enforced by the EFTA Surveillance Authority. Art. 23(1)(iii) of the 1972 EC-Switzerland Free Trade Agreement states: "The following are incompatible with the proper functioning of the agreement in so far as they may affect trade between the Community and Switzerland: ... any public aid which distorts or threatens to distort competition by favouring certain undertakings or the production of certain goods."
15. See Gross, "Subventionsrecht und 'schädlicher Steuerwettbewerb': Selektivität von Steuer vergünstigungen als gemeinsames Kriterium", [2002] *Recht der Internationalen Wirtschaft* 46 (49).
16. Wartenburger, "Die Bedeutung des Gemeinschaftsrechts für innergemeinschaftliche Steueroasen" [2001] Internationales Steuerrecht, 397 (399); Kahl in Callies/Ruffert, EUV/AEUV (4th edn, München, Beck, 2011) Art. 116 AEUV par. 10.
17. See ECJ, *Germany v. Commission*, Case No. 70/72 [1973] ECR 813 par. 13: "To be of practical effect, this abolition or modification may include an obligation to require repayment of aid

are intended to ensure free competition and to protect the competitors of those receiving the illegal State aid and such prohibitions are only effective if such recipients must disgorge the advantages they illegally obtained.[18] Thus, recovery forces such recipients to forfeit their competitive advantage, thereby restoring the status quo ante within the internal market. For State aid in the form of tax measures, the Commission Notice states that the amount to be recovered is calculated on the basis of a comparison between the tax actually paid and the amount which should have been paid if the generally applicable rule, and not the incompatible advantage, had been applied.[19] However, for tax incentives, recovery can be problematic as the number of beneficiaries can be quite large and the amount to recoup can be difficult to determine. For example, in calculating the difference between the amount actually paid and the amount that should have been paid in the absence of the illegal State aid, may a taxpayer rely on other tax advantages he would have been entitled to had he not benefited from the illegal State aid? In this regard, Commission policy seems to have shifted in favor of the taxpayer: Alternative tax advantages may now be taken into account when calculating the amount to be recovered.[20]

Afonso also asks whether a national measure incompatible with the State aid rules can be saved through tax measures of another Member State. By analogy to the *Amurta* judgment[21] where discrimination in the source State was neutralized by the actions of the resident State, it may be possible that an illegal tax benefit in one Member State may be absorbed by, and thereby neutralized by, the tax imposed in the residence State.

Joachim Englisch, in Chapter 5, concentrates on the application of State aid rules in the area of indirect taxation. For example, value added taxation (VAT) is almost completely harmonized within the European Union; in that regard, the Commission's Implementation Notice[22] states that "VAT reductions are subject to strict Community rules" and generally "conform to the principle of equality of taxation for similar products." Consequently, the Commission believes that VAT reductions are not typically caught by Article 107(1) TFEU. Excise duties, on the other hand, are not yet harmonized, such that, when considering indirect taxes, the Commission generally focuses its attention on them.

Englisch further highlights the main particularity of indirect taxes: They are "indirect" because the legal taxpayer is different from the economic taxpayer and such legal taxpayer is expected to simply pass on the tax burden to that economic taxpayer

granted in breach of the treaty." The Member State concerned does not have any discretion in implementing the decision of the Commission, it is obliged to recover the illegally obtained aid from the recipient. See ECJ, *Land Rheinland Pfalz v. Alcan*), Case No. C-24/95 [1997] ERC I-1591.

18. See Cremer in Callies/Ruffert, EUV/AEUV (4th edn, München, Beck, 2011) Art. 107 AEUV paras. 26 and 29.
19. Commission Notice para. 35.
20. See Commission Decision C 15/07, OJ L 237, 2008, 70.
21. ECJ, *Amurta*, Case No. C-379/05 [2007] ECR I-9569.
22. EC Commission Report of February 9, 2004 on the implementation of the Commission notice on the application of the State aid rules to measures relating to direct business taxation, C(2004)434 para. 72.

(i.e., the final consumer) while forwarding the taxes received to the tax authority. Thus, how can the Commission find a particular indirect tax constitutes illegal State aid, when the legal taxpayer does not receive any benefit (i.e., monetary advantage) from the illegal aid, an apparent prerequisite for a Commission finding that the particular advantage is incompatible with the internal market? The only conceivable advantage to the legal taxpayer is that, because of the particular indirect tax advantage, its goods or services become more popular thereby increasing its market share to the detriment of its competitors. But how does a Member State recover such a benefit? Englisch concludes that the increase in market share would have to be calculated and monetized with that amount reimbursed by the legal taxpayer. Englisch draws this conclusion from studying the inverse situation. If, for example, national VAT rules do not conform with the VAT directives, and the legal taxpayer was unlawfully obliged to charge a higher VAT rate, that legal taxpayer would not be entitled to a refund of the difference between the higher-but-unlawful VAT rate and the regular VAT rate. Rather, in this inverse case, the legal taxpayer is only compensated for its loss of market share resulting from having charged a VAT rate higher than necessary.[23] Englisch concludes that the final consumer-that is, the economic taxpayer—would not typically be an enterprise but even if it was an enterprise, it would most likely fall within the ambit of the de minimis rule. As a result, the final consumer would not have to repay any benefit received through an otherwise incompatible State aid VAT reduction.

Englisch then goes on to consider yet another interesting question which arises in connection with VAT: Whether reductions in VAT can legitimately be attributed to a Member State. Generally, in order to reduce VAT, a Member State must make use of an option already sanctioned by the EU in a VAT directive. But, a measure can only fall within the ambit of the State aid prohibitions if it is attributable to a Member State and not the European Union: Article 107(1) TFEU refers to "aid granted by a Member State" or "through State resources". Thus, in the case of optional VAT reductions, would such a reduction be covered by the State aid rules when the Member State only forgoes revenue after being invited to do so by the EU? In response to this question, Englisch suggests that the two provisions—the optional reduction and the State aid prohibitions—must be considered cumulatively, based on the relationship between the rule and the exception. For example, if the tax reduction is the default rule pursuant to the directive and a Member State only has discretionary power to revoke the tax

23. See, e.g., ECJ, *Weber's Wine World*, Case Nor. C-147/01 [2003] ECR I-11365 para. 80: "Also, in some border areas, the price increased by the duty may lead to a reduction in the volume of sales of Austrian retailers capable of adversely affecting profits"; para. 94: "there is only one exception to that obligation to make repayment. A Member State may resist repayment to the trader of a charge levied though not due only where it is established by the national authorities that the charge has been borne in its entirety by someone other than the taxable person and that reimbursement of the charge would constitute unjust enrichment of the latter. It follows that, if the burden of the charge has been passed on only in part, the national authorities are required to repay the amount not passed on."; and par. 99: "Even where the charge is wholly incorporated in the price the taxable person may suffer as a result of a fall in the volume of his sales... Accordingly, the existence and the degree of unjust enrichment which repayment of a charge which was levied though not due from the aspect of Community law entails for a taxable person can be established only following an economic analysis in which all the relevant circumstances are taken into account."

reduction, then the benefit is attributable to the Union and not to the Member State. On the other hand, if the Member State is entitled to opt to grant benefits and those benefits constitute an exception to a general rule that would tax the transaction (or tax it at a higher rate), then State aid prohibitions would apply as it is not the EU that has decided to grant the benefit, but it is the individual Member State. Notwithstanding his conclusions, Englisch still argues that optional benefits contained in a directive should never be regarded as State aid: By enacting the directive, including the optional benefits, the Commission, the Council, and the European Parliament have all approved that benefit and its effects on the internal market. Thus, if the Member State opts to grant such a benefit, the exercise of that option cannot later be determined to promote only the interest of that Member State or to distort the internal market.

Humbert Drabbe, in Chapter 6 discusses the aforementioned notion of "selectivity." He starts with an explanation of the three-step approach adopted by the ECJ: First, the general rule applicable in the Member State—the so-called "reference framework"—must be determined. As Member States are free to design their own system of taxation, the State aid rules do not refer to a general tax system applicable in all Member States or to a hypothetical general tax system but to the system in force in one Member State.[24] Next, the particular measure must be examined to determine if it deviates from the general rule. Finally, assuming the particular measure deviates from the general rule, the potential justifications for such a deviation must be reviewed to decide whether it can be justified by the nature or general scheme and logic of the tax system.

Drabbe then proposes that a proportionality requirement be introduced, asking if the Member State's goal could be achieved by less far reaching measures. Drabbe advocates making both an internal and external comparison. After his introductory remarks, Drabbe analyzes thoroughly the latest case law on selectivity.

Chapter 7, by Raymond Luja, illustrates the concept of sectoral aid, with a particular focus on investment fund regimes. In many countries, investment funds themselves benefit from complete tax exemption. Although such an exemption is an obvious deviation from the general corporate tax system, Luja suggests that it should be permissible as long as the vast majority of the income derived by the investment fund is passed on to its investors who are then taxed on the distributed or attributed income. However, advantages which go beyond such transparency should be subject to investigation under the State aid rules. Luja points out that the *Paint Graphos* judgment[25] shows that a substance-over-form approach is equally applicable to questions of State aid. Consequently, investment funds that are not, in reality, collective investment vehicles but are instead used to invest for the benefit of a single taxpayer might be questioned, in the future, under State aid rules.

24. For an example of the difficulties that can be encountered in trying to determine what is the "general tax system," see Surrey/McDaniel, *Tax Expenditures* (Harvard University Press 1985) (regarding United States tax expenditures).
25. Joined Cases ECJ, *Paint Graphos*, Cases No. C-78/08 to 80/08 not yet reported.

Luja also extensively discusses the recent *Gibraltar* judgment of the Court of Justice.[26] The tax at issue in the case, introduced by Gibraltar and based on payroll and business property, was regarded as a corporate tax because the tax liability was capped at 15% of profits earned. Luja argues that, without such a profit-based cap, a payroll tax, a business property tax, or even a combination of the two would not have violated the State aid rules. Although the profit-based cap was intended to benefit onshore businesses and thereby limit the inequality between onshore and offshore businesses, it was ultimately that cap that led to the tax's characterization as selective by the Court of Justice.

In Chapter 8, Edoardo Traversa first describes and then criticizes the concept of "regional" aid. Regional aid has two possible meanings: On the one hand, the term can refer to aid typically granted by a central government for the benefit of an underdeveloped region. On the other hand, this term can also refer to aid granted by a regional government. Although the ultimate effect of either type of "regional" aid is identical (with the only real difference being the donor of such aid), the ECJ has developed different criteria for the compatibility of these two types of regional aid. Aid granted by the central government is only permissible under the strict requirements of Article 107(2) and (3) TFEU, whereas aid granted by a regional government is compatible if (a) the region has a sufficiently autonomous status, (b) the central government does not have the power to interfere with the regional government's decision to grant the aid, and (c) the regional government bears the financial consequences of its decision. This last criterion requires that any revenue loss attributable to the tax benefit must be borne by the regional government and cannot be offset by revenue transfers from the central government.[27] According to the Court's reasoning, the reference framework will vary depending on which governmental institution grants the aid.

The requirements demanded by the Court are difficult to implement in practice: How far must a judge go to determine whether the financial consequences of the regionally-granted aid are actually borne by the region? Is the judge required to examine, in detail, the intricacies of all financial equalization schemes between the central and the regional governments? It may be difficult, if not impossible, to determine whether funds transferred by the central government to the regional government actually compensate for revenue losses attributable to a particular measure granted by the regional government. If the result of such an analysis is that any transfer from a central government to a regional government offering aid that reduces the region's tax revenue is to be considered illegal State aid, the consequence will be that only rich regions (which have no need for transfers from the central government) will be allowed to set their own reference framework. Poor regions, on the other hand, which rely most heavily on tax incentives to attract investment and development, will be cut off from that possibility.

A final problem stems from the fact that tax incentives are a peculiar type of State aid. Government subsidies, whether granted by the central or regional government, typically involve a direct transfer of money from public coffers to the recipient; they

26. Joined Cases ECJ, *Gibraltar*, Cases No. C-106/09 P and C-107/09 P not yet reported.
27. See ECJ, *Portugal v. Commission*, Case No. C-88/03 [2006] ECR I-7115 para. 67.

reflect a clear and unambiguous public expenditure. Tax incentives, on the other hand, do not require any direct outlay of public money; they only create a possibility that the ultimate tax revenue might be less than it would have otherwise been under the general tax system if those same taxpayers could have been convinced to invest in the region without the tax incentives—that is to say, the decrease in revenue is theoretical rather than actual, such that it is difficult to show an actual expenditure of public money. The new investment (and new taxpayers) attracted to the region may actually result in the growth of the region's coffers because it is highly unlikely that the investment would have been made in the absence of the incentive. How then should regional aid be qualified? Should that qualification depend on measure's success in attracting new investment to the region?

Frank Engelen and Anna Gunn, in Chapter 9, tackle the flaws associated with the selectivity test. They argue that, despite years of consideration and numerous court decisions addressing State aid, the applicability of the State aid rules remains uncertain for Member States and taxpayers alike. In that regard, the authors propose a more workable—and certain—approach.

After carefully considering the four requirements set out in Article 107(1) TFEU, they conclude that, in the context of tax incentives, it can simply be assumed that the "use of State resources" and the "distortion of competition" requirements have been satisfied. Thereafter, however, in connection with the remaining two requirements, the authors propose a balancing test. Thus, drawing inspiration from the discrimination test used in connection with impediments to the exercise of the four freedoms, the authors first ask whether certain taxpayers are treated in a more beneficial way than other taxpayers. If yes, they go on to ask whether the different treatment can be justified by a legitimate objective. If the different treatment can, in fact, be so justified, the authors suggest applying the proportionality principle, by asking whether the measure is a suitable means of achieving the objective pursued without going beyond what is necessary to do so. Finally, the authors distinguish between discrimination under the four freedoms and advantageous treatment which might be incompatible with the State aid provisions.

In Chapter 10, Claire Micheau and Gauthier Charles de la Brousse apply the selectivity test to two case studies. In the first case study, they analyze the so-called "patent box regime." In that regard, they determine that the decisive question is whether the partial exemption of royalty income for the use of a patent can be regarded as a general measure or whether it must be classified as an exception to the general corporate income tax system. Thus, for them, if the goal of a measure is to promote innovation, then the regime should not be limited to just patents but should be expanded to include all income derived from investment in the innovation. In its decision relating to Spain's patent box regime,[28] the Commission determined that the Spanish rules were not selective as they applied to all economic operators, thereby saving Spain's patent box regime from incompatibility with the State aid provisions.

28. Commission Decision N 480/2007, OJ C 80, 01.

In their second case study, the authors consider national provisions exempting foreign source income. An exemption of foreign income clearly constitutes a selective advantage; foreign income is treated more favorably than domestic income of the same type. However, under certain circumstances, the exemption of foreign income may be justified by the logic of the system. The authors argue that the proportionality test should be applied in connection with any such justification. The exemption of certain types of foreign income is generally intended to avoid juridical double taxation: Income should be taxed once, neither twice nor never. Consequently, an exemption system offered by a Member State goes beyond what is necessary (and, as such, is not proportionate) if the other country involved does not tax the income, either. In that regard, a more proportionate measure to avoid juridical double taxation would be the credit method, which effectively avoids juridical double taxation but does not lead to double non-taxation.

In the final chapter, Chapter 11, Keith O'Donnell and Ann Muller take a closer look at legal protections afforded to taxpayers. The authors rightly point out that, in the field of State aid, there is still a high degree of taxpayer uncertainty: It is difficult, if not impossible, to predict the outcome of a State aid case brought before the Court of Justice and, even after the *Gibraltar* judgment, the concept of selectivity remains murky, at best. The situation is equally untenable for tax professionals and advisors who remain, unfortunately, unable to give their clients clear and definitive advice with respect to the application of the State aid rules.

Moreover, if a taxpayer benefits from a particular tax incentive, that taxpayer's right to be heard in connection with a State aid case relating thereto is substantially compromised. According to Article 108(2) TFEU, it is the Commission that decides if a measure is incompatible and can require a Member State to abolish or alter the aid it offers. If the Member State does not comply, the Commission is entitled to start an infringement procedure against the Member State. The only parties to such an infringement procedure are the Commission and the Member State, while a taxpayer benefiting from the challenged aid has no role at all. Whether or not taxpayer input will even be considered is at the discretion of the Commission and the relevant Member State. Moreover, although any judgment issued by the Court of Justice will have immediate, and sometimes dire, consequences for taxpayers if a Member State is obliged to revoke the aid, taxpayers are not allowed to put forward their arguments during the infringement procedure or any appeal thereof to the Court of Justice. Thereafter, thc Court of Justice's judgment is binding on the Member State's national judges in any subsequent legal challenge to the manner in which the State aid is revoked. As a result, any arguments the taxpayer might have had concerning the legality of the State aid will never be heard, either before the Court of Justice or before the national court.

Moreover, suggestions that the relevant Member State will zealously, or even adequately, protect the interests of the taxpayer fall flat. If, for example, a substantial investment has already been made by the taxpayer in reliance on a particular tax incentive, and there is little chance that that investment will be withdrawn by the taxpayer, what incentive does a Member State have to fight for the taxpayer? If the tax incentive is found to be incompatible with the internal market, the Member State will be "forced" to recoup all of its foregone tax revenue while still benefiting from the economic investment the taxpayer made in reliance on the incentive. In such circumstances, it is clear that a Member State may not be particularly motivated to protect the taxpayer.

Finally, the authors note that the review procedures under the Code of Conduct and State aid are separated. A Commission decision according to which a measure does not constitute illegal State aid in no way prevents a separate proceeding attacking the measure before the Code of Conduct Group under the Code of Conduct, and vice versa. Thus, as the system currently works, no single proceeding can give taxpayers assurance that a particular measure is neither illegal State aid nor in violation of the Code of Conduct. As continuing uncertainty is not conducive to economic investment and growth, the authors propose to bundle both reviews into a single proceeding.[29] Further, the authors suggest that modifying the existing Treaties to give sole competence to decide both issues to either the Commission or the Code of Conduct Group. Such modification of authority and procedural consolidation would substantially increase legal certainty for taxpayers on which both the Member States and the EU rely to generate economic activity, growth and, of course, tax revenue.

29. For the German terminology of bundling several procedures, the so-called "Formale Konzentrationswirkung" see Bonk/Neumann in Stelkens/Bonk/Sachs, Verwaltungsverfahrensgesetz (7th edn, München, Beck, 2008) § 75 Verwaltungsverfahrensgesetz para. 14.

CHAPTER 2

Corporate Blackmail: State Tax Incentives in the United States

Tracy A. Kaye[*]

§2.01 INTRODUCTION

After almost 100 years in Illinois, the Modern Drop Forge Company has announced that it will be moving to Indiana.[1] The company's CEO cited the "poor business environment in Illinois," referring to the tougher worker's compensation laws and higher taxes in Illinois.[2] Modern Drop Forge Company is one of 13 companies that have pledged to relocate from Illinois to Indiana.[3]

Illinois offered the Modern Drop Forge Company further State and local incentives to remain in Illinois but the Indiana Economic Development Corporation (IEDC) produced a more lucrative package.[4] Based on Modern Drop Forge's job creation promises, the IEDC gave the company "up to USD 2 million in performance-based tax credits and up to USD 200,000 in training grants."[5] The local government designated the plant an Economic Revitalization Area, thus allowing for a 10-year tax abatement.[6] Thus, approximately 275 jobs will be lost in Illinois and 240 jobs gained in Indiana 35

* The author gratefully acknowledges the research assistance of Cheryl Ritter and Joel Plainfield.

1. K. Caffarini & S. Metsch, *Blue Island Forging Company Moving to Indiana*, Chi. Sun-Times, (Aug. 23, 2011), www.suntimes.com/business/7235414-418/blue-island-forging-company-moving-to-indiana.html, 5:47 PM .
2. *Ibid.*
3. J. Wernau, *Employing All Means for Creation of Jobs: Work Opportunities Front and Center as Indiana's Raids of Illinois Companies Are Exacting a Toll*, Chi. Trib. at C1 (Aug. 24, 2011).
4. K. Caffarini & S. Metsch, *supra* note 1.
5. *Ibid.*; see M.L. Nachbar et al., *Business Credits and Incentives: Idaho Through Mississippi*, *Tax Mgm't. (BNA)* No. 1460, at 1460.08 D-2, H-3 (2011) (hereinafter Nachbar, *Idaho Through Mississippi*).
6. K. Caffarini & S. Metsch, *supra* note 1; see M.L. Nachbar, *Idaho Through Mississippi*, *supra* note 5, at 1460.08 F-1 (citing Ind. Code Ann. § 6-3.1-19-1 and Ind. Code Ann. § 36-7-13-12).

miles away, resulting in a net job loss for the United States.[7] The Chief Financial Officer of the company reports that once "the Indiana plant is up and running and the Illinois facility closes, the company expects to have fewer employees, not more."[8] This scenario illustrates the compelling problem with the tax competition that takes place among the States in the US federal system.

In January 2011, Illinois raised its State corporate income tax rate from 4.8% to 7%[9] in an effort to lessen its budget deficit.[10] In response to this rate increase, various States began actively trying to lure away Illinois businesses. For example, New Jersey's Governor Chris Christie began running radio ads in Illinois as well as print ads in Illinois newspapers touting the benefits of New Jersey and promising not to raise any taxes.[11] South Dakota's governor began sending direct-mail postcards to Illinois businesses asking "'Tired of taxes? Call me.'"[12] In Michigan, however, the Michigan Economic Development Corporation "decrie[d] the 'one-upsmanship' that defines the US economic development game, in which States compete to offer the most aggressive tax incentives in an accelerating race to the bottom."[13]

The governor of Indiana declared that Illinois had been borrowing from its businesses and that Indiana's choices in governance had been wiser.[14] He even referred to Illinois as the entertaining, "dysfunctional family down the block."[15] The mayor of Indianapolis, ran full-page ads in Illinois newspapers (one of which was in Chicago) that encouraged Illinois businesses to consider the benefits of being located in Indianapolis.[16] The Northwest Indiana Forum and the Indiana Economic Development

---

7. The Associated Press, *Ill. v. Indiana, Not in Football, But in Jobs, Lincoln Courier* (Aug. 25, 2011), www.lincolncourier.com/news/x1153514554/Ill-vs-Indiana-not-in-football-but-in-jobs, 7:45 AM (hereinafter "*Ill. v. Indiana*").
8. J. Wernau, *supra* note 3.
9. Illinois Department of Revenue, "*Corporate Income Tax*," tax.illinois.gov/Businesses/TaxInformation/Income/corporate.htm, 24 Jan. 2011; see also R. Long, *Quinn on Tax Hike: Our Fiscal House Was Burning*, Chi Trib, (Jan. 12, 2011), newsblogs.chicagotribune.com/clout_st/2011/01/quinn-on-tax-hike-our-fiscal-house-was-burning.html, 12:01 PM. This rate is slated to decrease to 5.25% in 2015 and to eventually fall back down to 4.8% in year 2025. *Ibid.*
10. *Ill. v. Indiana*, *supra* note 7.
11. The Associated Press, *Gov. Christie to Launch Campaign Encouraging Illinois Businesses to Relocate to N.J.*, NJ. Com, (Jan. 24, 2011), www.nj.com/news/index.ssf/2011/01/gov_christie_to_launch_campaig.html, 9:09 PM; see also J. Bismarck, *Balls the size of musk melons: Chris Christie invites Illinois companies to move to New Jersey*, (Jan. 29, 2011), www.ihatethemedia.com/chris-christie-invites-illinois-companies-to-move-to-new-jersey.
12. *Ill. v. Indiana*, *supra* note 7.
13. N. Bomey, *Column: Caterpillar and Jimmy John's May Leave Illinois. Should Michigan Recruit Them?*, Ann Arbor, (Apr. 22, 2011), www.annarbor.com/business-review/caterpillar-and-jimmy-johns-may-leave-illinois-should-michigan-recruit-them, 11:45 AM.
14. D. Carden, *Daniels: Illinois Tax Hikes Good for Indiana*, Times of Nw. Ind, (Jan. 8, 2011) www.nwitimes.com/news/state-and-regional/illinois/article_27130bf0-6ebf-529f-9e40-4b8c9f205f93.html,12:00 AM.
15. Editorial, *Beware of Border Wars: Indiana Must Maintain Focus on Its Own Affairs*, Tribune-Star, (Jan. 14, 2011), tribstar.com/opinion/x233315185/TRIBUNE-STAR-EDITORIAL-Beware-of-border-wars.
16. R. James, *Legion of Leaders–Would Fill Void in Northwest Indiana Region*, Post-Tribune, (Jan. 23, 2011), posttrib.suntimes.com/opinions/3424498-474/indiana-lugar-tea-party-northwest.html, 1:30 PM. Mayor Ballard's ads read: "Dear Illinois business leader … As you consider the impact of large, new state tax increases on your company's bottom line and ability to hire, I invite you to take a serious look at Indianapolis. The nation's 13th largest city is right next door,

Corporation spent USD 200,000 to develop the slogans "Feeling Squeezed by Taxes?" and "Illinnoyed by Higher Taxes?" to attract Illinois businesses to Indiana.[17] A new website, www.solutionindiana.com, touts the benefits of being a business in Indiana.[18]

Illinois fights back with the EDGE (Economic Development for a Growing Economy) program, which was launched in 1999[19] and expanded in 2011 to keep up with the neighboring States.[20] The EDGE program offers "a special tax incentive to encourage companies to locate or expand operations in Illinois when there is active consideration of a competing location in another State."[21] The program provides tax credits to qualifying companies to offset their corporate income taxes. In general, companies must provide documentation attesting to a competing State offer, "make an investment of at least USD 5 million," and create at least "25 new full-time jobs in Illinois."[22] The EDGE credit has reduced corporate income tax revenues in Illinois by approximately USD 25 million each year.[23]

Interested companies must submit a written application to the Illinois Department of Commerce and Economic Opportunity; the actual amount of the Tax Credit granted is determined on a case-by-case basis.[24] For example, EDGE legislation in 2011 provided that Continental Tire will receive approximately USD 19 million worth of tax credits in return for the promise to make a capital investment of at least USD 200 million, add 350 full-time jobs, and abide by certain job retention requirements.[25] Furthermore, EDGE tax credits valued at greater than USD 100 million (over 10 years)

---

offering the same Midwestern work ethic and conveniences - but in a much more stable, affordable and pro-growth economic environment." *Ibid.*

17. C.S. Kirk, *NWI Forum, State Ask Businesses If They Are 'Illinnoyed' by Taxes*, Post-Tribune, (Feb. 15, 2011), www.indianaeconomicdigest.net/main.asp?SectionID=31&subsectionID=217&articleID=58506, 10:27 AM.
18. M. Odendahl, *Are Illinois Taxes Indiana's Gain?*, The Elkhart Truth, (Jan. 25, 2011), www.indianaeconomicdigest.com/Main.asp?SectionID=31&SubSectionID=124&ArticleID=58129, 6:16 PM.
19. A. Cancino & K. Bergen, *Incentives No Guarantee a Company Will Remain in Illinois*, Chi. Trib., (Mar. 5, 2011) articles.chicagotribune.com/2011-03-05/news/ct-biz-0306-incentives-exits-20110303_1_tax-credits-maytag-corporate-income.
20. See K. Erickson, *Quinn Signs EDGE Tax Credit Bill*, The S. Springfield Bureau, (May 7, 2011), thesouthern.com/news/local/article_3d3a3cc4-7864-11e0-ad9b-001cc4c002e0.html, 5:00 AM; M. Zawislak, *Big Incentives to Stay in Suburbs Quinn Cites Jobs Inlanding Motorola Arm's Headquarters in Libertyville*, Chi. Daily Herald, at 1 (May 7, 2011), available at 2011 WLNR 9247344; and K. Bergen and W. Wong, *Motorola Stays in Illinois ? for $100M; Expanded Tax Incentives Persuade Mobility to Keep Jobs, HQ in Libertyville*, Chi. Trib., (May 7, 2011) at C1, available at 2011 WLNR 8968731.
21. *Economic Development for a Growing Economy Tax Credit Program (EDGE)*, Ill. Dep't Commerce & Econ. Opportunity, (Jan. 24, 2011) www.commerce.state.il.us/dceo/Bureaus/Business_Development/Tax+Assistance/EDGE.htm.
22. *Ibid.* For a company with 100 or fewer employees, the company must agree to "make a capital investment of at least $1 million and must create a minimum of 5 new [full time] jobs" in Illinois. *Ibid.*
23. K. Bergen, A. Cancino & M. Harris, *State Business-incentive Program Falling Short of Promised Job Creation*, Chi. Trib., (Mar. 5, 2011), articles.chicagotribune.com/2011-03-05/business/ct-biz-0306-incentives-20110303_1_corporate-income-tax-tax-credits-job-creation.
24. *Economic Development for a Growing Economy Tax Credit Program (EDGE)*, *supra* note 21.
25. K. Erickson, *supra* note 20; see *Economic Development for a Growing Economy Tax Credit Act LexisNexis* (2011) 35 Ill. Comp. Stat. Ann. tit. 10/5-15 *amended by* S.B. 4, 97th Gen. Assemb., Reg. Sess. (Ill. 2011).

will be given to Motorola Mobility, Inc. to stay in Illinois and retain 3,000 jobs, while making its current facility in Libertyville, Illinois, its global headquarters.[26]

While both the United States and the European Union face the same problem of State tax competition, this article explains why this scenario would be extremely unusual in the European Union and examines whether any lessons can be learned from its experience. In *Investment Incentives and the Global Competition for Capital,* Professor Kenneth Thomas, documents how tax subsidies given to multinationals are increasing around the world.[27] However, the Europeans appear to be controlling the costs of these deals much better than the United States.[28] Thomas estimates total US State and local incentives at USD 46.8 billion in 2005[29] whereas "regional aid (the type most commonly used for investment incentives) in EU Member States" was only "EUR 9.6 billion (approximately USD 12.9 billion)."[30] According to the European Commission, the figure for regional aid has only grown to EUR 14.9 billion (approximately USD 19 billion in 2010 dollars)[31] in 2010 with the largest increase between 2007 and 2008 of EUR 3.2 billion.[32]

The level of regional aid in the EU remains far below the levels of US investment incentives because of the strict controls and procedures implemented in the EU.[33] Thomas suggests that because analogous rules in the US are lacking, bidding wars for incentives increase the size and number of incentives far beyond those encountered in the EU.[34] For example, "17 projects in the United States since 2002 have received over USD 100 million (EUR 74.1 million) in subsidies, compared to eight projects in the European Union."[35] The EU has also exhibited greater control in terms of the number

26. M. Zawislak, *supra* note 20; K. Bergen and W. Wong, *supra* note 20.
27. K.P. Thomas, *Investment Incentives and the Global Competition for Capital 2-3* [2011]. Because of the range of credits offered by US States and municipalities as well as the lack of a universal data collection and recordation procedure, it is extremely difficult to achieve an accurate total of investment incentives offered throughout the US. *Ibid.*, at 102–06.
28. D.C. Johnston, *On the Dole, Corporate Style*, 59 *St. Tax Notes* 127 (2011) (citing K. P. Thomas, *supra* note 27).
29. K.P. Thomas, *supra* note 27, at 106–07. Further, he estimated for 2005 total State and local subsidies to be USD 64.8 billion and USD 69.8 billion if accelerated depreciation is counted. *Ibid.*
30. *Ibid.*, at 96.
31. *Yearly Average Currency Exchange Rates*, IRS, (Jan. 24, 2012) www.irs.gov/businesses/small/international/article/0,,id=206089,00.html. In 2010, the yearly average exchange rate for converting Euros to US Dollars was 0.785. *Ibid.*
32. See *Commission Staff Working Paper: Autumn 2011 Update* [December 2011], at 13, 16, 23, 63, SEC 1487 final, ec.europa.eu/competition/state_aid/studies_reports/2011_autumn_working_paper_en.pdf, (Dec. 1, 2011); see also European Commission, *Table: Trend in State aid for regional development, by Member State, in million Euro*, (Jan. 24, 2012) ec.europa.eu/competition/state_aid/studies_reports/expenditure.html#1, (scroll to sub-section "3.4. State aid for regional development" and select the "Trend in State aid for regional development, by Member State, in million Euro" hyperlink).
33. K. P. Thomas, *supra* note 27, at 96. State aid is controlled through the adoption of overall regional aid guidelines. *Ibid.*, at 96–97, 101; see also European Commission, "Guidelines on National Regional Aid for 2007-2013" [2006] OJ C 54, 32. See *infra* notes 73–76 and accompanying text for a description of the State aid restrictions in the Treaty.
34. *Ibid.*, at 97–102.
35. *Ibid.*, at 100. *[M]arquee projects in the US receive more money than do similar projects in the EU. Ibid.*, at 98.

of State aid measures approved by reducing them from 96 in 2006 to 86 in 2009 and then to only about 50 in 2010.[36]

While competition to give money to companies is indeed a global problem, the problem is much worse in the United States.[37] For 2005, Thomas estimated that American State and local subsidies to businesses were much larger than the location subsidies found in 15 EU Member States.[38] The US also has markedly higher-aid intensity (the incentive amount as a percentage of the recipient's investment) and the locations granting these "investment incentives were substantially more prosperous than comparable EU regions."[39]

Both the US and the EU share the goal of economic unity[40] yet continue to struggle with the individual sovereignty of their subnational governmental units (their respective States and Member States).[41] This sovereignty includes the power to provide subsidies, such as tax incentives, to promote certain public policies.[42] However, the tax policy of one State cannot be discriminatory against other States in a way that interferes with commerce within the single market.[43] Despite their shared goal, the US and the EU have chosen different methods of restricting the ability of the States and Member States to provide subsidies through tax policy.

Congress has the authority to regulate State tax competition pursuant to the Commerce Clause of the US Constitution,[44] but rarely exercises this authority.[45] Generally, the federal government has adopted a laissez-faire attitude and has declined

36. European Commission, *Report on State Aid Contribution to Europe 2020 Strategy: Spring 2011 Update* [2011] COM, at 29, 356 final, ec.europa.eu/transparency/regdoc/recherche.cfm?CL=en, (Jun. 22, 2011) (enter "COM/2011/356" in the "Document search" form and select "final versions only"; select "search"; then follow "EurLex" hyperlink).
37. K.P. Thomas, *supra* note 27, at 1. "Alabama ... in 2002 gave Hyundai about $117,000 per job on a present value basis . ..." *Ibid.*
38. *Ibid.*, at 96; see also D. C. Johnston, *supra* note 28, at 127.
39. *Ibid.*, at 98–99.
40. The United States was founded in 1787, in hopes of a solution to "the mutual jealousies and aggressions of the States" that had led to economic retaliation. *Baldwin v. G.A.F. Seelig, Inc.*, 294 U.S. 511, 522 (1935) (citations omitted). See generally J. Madison, *The Federalist*, No. 42; M. Farrand (ed.), *The Records of the Federal Convention of 1787*, 308 [1911]; *ibid.* at 478, 547, 548. The European Economic Community was founded in 1958 with the establishment of a common market in the hopes of so intertwining their economies that future war would be avoided. See Treaty Establishing the European Economic Community Art. 2, March 25, 1957, 298 U.N.T.S. 11 (now Consolidated Version of the Treaty on European Union Art. 3, March 30, 2010, OJ (C 83) 1, 2010).
41. The Treaty of Maastricht established the European Union. Treaty on European Union Art. 1, (Feb. 7, 1992), OJ (C 191) 1, 1992. The Treaty of Lisbon was signed in December of 2007 and entered into force on 1 December 2009. Treaty of Lisbon Amending the Treaty on European Union and the Treaty Establishing the European Community, Dec. 13, 2007, OJ (C 306) 1, 2007 [hereinafter Treaty of Lisbon].
42. T. A. Kaye, *The Gentle Art of Corporate Seduction: Tax Incentives in the United States and the European Union*, 57 U. Kan. L. Rev. 93, 94 (2009). This article updates and expands *The Gentle Art of Corporate Seduction.*
43. See *infra* text accompanying notes 47–48, 68–72.
44. See U.S. Const. Art. I, § 8, cl. 3 [hereinafter Commerce Clause] (The Congress shall have Power To ... regulate Commerce ... among the Several States).
45. See K. Moore, *State and Local Taxation: When Will Congress Intervene*, 23 J. Legis. 171, 182–204 (1997) (reviewing the legislative history of various bills prohibiting State taxation).

to "to establish principles for state tax competition."[46] Dormant Commerce Clause doctrine is interpreted by the Supreme Court to deny the States the ability to tax or regulate in any manner that would unduly burden interstate commerce[47] and implicitly prohibits State discrimination of interstate commerce.[48] Modern Commerce Clause doctrine forbids nearly all discrimination on the basis of economic factors from sister-states and is designed to preclude States from engaging in economic protectionism.[49] Thus, tax subsidies that encourage investment within a State must comply with the dormant Commerce Clause.[50]

On the other hand, States are generally free to directly subsidize in-State activities under the "market-participant" exception.[51] "The 'market-participant' exception permits States acting as 'market participants' as opposed to 'regulators'—essentially when the State is engaged in ordinary buying or selling with taxpayer money—to make geographic distinctions the [dormant Commerce Clause Doctrine] would otherwise prohibit."[52] The Supreme Court has indicated that direct monetary subsidies to in-State companies do not usually violate the Commerce Clause.[53] A 1988 Supreme Court case explains that:

46. T.F. Field, *Tax Competition in Europe and America*, 27 St. Tax Notes 1211, 1213 (2003).
47. L.H. Tribe, *American Constitutional Law* § 6-2, at 1030 (3d ed., 2000) (Foundation Press). It is now established beyond dispute that "the Commerce Clause was not merely an authorization to Congress to enact laws for the protection and encouragement of commerce among the States, but by its own force created an area of trade free from interference by the States .... [T]he Commerce Clause even without implementing legislation by Congress is a limitation upon the power of the States". *Boston Stock Exch. v. State Tax Comm'n*, 429 U.S. 318, 328 (1977) (citing *Freeman v. Hewit*, 329 U.S. 249, 252 (1946)).
48. See M. Tushnet, *Rethinking the Dormant Commerce Clause*, 125 Wis. L. Rev. 130–31 (1979). (Beyond the proscription of purposeful discrimination, the commerce clause has been held to authorize judicial invalidation of State laws that unduly burden interstate commerce.)
49. D. Laycock, *Equal Citizens of Equal and Territorial States: The Constitutional Foundations of Choice of Law*, 92 Colum. L. Rev. 249, 269 (1992).
50. See generally E. Chemerinsky, *Constitutional Law: Principles and Policies*, 401 (2d ed., 2002) (Aspen Law & Business).
51. See, e.g., *Camps Newfound/Owatonna v. Town of Harrison*, 520 U.S. 564, 591 (1997) ("Direct subsidization of domestic industry does not ordinarily run afoul of [the Commerce Clause]." (citing *New Energy Co. of Ind. v. Limbach*, 486 U.S. 269, 278 (1988))). For an example of a prohibited subsidy, see *W. Lynn Creamery, Inc. v. Healy*, 512 U.S. 186, 204-05 (1994) (holding a Massachusetts tax on all milk dealers unconstitutional because its impact was identical to that of a discriminatory tax as the tax revenues were used to subsidize in-State dairy farmers).
52. B. Denning, *Is the Dormant Commerce Clause Expendable? A Response to Edward Zelinsky*, 77 Miss. L.J. 623, 626 n.17 (2007); see also D.S. Bogen, *The Market-Participant Doctrine and the Clear Statement Rule*, 29 Seattle U. L. Rev. 543 (2006) (According to the market-participant doctrine, however, the State does not violate the dormant Commerce Clause by favoring its own citizens and companies when it buys or sells goods or services). See generally D.T. Coenen, *Untangling the Market Participant Exception to the Dormant Commerce Clause*, 88 Mich. L. Rev. 395 (1989) (explaining the development of the rule, alternative approaches to the rule, and application of the rule).
53. See *W. L. Creamery*, 512 U.S. at 199 n.15 ("We have never squarely confronted the constitutionality of subsidies .... We have, however, noted that '[d]irect subsidization of domestic industry does not ordinarily run afoul' of the negative Commerce Clause. In addition, it is undisputed that States may try to attract business by creating an environment conducive to economic activity, as by maintaining good roads, sound public education, or low taxes." (citations omitted)).

> [t]he Commerce Clause does not prohibit all state action designed to give its residents an advantage in the marketplace, but only action ... *in connection with the State's regulation of interstate commerce.* Direct subsidization of domestic industry does not ordinarily run afoul of that prohibition; discriminatory taxation ... does.[54]

This dichotomy between the treatment of direct subsidies and tax subsidies under the dormant Commerce Clause has been severely criticized.[55]

Furthermore, the Supreme Court's jurisprudence is confusing and the case law on specific tax schemes does not establish a clear pattern of precedent.[56] While a tax on interstate commerce must meet four requirements to survive a constitutional challenge under the Commerce Clause;[57] the ban on discrimination against interstate commerce is the predominant basis upon which the Supreme Court has struck down State taxes in recent years.[58] In *Boston Stock Exchange,* the Supreme Court stated: "No State ... 'may impose a tax which discriminates against interstate commerce ... by providing a direct commercial advantage to local business.'"[59] Although this seems like an applicable standard that could produce consistent results, it has left much room for interpretation. This is demonstrated by the Court's general willingness to allow location tax incentives, which clearly favor one State's businesses over another.[60]

---

54. *New Energy Co. of Ind.*, 486 U.S. at 278.
55. See, e.g., E.A. Zelinsky, *Restoring Politics to the Commerce Clause: The Case for Abandoning the Dormant Commerce Clause Prohibition on Discriminatory Taxation,* 29 Ohio NUL Rev. 29 (2002). Professor Zelinsky has concluded "that the time has come to scrap the dormant Commerce Clause prohibition on discriminatory taxation. Since the judicially-created prohibition has served its historic purpose, to create a single common market of the United States, it can now safely be laid to rest." *Ibid.,* at 29. The Supreme "Court's distinction between discriminatory taxation (prohibited under the Court's Commerce Clause decisions) and equivalent direct government subsidies (generally permitted under those decisions) is" fundamentally incoherent because taxes and subsidies are often "similar in design and effect." *Ibid.,* at 30–31.
56. D.F. Shores, *State Taxation of Interstate Commerce—Quiet Revolution or Much Ado About Nothing?,* 38 Tax L. Rev. 127, 128–29 (1982). "This case-by-case approach has left 'much room for controversy and confusion and little in the way of precise guides to the States in the exercise of their indispensable power of taxation.'" *Boston Stock Exch.*, 429 U.S. at 329 (quoting *Nw. States Portland Cement Co. v. Minnesota,* 358 U.S. 450, 457 (1959)).
57. See R.D. Pomp & O. Oldman, *State and Local Taxation,* 1–15 (4th ed., 2001). The four requirements are: (1) the activity taxed has "a substantial nexus with the taxing [s]tate"; (2) the tax is fairly apportioned to reflect the degree of activity that occurs within the state; (3) the tax "does not discriminate against interstate commerce"; and (4) the tax "is fairly related to the services provided by the [s]tate." Complete Auto Transit, *Inc. v. Brady,* 430 U.S. 274, 279 (1977).
58. L.H. Tribe, *supra* note 47, § 6–16, at 1107.
59. *Boston Stock Exch.*, 429 U.S. at 329 (quoting *Nw. States Portland Cement Co.*, 358 U.S. at 458). "[A] tax which by its terms or operation imposes greater burdens on out-of-state goods, activities, or enterprises than on competing in-state goods, activities, or enterprises will be struck down as discriminatory under the Commerce Clause." W. Hellerstein & D.T. Coenen, *Commerce Clause Restraints on State Business Development Incentives,* 81 Cornell L. Rev. 789, 793 (1996).
60. See P.D. Enrich, *Saving the States from Themselves: Commerce Clause Constraints on State Tax Incentives for Business,* 110 Harv. L. Rev. 377, 407 (1996) [hereinafter P. D. Enrich, "Saving the States"].

State tax incentives reward a corporation's in-state activities and raise an important dormant Commerce Clause question that has yet to be answered by the Supreme Court.[61] While the Court consistently finds discriminatory tax schemes unconstitutional, it is reluctant to strike down positive tax incentives that favor local industry.[62] Until 2006, the Supreme Court had not seen "a challenge grounded in the claim that a State tax provision's primary purpose or effect is to attract business to locate or expand in the state."[63] Unfortunately, the Supreme Court refused to consider the merits in *DaimlerChrysler Corp. v. Cuno.*[64] In 2004, the Sixth Circuit had held that the Ohio investment tax credit violated the Commerce Clause because it "discriminates against interstate economic activity by coercing businesses already subject to the Ohio franchise tax to expand locally rather than out-of-state."[65] Although the Supreme Court ultimately limited its holding in *Cuno* to the issue of standing,[66] the discussion surrounding the case provides an excellent opportunity to compare and contrast the economic development policy in the US with the State aid law in the EU.[67]

Like the United States, the European Union bars tax discrimination.[68] Article 18 TFEU explicitly states that "any discrimination on grounds of nationality shall be prohibited."[69] Generally, Member States are not permitted to pass national legislation that distinguishes between domestic and foreign persons, goods, services or capital (the four fundamental freedoms espoused by the Treaty).[70] According to the jurisprudence of the

61. P.M. Tatarowicz, *Federalism, The Commerce Clause and Discriminatory State Tax Incentives: A Defense of Unconditional Business Tax Incentives Limited to In-State Activities of the Taxpayer*, 60 Tax Law. 835, 837 (2007).
62. P.D. Enrich, "Saving the States," *supra* note 60, at 407–08. "The Supreme Court's calendar has included a steady diet of state tax cases raising Commerce Clause issues, but to date, the Court has not applied its Commerce Clause doctrine to a state [investment tax credit], to a jobs credit, or to any of the other characteristic location incentives." *Ibid.*, at 407 (citations omitted).
63. *Ibid.*, at 381.
64. *DaimlerChrysler Corp. v. Cuno*, 547 U.S. 332 (2006), *reh'g denied*, 548 U.S. 920 (2006).
65. *Cuno v. DaimlerChrysler, Inc.*, 386 F.3d 738, 743, 746 (6th Cir. 2004), *cert. granted*, 545 U.S. 1165 (2005), *vacated in part and remanded*, 547 U.S. 332 (2006).
66. *Cuno*, 547 U.S. at 338.
67. See, e.g., R.S. Avi-Yonah, *Passport to Toledo: Cuno, the World Trade Organization and the European Court of Justice*, Tax Notes, at 1661 (Dec. 26, 2005); D.H. Schenk, *The Cuno Case: A Comparison of U.S. Subsidies and European State Aid*, 1 Eur. St. Aid Q. 3 (2006); J.R. Rogers, *The Law and Policy of State Tax Competition: Much Ado About Nothing?*, 4 Geo. JL & Pub. Pol'y 101 (2006); D.P. Wood, Cuno v. DaimlerChrysler, Inc.*: State "Aids" from an American Perspective*, 1 Eur. St. Aid Q. 3 (2007).
68. T.A. Kaye, *Tax Discrimination: A Comparative Analysis of U.S. and EU Approaches*, Comparative Fiscal Federalism: Comparing the European Court of Justice and the US Supreme Court's Tax Jurisprudence, R.S. Avi-Yonah et al. (eds.), 191, 212–13 (2007) [hereinafter T.A. Kaye, *Tax Discrimination*].
69. Consolidated Version of the Treaty on the Functioning of the European Union Art. 18, Mar. 30, 2010, OJ (C 83) 47 2010 [hereinafter TFEU]. See generally T.A. Kaye, *Tax Discrimination, supra* note 68.
70. W. Schön, *EC State Aids*, 241, 244 (3rd ed., L. Hancher et al. eds., 2006) (Sweet & Maxwell); see also Art. 26 TFEU.

Court of Justice, the "Four Freedoms" are directly applicable,[71] permitting economic operators to challenge the validity of national law, including a tax law.[72]

Unlike the US Constitution, the Treaty also explicitly prohibits State aid because the founders believed that State aid distorts competition within the internal market.[73] "State aid control comes from the need to maintain a level playing field for all undertakings active in the Single European Market, no matter in which Member State they are established."[74] Specifically, "any aid granted by a Member State or through State resources in any form whatsoever which distorts or threatens to distort competition by favouring certain undertakings or the production of certain goods shall, in so far as it affects trade between Member States, be incompatible with the internal market."[75] Therefore, State aid that selectively favors *certain* undertakings or the production of *certain* goods is prohibited, while general aid that assists all sectors or industries is not.[76]

Although tax incentives were not the initial focus of the State aid restrictions, the Court of Justice made it clear in dictum in *Italy v. Commission* that these restrictions apply to aid in any form.[77] Thus, unlike in the US, there is no incoherence in EU law with respect to the treatment of tax measures versus direct subsidies. The analysis and the outcome will be the same regardless of the aid instrument that is chosen. Tax measures are State aid if the State grants the recipients a fiscal advantage that affects competition and trade between the Member States.[78] The tax measure must also be specific or selective and not a part of the general overall tax system.[79]

71. ECJ, *NV Algemene Transport–en Expedite Onderneming van Gend & Loos v. Nederlandse Administratie der Belastingen*, Case No. 26/62, [1963] ECR. 1, para. 12.
72. S. van Thiel, *EU Case Law on Income Tax*, at 4–9 (2001); see also B.J.M. Terra & P.J. Wattel, *European Tax Law*, 32–34 (5th ed., 2008) (Wolters Kluwer Law & Business).
73. Article 107 TFEU.
74. P. Nicolaides, *EC State Aids*, 17, 19 (3d ed., L. Hancher et al. eds., 2006) (Sweet & Maxwell) (citing European Commission, *State Aid Action Plan: Less and Better Targeted State Aid* (2005), COM 107 final (Jun. 7, 2005)). In general, State aid is financial support given by a government to a certain business sector, enterprise or geographic region through either direct or indirect transfer of resources. C. Pinto, *Tax Competition and EU Law*, 100 (2003) (Kluwer Law International).
75. Article 107 TFEU, para. 1; see also W. Schön, *Taxation and State Aid Law in the European Union*, 36 Comm. Mkt. L. Rev. 911, 919 (1999).
76. See F.C. de Hosson, *Tax Facilities for State-Induced Costs under the EC State Aid Rules*, 35 Intertax 719, 720 (2007).
77. "The aim of Article 92 [now Article 107] is to prevent trade between Members States from being affected by benefits granted by the public authorities which ... distort or threaten to distort competition by favouring certain undertakings or the production of certain goods. Accordingly, Article 92 does not distinguish between the measures of State intervention concerned by reference to their causes or aims but defines them in relation to their effects. Consequently, the alleged fiscal nature or social aim of the measure in issue cannot suffice to shield it from the application of Article 92." ECJ, *Italy v. Commission*, Case No. C-173/73[1974] ECR I-709, para. 13.
78. P. Rossi-Maccanico, *A Review of State Aid in Multinational Tax Regimes*, 46 Tax Notes Int'l 941, 943 (2007).
79. *Ibid.* "Selectivity may derive from a legislative, regulatory, or administrative provision, or from a discretionary practice on the part of the tax authorities." *Ibid.* The ECJ has clarified that tax measures are specific if they differentiate between enterprises that are in legally and factually

§2.02 USE OF TAX INCENTIVES IN THE UNITED STATES

In the United States, there is no obligation on the individual States to impose sales, individual, or corporate taxes; State sovereignty over fiscal matters is broad.[80] Such sovereignty makes it possible for the individual States to engage in a substantial amount of tax competition as a means of attracting or retaining businesses.[81] "Our states are not united when it comes to taxation. Each merrily goes its own way, angling for an economic advantage, their leaders hoping their actions will translate into votes on election day."[82] Over the years, the states have become "more and more aggressive tax competitors."[83]

Since at least 1791, when New Jersey granted a tax exemption to Alexander Hamilton's new manufacturing company, States have used tax incentives to lure businesses inside their borders.[84] Today, States are demonstrating extraordinary creativity with respect to the tax policies designed to influence business decisions.[85] As of 2011, almost every state offered some type of tax credit or tax incentive to persuade businesses to locate, maintain, or expand their operations within the State.[86] Although interstate competition to attract economic development has raised concerns regarding the smooth functioning of the national economy,[87] the proliferation of tax credits and incentives has continued relatively unabated despite the dire financial condition of many of the States.[88]

comparable situations. *Ibid.*, at 957 (citing ECJ, *Adria-Wien Pipeline GmbH and Wietersdorfer & Peggauer Zementwerke GmbH v. Finanzlandesdirektion für Kärnten*, Case No. C-143/99[2001] ECR. I-8365.

80. T.F. Field, *supra* note 46, at 1213.
81. *Ibid.*
82. M.A. Sullivan, *Economic Analysis: Lessons from Europe on U.S. Corporate Taxes*, 111 Tax Notes 420 (2006).
83. T.F. Field, *supra* note 46, at 1214.
84. M.L. Nachbar et al., *Business Credits and Incentives: Alabama Through Hawaii*, Tax Mgm't. (BNA) No. 1450, at 1450.01 (2011) [hereinafter M. L. Nachbar, "Alabama Through Hawaii"] (citing P. W. Bernstein, *States Are Going Down Industrial Policy Lane* [Mar. 5, 1984], Fortune, at 112).
85. P.D. Enrich, *The Future of State Taxation*, 73–74 (D. Brunori ed., 1998) (Urban Institute Press).
86. M.L. Nachbar, *Alabama Through Hawaii*, *supra* note 84, at 1450.01-1450.02; see also M.L. Nachbar et al., *Business Credits and Incentives*, Tax Mgm't. (BNA) Nos. 1450, 1460, 1470, and 1480 (2011) [hereinafter M. L. Nachbar, "Credits and Incentives"].
87. See, e.g., D. Brunori, *Introduction to The Future of State Taxation*, 6 (1998) [hereinafter D. Brunori, *State Taxation*] (stating that "[c]ommentators generally agree that incentives violate the most basic principles of sound tax policy"); D. Brunori, *"The Politics of State Taxation": Thou Shalt Not Use Tax Incentives*, St. Tax Today 557 (2002) [hereinafter D. Brunori, *Thou Shalt Not Use Tax Incentives*] (stating tax incentives violate "the cardinal rule that tax systems should be designed so that they have a minimal impact on economic activity").
88. See D. Brunori, *Thou Shalt Not Use Tax Incentives, supra* note 87, at 557 (describing States, corporations, and consultants as actively in pursuit of granting and obtaining tax breaks); see also D. Brunori, *State Taxation, supra* note 87, at 6 (stating that tax incentives have increased "primarily because political leaders lack the will to reject them").

Illinois ended fiscal 2010 financially insolvent, owing USD 37.9 billion more than its combined assets.[89] But given the high unemployment nationwide, there is extreme pressure on "state governments to keep large employers happy as they look to recover some of the more than seven million jobs lost during the recession, and retain those remaining within their borders."[90] However, the State that wins the incentive wars also "loses" because as Enrich notes, "[b]usinesses have become increasingly adept at playing the states off against one another to stimulate more attractive offers."[91] For example, Caterpillar Inc.'s CEO sent a letter to Illinois' governor "warning that Texas, Nebraska, Virginia, and South Dakota were wooing the … firm to relocate its headquarters." However, the company's profitability and size make it unlikely that it would actually leave Illinois where it has been located since 1909.[92] On the other hand, Caterpillar does operate globally so the poor economic conditions and unemployment situation give it leverage.[93] Unfortunately, the economic conditions are leading to more subsidies "'even if there is no tangible economic benefit to society of giving them out.'"[94] Professor Thomas has estimated that States doled out about USD 64.8 billion in total State and local subsidies to businesses in 2005[95] and predicts increases for 2011.[96]

In 2010, Illinois granted USD 272.7 million in tax breaks to 67 companies entertaining offers from other States.[97] This was more than quadruple the incentive packages 44 companies received in 2006 and more than a doubling of the amounts received in 2009.[98] By mid-2011, the State had already "committed to USD 230 million in subsidies to 27 companies, including a USD 100 million deal for electronics manufacturer Motorola Mobility."[99] A deal with Sears was also negotiated because the company had threatened to "move its headquarters and 6,200 jobs out of Hoffman Estates, Illinois, when its current tax subsidies expire."[100] State officials agreed to these tax breaks while Illinois was grappling with its huge budget deficit.[101]

---

89. Illinois Statehouse News, *Auditor: Illinois Is Broke, Really*, WJBC, (Jul. 29, 2011), wjbc.com/auditor-illinois-is-broke-really. Three other States including New Jersey had deficits when comparing debts to all assets. *Ibid.*
90. M. Hirsch, *Business to States: Make Us an Offer We Can't Refuse*, The Fiscal Times, (Jun. 13, 2011), www.thefiscaltimes.com/Articles/2011/06/13/Business-to-States-Make-Us-an-Offer-We-Cant-Refuse.
91. P.D. Enrich, *Saving the States*, *supra* note 60, at 395.
92. M. Hirsch, *supra* note 90. "[C]ompanies asking for tax breaks or subsidies often … are just jockeying for the best deal. …" *Ibid.*
93. *Ibid.*
94. *Ibid.*
95. K.P. Thomas, *supra* note 27, at 107.
96. M. Hirsch, *supra* note 90. Professor Thomas "has assembled data showing that states doled out USD 70 billion worth of fiscal incentives and subsidies to businesses in 2010. He has no estimates yet for 2011, but anticipates the dollar amounts will increase." *Ibid.*
97. M. Hirsch, *supra* note 90; see also D. Mercer, *Illinois Businesses Reap Huge Tax Breaks*, Chi. Sun-Times, (May 21, 2011), www.suntimes.com/business/5519860-420/illinois-businesses-reap-huge-tax-breaks.html.
98. D. Mercer, *supra* note 97.
99. M. Hirsch, *supra* note 90.
100. *Ibid.* "Gov. Pat Quinn signed tax-break legislation … aimed at keeping CME Group Inc. and Sears Holdings Corp. from leaving the state, [and] those two major employers announced they would stay put." K. Bergen, *Quinn Signs Sears–CME Tax Breaks Into Law*, Chi. Trib.,

This proliferation is occurring throughout the United States despite criticism regarding the effectiveness of state tax incentives coming from a myriad of economic studies.[102] While "[s]tate and local governments continue to demonstrate a seemingly limitless enthusiasm for economic development incentives ... economists deride [such incentives] as fiscally irresponsible and irrational."[103] At the National Economic Policy Implications of State Tax Incentive Competition Senate Subcommittee Hearing, Professor Fisher testified that the tax incentive competition engaged in by the states is, at its best, a zero-sum game because it "merely move[s] economic activity from one state to another" with no net gain on either the national or local level.[104] Any influx of jobs and investment "won" through incentive wars by one locality is offset by a corresponding loss to another as seen in the Illinois story. Tax incentive competition quite possibly can be a negative-sum game that produces a net loss.[105]

Several studies described in *Unleashing Capitalism*[106] examine whether the benefits of these kinds of tax incentives outweigh the costs.[107] Arguably, development

---

(Dec. 16, 2011), articles.chicagotribune.com/2011-12-16/business/chi-quinn-signs-searscme-tax-breaks-into-law-20111216_1_cme-and-cboe-sears-cme-employee-income-taxes; see also D. McKinney, *Quinn Signs Tax Break Bill to Keep Sears*, CME in State, Chi. Sun-Times (Dec. 16, 2011), www.suntimes.com/news/metro/9487172-418/quinn-signs-tax-break-bill-to-keep-sears-cme-in-state.html, 4:52 PM.

101. D. Mercer, *supra* note 97.

102. See K.J. Stark & D.J. Wilson, *What Do We Know About the Interstate Economic Effects of State Tax Incentives?*, 4 Geo. J.L. & Pub. Pol'y 133, 163 (2006) for an excellent introduction to the literature.

103. N.S. Garnett, *The Neglected Political Economy of Eminent Domain*, 105 Mich. L. Rev. 101, 140 (2006). "A sampling of studies that have focused on individual tax incentive plans ... found little correlation between the amount of tax benefit received and growth in employment which resulted." S.L. Jarrell et al., *Law and Economics of Regulating Local Economic Development Incentives*, 41 *Wake Forest L. Rev.* 805, 826 (2006) (citations omitted). Enrich describes the States as being:" caught in a classic prisoners' dilemma. If all the states would refrain from deploying location incentives for business, then they all could retain more robust tax bases to support other governmental functions. But, if the other states are going to offer a widening array of tax breaks, then none can afford the costs – more political than economic – of abstaining. As a result, incentives proliferate, leaving all the states worse off." P.D. Enrich, *Saving the States*, *supra* note 60, at 396.

104. P. Fischer, *The National Economic Policy Implications of State Tax Incentive Competition: Hearing on "Cuno and Competitiveness: Where to Draw the Line" Before the Subcomm. on Int'l Trade of the S. Comm. on Finance*, [2006], 109th Cong. 2 (statement of Peter Fisher) [hereinafter Statement of P. Fisher]. A 2004 study concluded that selective incentives merely reallocate resources rather than generate real economic growth. P.T. Calcagno & F. Hefner, *State Targeting of Business Investment: Does Targeting Increase Corporate Tax Revenue?*, 37 J. Regional Analysis & Pol'y 90 (2007).

105. Brief of Amicus Curiae Economics & Public Policy Professors et al. in Support of Respondents at 10 *DaimlerChrysler Corp. v. Cuno*, 547 U.S. 332 (2006) (Nos. 04-1704, 04-1724), 2006 WL 189794 at *10.

106. P.T. Calcagno (ed.), *Unleashing Capitalism: A Prescription for Economic Prosperity in South Carolina*," 129–149 (2009) [hereinafter P. T. Calcagno, "Unleashing Capitalism"].

107. See, e.g., M.L. Burstein & A.J. Rolnick, *Congress Should End the Economic War Among the States*, Fed. Reserve Bank of Minneapolis, (Jan. 1, 1995), www.minneapolisfed.org/publications_papers/ar/index.cfm, (under "Annual Report Essays" for 1994); Weekly Letter by J. Mauey & M.M. Spiegel, *Is State and Local Competition for Firms Harmful?*, Fed. Reserve Bank of S.F., (Aug. 4, 1995), www.minneapolisfed.org/publications_papers/studies/econwar/frbsf.cfm; T.J. Bartik, *Evaluating the Impacts of Local Economic Development Policies on Local*

incentives provide the greatest benefit to high unemployment areas, yet State governments often attract firms to areas with low unemployment.[108] Although the ultimate goal of targeted incentives is to create jobs[109] and to increase economic growth, a 2001 study found no evidence of overall economic growth in-state GDP or employment in measuring over 2,000 programs across all States.[110] The study by Peters and Fisher suggests that "many public officials appear to believe that they can influence the course of their state or local economies through incentives and subsidies to a degree far beyond anything supported by even the most optimistic evidence."[111]

As one example, States compete heavily to attract business from the film industry believing that the production company's activities produce a ripple effect of income and subsequent tax revenue from the local economy.[112] However, studies of the various State tax incentives granted to the film industry do not support this assertion. The Connecticut Department of Economic and Community Development found that the State only received about USD 0.08 in tax revenue per dollar spent on 13 projects between the beginning of July 2006 and the end of September 2007.[113] The State Senate Fiscal Agency of Michigan reported that in 2008, the generation of USD "10 million in tax receipts" from films cost the State about USD 127 million[114] and the Department of Revenue in Wisconsin determined "that the state would likely see a net loss in revenue" from their tax incentive bill proposal.[115]

Previously, few States were performing cost-benefit analyzes of their Economic Development Incentive programs as it was "in the local and state politicians' interests to bid for the businesses ... to stay in the economic development game."[116] However, the growing trend is for States to increase reporting and oversight requirements and to perform more rigorous analysis.[117] "Over the past few years, nearly every State has

---

Economic Outcomes: What Has Been Done and What Is Doable?, (W.E. Upjohn Inst. for Employment Research, Working Paper No. 03-89 (2002)).

108. T.J. Bartik, *Jobs, Productivity, and Local Development: What Implications does Economic Research have for the Role of Government?*, 47 Nat'l Tax J 847 (1994).
109. A 2002 study of selective incentives in Ohio found that the number of new jobs promised by a targeted business was the major factor in determining whether or not that firm received the incentive. T.M. Gabe & D.S. Kraybill, *The Effect of State Economic Development Incentives on Employment Growth of Establishments*, 42 J. Regional Sci. 703 (2002).
110. M. Saiz, *Using Program Attributes to Measure and Evaluate State Economic Development Strategies*, 15 Econ. Dev. Q 45 (2001).
111. A. Peters & P. Fisher, *The Failures of Economic Development Incentives*, 70 J. Am. Plan. Ass'n 27, 35 (2004).
112. K. Cobb, *Roll the Credits... and the Tax Incentives*, FedGazette, (Sep. 1, 2006), www.minneapolisfed.org/research/pub_display.cfm?id=1309.
113. P.T. Calcagno, *Unleashing Capitalism*, *supra* note 106, at 143 (citing S. Christopherson & N. Rightor, *The Creative Economy as 'Big Business': Evaluating State Strategies to Lure Film Makers*, 29 J. Plan. Educ. & Res. 336).
114. P. T. Calcagno, *Unleashing Capitalism*, *supra* note 106, at 143.
115. K. Cobb, *supra* note 112.
116. S. L. Jarrell et al., *supra* note 103, at 823. "While billions of dollars have been spent on EDI across the country in the last ten to fifteen years, states prefer not to evaluate tax incentive programs." *Ibid.*, at 822-23.
117. R. Weiss, *States Seek to Manage the Cost of Tax Credits in the Current Economic Environment*, 20 J. Multistate Tax'n & Incentives 6 (2011). States such as California, Colorado, Iowa, Kansas,

examined its tax credit and incentives programs—the savviest States have ... adjust[ed] their programs to reflect a new reality for job creation and investment projects . ...."[118] In the aftermath of the economic crisis and the budget deficits that followed, "efforts are directed at either (1) reducing or limiting the extent to which taxpayers may claim credits, or (2) evaluating existing incentive programs to determine whether the tax credits provided are accomplishing essential goals."[119] Moreover, States are establishing Incentive Review Commissions to provide additional oversight for incentive programs such as ongoing analysis of the efficacy of incentives and the performance of recipients (essentially continuing cost-benefit analysis).[120]

Forty-three States and the District of Columbia now produce their own tax expenditure reports;[121] however, these reports vary greatly in the usefulness of their information.[122] Most States' reports omit some piece of essential information, such as major taxes, the actual law authorizing the tax expenditure, the tax expenditures' cost, or the number of companies that actually benefit from these tax expenditures.[123] "Two States, Arkansas and New Hampshire, fail to make their report accessible to the public through means such as posting it on the Internet."[124]

"Estimating aggregate state and local subsidies in the US is a difficult proposition because of the lack of transparency at all subnational levels of government."[125] Historically, the approval process for many of the tax credit and other subsidy programs had been conducted behind closed doors "with little opportunity for community input."[126] However, Good Jobs First reports that some States are now holding public hearings to provide for resident participation and facilitate accountability.[127] Minnesota, Connecticut, and Kansas, for example, have opened up the approval process of subsidy grants to the public and set out qualifications such as minimum

---

New Jersey, New York, Ohio, Oklahoma, and Texas undertook studies of their incentive programs and modified legislation to reduce and eliminate ineffective credits and establish better qualifications. *Ibid.*

118. M.F. LaFaver & J. Hoffman, *Credits and Incentives: Where Have We Been and Where are We Going?*, 21 J. Multistate Tax'n & Incentives 14 (2011).
119. R. Weiss, *supra* note 117, at 6.
120. *Ibid.*, at 18–44. Arizona, Missouri, Oklahoma, and Washington have recently created such Commissions. *Ibid.*
121. M. Leachman, D. Grundman & N. Johnson, *Center on Budget and Policy Priorities, Promoting State Budget Accountability Through Tax Expenditure Reporting*, 3 (2011) www.cbpp.org/cms/index.cfm?fa=view&id=3491 (select "PDF of this report"). The seven States that "produce no regular tax expenditure report" are "Alabama, Alaska, Indiana, Nevada, New Mexico, South Dakota, and Wyoming." *Ibid.*, at 5. In 2011, although both legislative houses in New Mexico unanimously passed "a bill to create a tax expenditure budget," the governor ultimately vetoed it. *Ibid.*
122. *Ibid.*, at 3.
123. *Ibid.*, at 4.
124. *Ibid.*
125. K.P. Thomas, *supra* note 27, at 102. Professor Thomas concluded that total State and local subsidies for the US in 2005 was USD 64.8 billion with investment incentives accounting for approximately USD 46.8 billion. *Ibid.*, at 107.
126. *Key Reforms: Accountability in the Approval Process*, Good Jobs First, (Jan. 24, 2012), www.goodjobsfirst.org/accountable-development/key-reforms-accountability-approval-process.
127. *Ibid.*

contribution and job creation.[128] A majority of States are setting out qualification metrics for subsidy and tax credit eligibility.[129]

States are increasingly interested in more than just job creation and are examining the quality of jobs a subsidy will create.[130] Job quality standards are the most widely enacted subsidy reform with over 42 States requiring that jobs created by subsidized companies meet certain wage levels, be full-time or provide health insurance.[131] "Clawbacks," recapture provisions requiring taxpayers "to recapture or reimburse the [state] for benefits" received if they fail to meet certain requirements, are also becoming a more prominent feature in many States' economic incentive legislation.[132] Almost 30 States utilize clawback provisions, including Kentucky, South Carolina, Vermont, Nebraska, and Indiana.[133] These clawback provisions range in effect from simple penalties to severe or proportional demands for repayment due to the failure to meet expectations.[134] Provisions also differ in the scope of their application. Minnesota, for example, uses recapture provisions for all business subsidies at the State and local level.[135]

Although current econometric research does not provide a definitive conclusion concerning the economic effects of State tax incentives, I agree with the European Commission that harmful tax competition exists. A 1996 Commission Report dealing with tax competition showed a higher relative weight of taxes on less-mobile personal income as compared to taxes on corporate income and consumption and stated that this was partly due to harmful tax competition.[136] In 1997, the Commission proposed the adoption of a common policy to tackle harmful tax competition.[137] The Code of

128. *Ibid.*; see also T. Anderson, *Question of the Month: What Mechanisms do States Use to Review the Efficacy and/or Oversee the Use of Their Tax Incentives for Businesses?*, (May 2011), *Stateline Midwest* (Midwestern Office of The Council of State Governments, Illinois), at 5, www.csgmidwest.org/publications/documents/0511slmw.pdf.
129. M.L. Nachbar, "Credits and Incentives," *supra* note 86.
130. *Key Reforms: Job Quality Standards*, Good Jobs First, www.goodjobsfirst.org/accountable-development/key-reforms-job-quality-standards, (Jan. 24, 2011).
131. *Ibid.* "Only 51 programs (in 28 states) require that a subsidized employer make available healthcare coverage of some kind, and only 31 of these require that the employer contribute to the cost of the premium." *Ibid.*
132. M.L. Nachbar, *Alabama Through Hawaii*, *supra* note 84, at 1450.05 B. An increasing number of states are both adopting and strengthening clawback provisions in their subsidy programs. *Ibid.*
133. *Ibid.*; see also *Key Reforms: Clawbacks*, Good Jobs First, www.goodjobsfirst.org/accountable-development/key-reforms-clawbacks, (Jan. 24, 2011). Ohio legislated a clawback provision with respect to its Enterprise Zone Credits and Incentives that allows a municipality to assert a tax lien against the taxpayer's property. M.L. Nachbar et al., *Business Credits and Incentives: Missouri Through Oklahoma, Tax Mgm't.* (BNA) No. 1470 (2011), at 1470.16 D-1.
134. *Key Reforms: Clawbacks*, *supra* note 133.
135. *Ibid.*; see also M.L. Nachbar, *Idaho Through Mississippi*, *supra* note 5; T. Anderson, *supra* note 128, at 5.
136. European Commission, *Taxation in the European Union: Report on the Development of Tax Systems* (1996), COM 546 final (22 Oct. 1996) reprinted in 25 Intertax 23, 26 (1997). Harmful tax competition had forced Member States to reduce taxes on capital and increase taxes on labor. *Ibid.*
137. W. Schön, *supra* note 70, at 242 (citing European Commission, *Towards Tax Coordination in the European Union; A Package to Tackle Harmful Tax Competition* (1997), COM 495 final (15 Oct. 1997).

Conduct for Business Taxation was established by the Economy and Finance Council[138] based on this recommendation from the European Commission with regard to the elimination of harmful tax competition.[139] The Code of Conduct is not binding on the Member States, but those adopting it agree to reduce any existing tax measures that constitute harmful competition and to refrain from instituting any similar measures in the future.[140] Although not a legally binding document, the Code of Conduct carries great political force.[141]

In the United States, residents of the States granting such harmful tax incentives have started challenging these programs in court.[142] One of their claims is that the resulting tax revenue reductions shift the tax burden to them.[143] The plaintiffs also attack the constitutionality of these State tax subsidies used to encourage investment within a State, using the dormant Commerce Clause.[144] In §2.03, I analyze whether effective challenges to these targeted tax incentives can be brought in the United States given the current standing doctrine.

---

138. Conclusions of the ECOFIN Council Meeting on December 1, 1997 Concerning Taxation Policy, OJ (C 2) 1,1, 1998:
"The Council of Ministers is comprised of representatives of the Member States, usually the ministers responsible for the subject matter under discussion .... [T]he Member States' Finance Ministers meet with respect to tax and other economic matters and are known as the Economy and Finance Council (ECOFIN) .... In tax matters, the Council is the principal lawmaking body of the Community, but it can only act on a proposal from the Commission". T.A. Kaye, *Tax Discrimination*, *supra* note 68, at 201 (citations omitted).
139. Resolution of the Council and the Representatives of the Governments of the Member States, Meeting Within the Council of December 1, 1997 on a Code of Conduct for Business Taxation, OJ (C 2) 2,2, 1998 [hereinafter Code of Conduct].
140. *Ibid.*, at 4. Generally speaking, the Code of Conduct requires the following: (1) Member States must refrain from creating new "harmful" tax measures (known as standstill); (2) all existing tax policies must be examined for compliance–those policies that would be categorized as "harmful" by the Code must be amended to conform (known as rollback); (3) the signatories to the Code must inform other signatories of "harmful" policies–there must be transparency; and (4) the signatories to the Code and the Council participate in ongoing evaluation of policies by a tax policy group known as the Primarolo group. *Ibid.*
141. For example, Ireland repealed its preferential 10% tax rate for certain manufacturing activity and replaced the targeted incentive with an overall corporate tax rate of 12.5% in 2003. M. Mikiciuk, *Foreign Direct Investment Success in Ireland: Can Poland Duplicate Ireland's Economic Success Based on Foreign Direct Investment Policies?*, 14 *U. Miami Int'l & Comp. L. Rev.* 65, 106 (2006).
142. See S. L. Jarrell et al., *supra* note 103, at 809 (Lawsuits around the country have challenged the legality of EDI under state constitutions and other local laws.).
143. See, e.g., *Blinson v. State*, 651 S.E. 2d 268, 273 (N.C. App. 2007) (Plaintiffs contend that their status as taxpayers, suffering an increased tax burden as a result of the Dell incentives, is sufficient to provide plaintiffs with standing.).
144. *Ibid.* ([T]he disputed incentives and subsidies ... discriminated against interstate commerce in violation of the [d]ormant Commerce Clause.). The dormant Commerce Clause is a doctrine that has been read into the Constitution's affirmative grant of Congress's power to regulate commerce. See U.S. CONST. Art. I, § 8, cl. 3. See generally L.H. Tribe, *supra* note 47, § 6-2, at 1030 (discussing the dormant Commerce Clause).

§2.03 PROCEDURES FOR CHALLENGING TAX INCENTIVES

[A] United States Standing Doctrine

In *Cuno v. DaimlerChrysler, Inc.*, the Sixth Circuit Court of Appeals invalidated Ohio's investment tax credit, finding it discriminatory against interstate commerce.[145] Although the US Supreme Court heard the case,[146] it ultimately concluded that the "state taxpayers have no standing under Article III to challenge State tax or spending decisions simply by virtue of their status as taxpayers."[147] Thus, in May 2006, the Supreme Court dismissed the plaintiffs' challenge to the Ohio tax credit without discussing the merits of the case.[148] Therefore, questions regarding the constitutionality of State investment tax credits and other corporate tax incentives remain unanswered.

The *Cuno* decision clarifies that being a State taxpayer is not sufficient for standing under Article III of the US Constitution to challenge the State's tax incentive programs as Commerce Clause violations.[149] A State taxpayer must establish that he has sustained a direct injury as a result of the challenged tax scheme before such a taxpayer may bring suit in federal court.[150] The injury cannot be one that is common with people generally, nor can it be an injury that is hypothetical. The States themselves may be in the best position to bring a challenge to State tax incentives because they are the "most direct losers in the ongoing incentive competition."[151] However, it appears that the States have no interest in challenging tax incentives as more than half the States filed an amicus brief together in support of petitioners'

145. *Wilkins v. Cuno*, 386 F.3d at 746. In *Cuno*, the Sixth Circuit ruled on two Ohio tax incentives granted to DaimlerChrysler to build a plant in Toledo. *Ibid.* The court held that the property tax exemptions did not violate the dormant Commerce Clause because it did not favor in-state activity. *Ibid.*, at 747.
146. *Wilkins v. Cuno*, 547 U.S. at 338, 340.
147. *Ibid.*, at 346.
148. *Ibid.*, at 338 ("We are obligated before reaching this Commerce Clause question to determine whether the taxpayers who objected to the credit have standing to press their complaint in federal court. We conclude that they do not, and we therefore can proceed no further.").
149. Plaintiffs in *Wilkins v. Cuno* argued that they had standing as state taxpayers pursuant to the Court's holding in *Flast v. Cohen*, 392 U.S. 83, 105-06 (1968). *Wilkins v. Cuno*, 547 U.S. at 347. Plaintiffs argued that there was a "sufficiently close nexus between the plaintiffs' taxpayer status and the claims that they assert." Respondents' Brief at 11, *Cuno*, 547 U.S. 332 (Nos. 04-1704 & 04-1724).
150. *Wilkins v. Cuno*, 547 U.S. at 345 (citing *Doremus v. Bd. of Educ. of the Borough of Hawthorne*, 342 U.S. 429, 433-34 (1952)).
151. P.D. Enrich, *Saving the States*, *supra* note 60, at 418–419 (stating that the incentive system leaves the States "with diminished and distorted revenue capacities and without appreciable compensating economic gains"). Professor Enrich also notes that the Commerce Clause's "primary focus concerns the structural dangers posed to the federal system by excessive state interference with the dynamics of the national economy." *Ibid.*, at 419. Thus, "the states have a peculiarly direct and compelling interest in the enforcement of this structural safeguard of federalism." *Ibid.*

argument that Ohio's investment tax credit did not violate the dormant Commerce Clause.[152]

State court is the alternative venue to pursue these challenges and the requirements to sue in-state court may not be quite as stringent. In *Asarco, Inc.*, the Court distinguished between a State taxpayer's standing in-state court and federal court,[153] explaining that "the constraints of Article III do not apply to state courts ... [which] are not bound by the limitations of a case-or-controversy or other federal rules of justiciability even when they address issues of federal law, as when they are called upon to interpret the Constitution."[154] Because States are not bound to adhere to the "case-or-controversy" doctrine, a State court may be more likely to address the merits of a state taxpayer's challenge to a State tax incentive.[155]

Of course, the standing rules vary from State to State.[156] For example, it appears that the rules for taxpayer standing in New York State courts are relatively lax, requiring only that "the litigant have something truly at stake in a genuine controversy."[157] Furthermore, "citizen-taxpayers need not demonstrate an injury-in-fact to acquire standing ... [but] may bring suit to prevent the unlawful expenditure of State funds 'whether or not such person is or may be affected or specially aggrieved' by the challenged action.... [However,] a plaintiff's claims must have a 'sufficient nexus to fiscal activities of the State' in order to confer standing."[158] Thus, in what is known as "The Pork Lawsuit," taxpayers in New York are claiming "that the appropriation and use of State funds to promote economic development through private entities violates Article VII § 8 of the New York State Constitution."[159] However, the New York Court of Appeals (the highest NY State court) issued a decision on November 21, 2011, basically dismissing the lawsuit (although not on the basis of lack of standing).[160] Two judges

152. Brief of Florida et al. as Amici Curiae Supporting Petitioners, *Wilkins v. Cuno*, 547 U.S. 332 (2006) (No. 04-1724) (decided together with *DaimlerChrysler Corp. v. Cuno* (No. 04-1704)). The list of state signatories to this amicus brief is as follows: Florida, Alabama, Arizona, Arkansas, California, Colorado, Connecticut, Delaware, Georgia, Guam, Hawaii, Idaho, Illinois, Indiana, Iowa, Kentucky, Maine, Maryland, Massachusetts, Michigan, Missouri, Nebraska, Nevada, New York, North Dakota, Northern Mariana Islands, Oklahoma, Oregon, Pennsylvania, Puerto Rico, South Carolina, South Dakota, Tennessee, Texas, Utah, Vermont, Washington, and Wisconsin. *Ibid.*
153. *Asarco Inc. v. Kadish*, 490 U.S. 605 (1989).
154. *Ibid.*, at 617.
155. K.L. Dietrich, *Saving the States from Unsuitable Plaintiffs: Uncovering the Lack of Standing in Challengers to State Income Tax Credits for Business Development*, 36 Cumb. L. Rev. 343, 345.
156. See generally H. Hershkoff, *State Courts and the "Passive Virtues": Rethinking the Judicial Function*, 114 *Harv. L. Rev.* 1833 (2001). "[J]udicial practice in some states differs—and differs radically—from the federal model .... Many state courts do conform ... to the Article III model." *Ibid.*, at 1836.
157. *Saratoga County Chamber of Commerce, Inc. v. Pataki*, 798 N.E.2d 1047, 1052 (N.Y. 2003). See generally J. Carr & C. Griffith, *Establishing Standing in the Ohio Incentives Case: An Insurmountable Task?*, 39 *St. Tax Notes* 651 (2006).
158. *Pataki*, 798 N.E.2d at 1053 (quoting *Rudder v. Pataki*, 711 N.E.2d 978, 982 (N.Y. 1999)); see also N.Y. STATE FIN. LAW § 123-b (McKinney 2012).
159. In the Matter of the Application of *Lee Bordeleau, et al. v. New York*, 881 N.Y.S.2d 362, 362 (N.Y. Sup. Ct. 27 February 2009), *aff'd in part* and *rev'd in part*, 905 N.Y.S.2d 307, *rev'd and claim dismissed*, No. 190, slip op. 8444 (N.Y. Nov. 21, 2011).
160. *Bordeleau*, No. 190, slip op. 8444.

dissented with Judge Smith stating: "It is an illusion—one that seems to have the persistence of original sin—that prosperity can be attained by taking money from taxpayers and handing it to favored businesses."[161] He further complained: "[W]hen our Legislature commits the precise folly that a provision of our Constitution was written to prevent, and this Court responds by judicially repealing the constitutional provision, I think I am entitled to be annoyed."[162]

Litigation over State tax laws that provide tax advantages to in-state business activity is underway in many states. In North Carolina, taxpayers challenged the USD 279 million tax incentive package given to Dell Inc., to build a computer manufacturing and distribution facility in the state.[163] Taxpayers relied on the Commerce Clause and various State constitutional arguments to challenge the tax incentive package.[164] The North Carolina Superior Court dismissed the complaint due to lack of standing, the Court of Appeals affirmed the trial court's conclusion,[165] and the Supreme Court of North Carolina denied the petition for discretionary review.[166] The challenge to a USD 165 million economic development incentive package[167] granted to a wholly owned subsidiary of Google, Inc.[168] alleged violations of numerous provisions of the North Carolina Constitution.[169] On February 3, 2011, the Supreme Court of North Carolina affirmed that the plaintiffs lacked standing to assert the discrimination claims.[170] Notwithstanding that the procedural rules in some States are more lenient, these types of cases may have a fate similar to those in North Carolina, where State trial judges have ruled that plaintiffs lacked standing to challenge the tax incentives.[171] Thus, it is unclear whether the US Supreme Court will ever send a clear message to the States on whether positive location incentives pass the constitutional test.

161. *Ibid.*, at 11 (Smith, J. dissenting). "A recent article restates well-established economic doctrine: 'The idea of government intervention to influence the composition of a country's output has long been derided by economists for breeding inefficiency, reducing competition, encouraging lobbying and saddling countries with factories producing products nobody wants.'" *Ibid.*, (quoting Tinker, Tailor: Economists Reconsider the Merits of Industrial Policy, but "Some Flaws Are Hard to Fix," *The Economist*, Oct. 1, 2011, www.economist.com/node/21530958).
162. *Bordeleau*, No. 190, slip. op. at 12 (Smith, J. dissenting).
163. *Blinson v. North Carolina*, 651 S.E.2d 268 (N.C. Ct. App. 2007).
164. K.M. Hobart, *Judge Dismisses Lawsuit over Dell Incentives Package*, 40 St. Tax Notes 669 (2006). The judge was "not content to base his decision on standing alone," and "went on to dismiss the Commerce Clause claims as lacking substantive merit." *Ibid.*
165. *Blinson*, 651 S.E.2d at 273.
166. *Blinson v. North Carolina*, 661 S.E.2d 240, (N.C. 2008).
167. NC Institute for Constitutional Law, *The Incentive Game: North Carolina Local Economic Development Incentives* (2007), 8 (on file with author).
168. M. Blocher, *NCICL Files Lawsuit Challenging the Constitutionality of State Economic Subsidies to Google, Inc.*, (Jul. 25, 2007), /blog.news-record.com/staff/capblog/ncccl072507.doc; see also North Carolina Institute for Constitutional Law, *supra* note 167, at 8.
169. M. Blocher, *supra* note 168.
170. *Munger v. North Carolina*, No. 130PA10, (N.C. February 4, 2011), ncicl.org/litigation/6.
171. D. Brunori, *Cuno—The Right Decision? Unfortunately*, 40 St. Tax Notes 723 (2006).

[B] Comparative Analysis

Both the European Union and the United States have procedures in place to allow challenges to tax incentives that might obstruct the efficient functioning of the internal market.[172] But in the EU, the Member State bears the burden of proving that the proposed tax incentive does not distort the internal market.[173] Any new incentive is subject to a formal investigation by the European Commission to determine whether it is compatible with the internal market.[174]

The United States does not, however, have a governmental entity that is analogous to the European Commission. The closest analogy would be the Multistate Tax Commission (MTC) that was formed in 1967 by the States "in response to the threat of federal legislation to restrict and regulate state business taxation."[175] Its purpose is "to study state tax issues and to recommend uniform tax laws and regulations to the states."[176] This entity was not Congressionally-sanctioned and does not have binding regulatory authority.[177]

Appropriate parties have access to a Member State's national court system as well as to the European Commission.[178] Although the Commission has exclusive jurisdiction to decide whether or not State aid is compatible with the internal market and the Treaty,[179] the national courts have the authority to determine whether or not a certain

172. G.A. Bermann et al., *Cases and Materials on European Union Law*, 1079–80, 1085–86 (3d ed., 2011) (Thomson West); see Art. 108 TFEU.

173. Article 108 TFEU; G.A. Bermann, *supra* note 172, at 1079. For example:
"If, after giving notice to the parties concerned to submit their comments, the Commission finds that aid granted by a State or through State resources is not compatible with the internal market ... it shall decide that the State concerned shall abolish or alter such aid within a period of time to be determined by the Commission". Art. 108 TFEU, para. 2.

174. Article 108 TFEU, para. 3:
"The Commission shall be informed, in sufficient time to enable it to submit its comments, of any plans to grant or alter aid. If it considers that any such plan is not compatible with the internal market having regard to Article 107, it shall without delay initiate the procedure provided for in paragraph 2. The Member State concerned shall not put its proposed measures into effect until this procedure has resulted in a final decision". *Ibid.*

175. M.A. Sullivan, *supra* note 82; see W.B. Hildreth et al., *Interstate Tax Uniformity and the Multistate Tax Commission*, 58 Nat'l Tax J. 575 (2005) (describing the origins of the MTC).

176. M.A. Sullivan, *supra* note 82.

177. However, it was found to be constitutional. W.B. Hildreth, *supra* note 175 (citing U.S. *Steel Corp. v. Multistate Tax Comm'n*, 434 U.S. 452 (1978)).

178. Article 108 TFEU, para. 2. "If the State concerned does not comply with this decision within the prescribed time, the Commission or any other interested State may, in derogation from the provisions of Articles 258 and 259, refer the matter to the Court of Justice of the European Union direct." *Ibid.* "If the Member State fails to comply, the Commission or an interested Member State may refer the matter to the Court of Justice." G.A. Bermann et al., *supra* note 172, at 1079.

179. ECJ, *Steinike und Wenlig v. Germany*, Case No. 78/96 ECR 595. The Court held that the purpose of Art. 88 (now Art. 108) was to keep aid under the constant scrutiny of the Commission and that a finding of incompatibility was to be a result of a procedure that is the Commission's responsibility to initiate. *Ibid.*

proposal constitutes State aid.[180] Furthermore, the Commission may bring a Member State to the Court of Justice.[181]

In the United States, it appears that the standing doctrine is effectively keeping most parties from challenging the various States' tax incentives.[182] Although, some commentators believe that the standing rules are less stringent in the State courts, taxpayers have failed to overcome the "standing" barrier in North Carolina.[183] The same fate has befallen cases filed in Minnesota and Nebraska.[184] Furthermore, even when standing is not a barrier to consideration of these issues, there is no guarantee that the courts will find a violation of the dormant Commerce Clause.[185]

§2.04 LESSONS LEARNED FROM THE EUROPEAN UNION

European Union State aid policy enables Member States to resist protectionist pleas from their companies. As eloquently phrased by Professor Maduro, State aid controls can "be seen as an instrument of external discipline self-imposed by the States to thwart instances of likely malfunction in their political processes that cannot be domestically prevented."[186] The EU is experiencing a downward trend in the use of tax incentives and much less use of the targeted tax incentives utilized so widely by the American States due to the procedures that have been put in place. What are the options for the United States given our longstanding policy of no national subsidy control?[187]

---

180. C. Bellamy et al., *European Community Law of Competition*, 1271 (5th ed., P.M. Roth ed., 2001) (Sweet & Maxwell, Ltd.).
181. If, after giving notice to the parties concerned to submit their comments, the Commission finds that aid granted by a State ... is not compatible with the internal market having regard to Article 107 ... it shall decide that the State concerned shall abolish or alter such aid .... If the State concerned does not comply with this decision within the prescribed time, the Commission or any other interested State may, in derogation from the provisions of Articles 258 and 259, refer the matter to the Court of Justice of the European Union direct. (Art. 108 TFEU, para. 2).
182. Respondents' Brief at 7, *Cuno*, 547 U.S. 332 (Nos. 04-1704 and 04-1724). *Cuno*, 547 U.S. at 347.
183. K.M. Hobart, *supra* note 164 (citation omitted).
184. *Olson v. Minnesota*, 742 N.W.2d 681 (Minn. Ct. App. 2007). Similarly, a former Nebraska State Senator challenged Nebraska's law that gave "tax credits to companies that invest at least $3 million and create at least [thirty] new full-time jobs in-state." C. Atkins & J.D. Henchman, *The Ohio Incentives Decision and the Quest for a 21st Century Tax System*, 40 *St. Tax Notes* 945, Doc. No. 2006-11356 (LEXIS). The challengers contended that the bill promotes discrimination against small businesses and favors in-state over out-of-state businesses. *Ibid.* Their challenge rested on both the Commerce Clause of the U.S. Constitution and the Nebraska Constitution's guarantee of proportionate taxation. *Ibid.* This case was dismissed. *DeCamp v. Nebraska*, No. C1041981 (dismissed Mar. 7, 2005).
185. See e.g., *DIRECTV v. Treesh*, 487 F.3d 471 (6th Cir. 2007); see also *Commonwealth Edison Co. v. Montana*, 453 U.S. 609 (1981). The Supreme Court upheld a State's transparent and politically controversial attempt to shift tax burdens to outsiders by simultaneously reducing various in-state taxes and increasing a coal severance tax that out-of-state consumers principally paid, at least in the short run. *Ibid.*
186. M.P. Maduro, *Passion and Reason in European Integration*, 6 (2010), papers.ssrn.com/sol3/papers.cfm?abstract_id=1709950. "EU law on state aids is in fact aiding the states." *Ibid.*, at 6.
187. Two exceptions are the prohibition of discriminatory subsidies that impose a burden on interstate commerce and the requirements of the GATT/WTO. See Avi-Yonah, *supra* note 67, at 1666.

[A] The Congress

Although the Commerce Clause confers to Congress the authority to regulate State tax competition, Congress has for the most part declined to exercise such authority.[188] Occasional interventions have occurred such as in 1976, when "to prevent states from imposing ... potentially destructive taxes on interstate businesses such as railroads and airlines,"[189] Congress passed the Railroad Revitalization and Regulatory Reform Act. This law prohibited States from placing higher tax rates on property owned by railroads than on property owned by other commercial enterprises within the same jurisdiction.[190] In 1998, Congress passed the Internet Tax Freedom Act (ITFA), a law intended to curb state taxes on an "emerging technology" and "achieve neutrality in the taxation of electronic commerce."[191]

However, in response to the constitutional challenge raised in *Cuno,* some Members of Congress introduced the Economic Development Act of 2005 in the US House and Senate.[192] It allowed for "any State to provide to any person for economic development purposes tax incentives that otherwise would be the cause or source of discrimination against interstate commerce under the Commerce Clause of the United States Constitution...."[193] As demonstrated by this Congressional response to the potential finding of unconstitutionality of a state tax credit, it appears that Congress is only interested in legislation that reduces State taxes. Thus, it is unlikely that Congress will be willing to prevent a "race to the bottom" with any federal legislation. As I have written previously, unfortunately when State taxpayers turn to Congress, the result is that no one pays taxes.[194]

[B] The Judiciary

Given this historic reluctance of Congress to intervene in-state taxation, the US Supreme Court has been forced to examine issues similar to those now confronting the European Union. Thus, the US Supreme Court has intervened on occasion with State tax regimes through its jurisprudence. For example, in *Bacchus Imports, Ltd. V. Dias,* the Court struck down a Hawaiian law that granted a tax exemption for certain locally

---

188. See generally P.D. Enrich, "Saving the States," *supra* note 60.
189. T.F. Field, *supra* note 46, at 1213.
190. *Ibid.*, at 1213 n.13 (citing 49 U.S.C. § 11503).
191. *Ibid.*, at 1213; see also T.A. Kaye, *Tax Discrimination, supra* note 68, at 208. The Act ended up costing the States "billions in foregone revenues." *Ibid.* The Internet Freedom Act Amendments Act of 2007 extended the moratorium that had been imposed by the ITNA through November 2014. The Internet Tax Freedom Act Amendments Act of 2007, Pub. L. No. 110-108, 121 Stat. 1024 (2007).
192. H.R. 2471 and S.1066, 109th Cong. (2005). In the 110th Congress, the Senate has reintroduced the bill. S.914, 110th Cong. (2007); see M. A. Sullivan, *State Tax Incentives: Who Will Clean Up the Mess?*, 40 *St. Tax Notes* 331 (2006).
193. ABA Tax Section, *SALT Incentives–Will They Last in Light of Cuno?*, 9 (2006) "Because the Supreme Court dismissed the constitutional challenge in *Cuno*, it is unlikely this legislation will move forward until similar credits and incentives are endangered at a point in the future." *Ibid.*
194. T.A. Kaye, *Show Me the Money: Congressional Limitations on State Tax Sovereignty*, 35 Harv. J. on Legis. 149, 167 (1998).

produced liquors. The Court concluded that because the law had both "the purpose and effect of discriminating in favor of local products," it violated the Commerce Clause.[195] The Court rejected Hawaii's argument that the law was not intended to burden out-of-state suppliers of alcohol but instead to benefit local business. In doing so, the Court concluded that such discriminatory laws constituted nothing more than economic protectionism and thus were violative of a "central tenet of the Commerce Clause."[196]

Unfortunately, the Judiciary is not the solution either because the US Supreme Court is not obligated to hear every case.[197] The Supreme Court only grants certiorari in about 100 cases of the approximately 10,000 petitions filed per Term.[198] The Court's denials of certiorari show a lack of enthusiasm for State tax cases,[199] even though the Court's review is particularly significant in a constitutional challenge to a State tax system in order to send appropriate messages to the State legislatures.[200] Besides the seemingly insurmountable barrier that has been erected to keep challenges of State tax incentives from being heard, it was not clear that the Supreme Court would have found the Ohio tax credit unconstitutional even if they had agreed to consider the merits of the case. In fact, some commentators were predicting a finding of constitutionality by the Supreme Court.[201]

[C] "Soft Law"

Because of the difficulty of reaching unanimous agreement on EU tax legislation,[202] the use of non-legislative approaches, "soft law," has become accepted in the European Union.[203] The EU's Code of Conduct for Business Taxation is the first example of "soft

195. Bacchus Imports, *Ltd. v. Dias*, 468 U.S. 263, 273 (1984).
196. *Ibid.*, at 276.
197. The Court of Justice is obligated under the Treaty to take every case that is referred to it under Art. 267. TFEU: "Where any such question is raised in a case pending before a court or tribunal of a Member State against whose decisions there is no judicial remedy under national law, that court or tribunal shall bring the matter before the Court." *Ibid.*
198. Supreme Court of the U.S, "The Justices' Caseload," www.supremecourt.gov/about/justicecaseload.aspx, (Jan. 24, 2012).
199. See, e.g., *Lanco, Inc. v. Dir of Div. of Taxation*, 908 A.2d 176 (N.J. 2006), *cert. denied* 551 U.S. 1131 (2007); Tax Comm'r of the State of *W. Va. v. MBNA. Am Bank*, N.A., 640 S.E.2d 226 (W. Va. 2006), *cert. denied,* 551 U.S. 1141 (2007).
200. W.J. Quirk & C.R. Shaver, *Does Congress Put Federalism at Risk When It Limits the States' Power to Tax?*, 21 *St. Tax Notes* 649, 650–651 (2001) (citations omitted).
201. See, e.g., M. Coyle, *High Court to Hear Challenge to Company Tax Breaks* NAT'L L.J. (February 12, 2006), (explaining Walter Hellerstein's prediction that Ohio would prevail in the United States Supreme Court)(on file with author).
202. "[T]he Council shall, acting unanimously in accordance with a special legislative procedure and after consulting the European Parliament and the Economic and Social Committee, issue directives for the approximation of such laws, regulations or administrative provisions of the Members States as directly affect the establishment or functioning of the internal market". (Art. 115 TFEU)
203. *Communication from the Commission to the Council, the European Parliament and the Economic and Social Committee: Tax Policy in the European Union–Priorities for the Years Ahead* (2001), at 10, 22–23, COM 260 final, eur-lex.europa.eu/LexUriServ/LexUri

law" in the area of corporate taxation.[204] This effort was successful in that the Code provided a system to tackle the issue of harmful tax competition and the criteria in the Code made evaluation of specific tax regimes possible. The method of peer review performed by the Primarolo Group was an innovation for tax policy.[205] There is evidence of actual effects on Member States' tax policies.[206] "It would be politically difficult now to propose the same type of beggar-thy-neighbour regimes which were so popular until the mid-1990s."[207]

As the Multistate Tax Commission has been somewhat successful in its promotion of tax uniformity,[208] I previously suggested that the promulgation of a State Code of Conduct analogous to the European Union's Code of Conduct would be an appropriate and worthwhile project for the MTC.[209] The States have shown some willingness to cooperate when their revenue base is at stake as the Streamlined Sales and Use Tax Agreement (SSUTA) demonstrates.[210]

The Supreme Court has ruled that an out-of-state vendor is not obligated to "collect sales taxes for states in which they (the vendors) do not have nexus . . . ."[211] With the growth of Internet commerce, States became concerned that the Court's ruling would lead to substantial sales tax revenue loss, leading them to support the drafting of the SSUTA.[212] Although not a perfect solution,[213] it will reduce tax compliance and simplify sales and use tax administration among the SSUTA Member States.[214] The central focus of the SSUTA was to simplify the current sales and use tax systems, relying on an optional "agreement among the states to collect and remit sales tax to the taxing state."[215]

Serv.do?uri=COM:2001:0260:FIN:EN:PDF, (May 23, 2001); see also A.J. Rädler, *In Memoriam Kari S. Tikka 1944–2006*, 422–423 (E. Andersson et al. eds., 2007) (Suomalainen Lakimiesyhdistys).

204. C. Radaelli, *The Code of Conduct against Harmful Tax Competition: Open Method of Coordination in Disguise?*, 81 Pub. Admin. 513, 521 (2003).
205. *Ibid.*, at 526.
206. "[R]ecent changes in The Netherlands' intermediate royalty and interest companies, advance pricing agreements and advance ruling practices have been linked to the intention of the Dutch government to comply with the criteria listed by the code." *Ibid.*, at 527.
207. *Ibid.*, listed by the code." *Ibid.*, at 527.
208. W.B. Hildreth, *supra* note 175, at 583.
209. T.A. Kaye, *supra* note 42, at 153.
210. See K. Setze, *Federal Action Necessary for State Tax Uniformity, Say National Tax Association Speakers*, 36 St Tax Notes 630 (2005), Doc. No. 2005-11376 (LEXIS).
211. S. Maguire, *Cong. Research Serv.*, State Taxation of Internet Transactions, (R 41853, 2011), p.1.
212. *Ibid.* As of Jan. 1, 2011, 20 States are in compliance with the SSUTA through their laws, rules, regulations and policies, with 4 more States considered "associate members." Nineteen States are participating in the streamlining project but have not made sufficient changes in their state sales tax law to be considered "associate" members. *Ibid.*, at 5–6. For an up-to-date status report on membership, see *State Info, Streamlined Sales Tax Governing Board*, www.streamlinedsalestax.org/index.php?page=state-info.
213. B. Galle, *Designing Interstate Institutions: The Example of the Streamline Sales and Use Tax Agreement (SSUTA)*, 40 U.C. Davis L. Rev. 1381, 1401 (2007).
214. J.A. Swain, *State Sales and Use Tax Jurisdiction: An Economic Nexus Standard for the Twenty-First Century*, 38 Ga. L. Rev. 343, 371–373 (2003).
215. E.A. Ess, *Internet Taxation without Physical Representation?: States Seek Solution to Stop E-Commerce Sales Tax Shortfall*, 50 St Louis U.L.J 893, 907 (2006). The Agreement "establishes uniform definitions for taxable goods and services and requires that a participating state and

I previously proposed the formation of a group under the auspices of the MTC to promulgate a State Code of Conduct for Business Taxation analogous to the EU's Code of Conduct.[216] This State Code of Conduct would require abstention from targeted tax incentives. Given the State autonomy issues that exist in the United States, I think it would be impractical to advocate the prohibition of all subsidies. However, a prohibition on targeted tax incentives will still accomplish the goal of transparency and encourage States to compete on the basis of tax rates.

I believe that this proposal will indirectly reduce the size of direct subsidies. Take the example of the subsidy package offered ThyssenKrupp AG by Alabama in 2007 to build a USD 3.7 billion steel mill.[217] The USD 461 million in direct subsidies included land acquisition, site preparation, worker training, and road improvements.[218] An additional USD 350 million tax subsidy included relief from sales, property, and utility taxes by the State and local governments.[219] Perhaps the voters could swallow that package. But if the German company was also offered an additional cash grant of USD 350 million in lieu of the tax subsidy, I believe that there would have been a greater outcry from the Alabamans. Actually the check would have to be in excess of USD 350 million as the deal included a promise that the company will not have to pay any state corporate income tax "for the next thirty years unless its tax liability exceeds USD 185 million in any year."[220]

It will be harder for States to generate this large of a direct subsidy package given the procedural constraints that exist on appropriations. Relief from sales, property, income and utility taxes by the State and local governments usually bypasses the budgetary process in most States. For example, in Connecticut the amount spent through tax expenditures exceeds the amount spent in any other budgetary category. Nevertheless, the State's tax expenditure budget is not integrated into the budgetary process.[221]

"Although tax exemptions and subsidies serve similar ends, they differ in important and relevant respects . . . ."[222] The Supreme Court is right when it comes to the different perceptions and procedural rules that pertain to direct expenditures versus tax expenditures.[223] Explicit subsidies are easier to monitor than tax expenditures.[224]

local government have only one statewide tax rate for each type of product." S. Maguire & N.A. Noto, Cong. Research Serv., *Internet Taxation: Issues and Legislation in the 109th Congress* (RL 33261, 2006), 10.

216. See M.A. Sullivan, *supra* note 82, at 421 (making a similar proposal based on the European Union as a model).
217. B. Hamilton, *Saving the States from Themselves*, 45 St Tax Notes 131 (2007). In May 2007, ThyssenKrupp AG of Dusseldorf, Germany chose Alabama for the site of a USD 3.7 billion steel mill ending a bidding war for the mill between Alabama and Louisiana. *Ibid.*
218. *Ibid.*
219. *Ibid.*
220. *Ibid.*
221. R.D. Pomp, *Ruminations on Reforming Aspects of Connecticut's Tax Structure*, 41 St. Tax Notes 647, 671 (2006).
222. *Camps Newfound/Owatonna, Inc.*, 520 U.S. at 589 (1997).
223. See generally E.A. Zelinsky, *Are Tax "Benefits" Constitutionally Equivalent to Direct Expenditures*, 112 Harv. L. Rev. 379 (1998).
224. M. Gergen, *The Selfish State and the Market*, 66 Tex. L. Rev. 1097, 1110 (1988).

Although most of the States now enact tax expenditure budgets,[225] few States mandate the use of these reports in their annual budget processes.[226]

§2.05 CONCLUSION

The provision of subsidies is firmly entrenched in the economic culture of the individual American States. Thus, outright prohibition of such subsidies is unrealistic. Even the European Union has not completely foregone all such State aid. The goal of my proposal is to make the provision of such subsidies more transparent by taking away the one aid instrument, the State tax system, that is the most difficult for the public to understand and is the most easily hidden from scrutiny. The States should be encouraged to compete on the basis of tax rates, infrastructure, etc.

The SSUTA demonstrates that the States have the capability to solve this problem themselves. Agreeing to a State Code of Conduct for Business Taxes that requires the states to abstain from targeted tax incentives, will force those that continue to bid for companies to use direct subsidies. Direct subsidies are more readily understood by the average citizen, who will then be able to demand restraint from their public officials if they do not perceive sufficient benefits as arising from such spending. This proposal will not prevent all corporate blackmail but it will serve to increase public scrutiny of targeted State tax incentives.

225. M. Leachman, *supra* note 121.

226. J. Levitis, N. Johnson & J. Koulish, *State Budget Accountability Through Tax Expenditure Reports*, 52 St Tax Notes 641 (2009). New Jersey has enacted a law that requires corporations receiving subsidies to report on jobs created, retain, or lost, average annual pay rates, and the number of employees receiving health benefits. J. Buhl, *New Jersey Enacts Tax Subsidy Accountability*, 46 St. Tax Notes 526 (2007). A Good Jobs First research director described the law as a major advance for corporate tax subsidy accountability. *Ibid.*

CHAPTER 3

Fiscal Aid Review and Tax Competition

Pierpaolo Rossi-Maccanico, Esq.[*]

§3.01 INTRODUCTION

International tax competition was not the original focus of the State aid control foreseen by Articles 107 and 108 TFEU. Since more than 35 years, however, the European judicature has made it clear that the application of State aid rules to measures relating to business taxation could also concern tax preferences with cross-border effects, as it was the case for an Italian scheme aimed at improving social contribution charges for the textile sector vis-à-vis the foreign comparative standard for the industry.

Moreover, the Commission practice first and the Court of Justice later have confirmed that the notion of selective aid includes certain tax preferences irrespective of whether these are internationally harmful or not. Starting with its 1998 Notice on the application of State aid rules to direct tax measures, the Commission has been active in policing the tax regimes relating to the 1997 Code of Conduct on business taxation to tackle international tax competition.

Against this background, this chapter provides a reasoned review of the application of State aid rules to international tax preferences and of the selectivity criterion. The article considers that, in the case of direct business tax measures, State aid review implies appraisals, under a rule of reason, of the effects of such measures under the nature and scheme of the respective tax systems as illustrated by the *Gibraltar* case law. The recent case law accrues legal certainty and opens the way to a new phase in State aid review of national tax preferences.

---

* Any opinion expressed by the author is personal and does not necessarily reflect the views of any institution.

§3.02 BACKGROUND ON FISCAL AIDS: THE INTERPLAY BETWEEN STATE AID REVIEW AND DIRECT TAXATION

There are two fundamental issues concerned with State aid review of measures relating to direct business taxation. The first issue relates to the notion of selective tax preference as opposed to general tax policy measure. The notion of State aid within the meaning of Article 107(1) TFEU[1] is a complex one, including several elements, which shall cumulatively be fulfilled, such as the selectivity criterion, the most significant one when examining a tax measure. Since the latter criterion is assessed, in line with the rather undefined and broad notion of State aid, on the basis of the effects of a measure, this by definition implies that any tax preference is selective because it introduces differentiations in the tax system. Even the tax preferences that are very general and do not entail significant differentiations between undertakings covered by the same tax system are selective, unless these distinctions are justified by the nature or scheme of that system. Such justified measures, although creating differential tax burdens for distinct classes of undertakings, should not be subject to the special review procedures foreseen by Article 108 TFEU[2] because these are not State aid within the meaning of Article 107(1) TFEU.

The second issue is specific to the methodology of State aid review of tax measures in itself. It relates to the interplay between the legitimate prerogatives of Member States in the area of direct taxation and their obligation not to set into effect State aid without prior authorization from the Commission. On this jurisdictional point, the system of State aid review likens a *scheme for advance rulings*, which is also typical in certain tax legislations to manage fiscal benefits or waiving the application of anti-avoidance rules. Under the ordinary review procedure for new aid,[3] Article 108(3) TFEU requires Member States to notify the Commission of any plan to grant State aid, which also applies to tax aid. However, a Member State can notify a tax measure to the Commission also for reasons of legal certainty in order to obtain a formal exclusion of the measure from State aid. Moreover, anybody can flag a possible tax aid to the Commission and demand that the Commission carries out a formal review procedure in case of doubts. If the Commission finds that a tax measure is *prima facie* aid it opens a formal review procedure to verify whether it can qualify for any of the exemptions provided for in the Treaty to be declared compatible with the internal market. If a State

1. Article 107(1) TFEU, former Art. 87(1) EC and Art. 92(1) EEC, provides: "Save as otherwise provided in the Treaties, any aid granted by a Member State or through state resources, in any form whatsoever, which distorts or threatens to distort competition by favouring certain undertakings or the production of certain goods is, in so far as it affects trade between Member States, incompatible with the internal market."
2. Article 108 TFEU, former Art. 88 EC and Art. 93 EEC, sets the procedural rules for the Commission to review State measures within the meaning of State aid.
3. Under the other procedure foreseen for existing aids, Art. 108(1) TFEU provides that the Commission keeps under constant review all systems of existing aid in cooperation with Member States. Such review extends to State aid in the form of tax measures. Following the information exchanged with Member States on this subject, the Commission may, if it considers that the scheme is not or is no longer compatible with the internal market, propose that the Member State amend or abolish it.

aid has been put into effect in breach of the obligation to notify, it requires the Member State to recover it, except where that would be contrary to a general principle of EU law, in particular with regard to legitimate expectations to which the Commission's behavior can give rise. In the case of State aid in the form of tax measures, the amount to be covered is calculated on the basis of a comparison between the tax actually paid and the amount which should have been paid if the generally applicable rule had been applied. Interest is added to this basic amount. The interest rate to be applied is equivalent to the reference rate used to calculate the grant equivalent of regional aid. However, if a measure has been notified or otherwise signaled to the Commission for ruling and the Institution fails to assess its aid nature or generates sufficient expectations as to its compatibility with the internal market, although the unlawful tax aid cannot be recovered. Under that ex-ante review procedure, the implementation of tax aid is subject to Article 108 TFEU, so that the freedom for Member States to set up business tax schemes, in case of suspect conflict with Article 107 TFEU, is conditional upon an official notification of the scheme to the Commission and the demonstration that the scheme is not State aid because justified, or alternatively that the scheme is State aid but that the Commission should find it compatible with the internal market under one of the derogations foreseen by Article 107(2) and (3) TFEU. The ex-ante review procedure is therefore conducive to legal certainty.

Against the above background, it is appropriate to examine the two said issues by reference to the clarifications provided by the most recent case law of the European Court of Justice, which currently comprises, for State aid review purposes, the General Court (GC), as first grade, and the Court of Justice (CJ), as appellate grade, on the notions of selective advantage and justification and about the methodology to review tax measures under the State aid discipline, examining first the jurisdictional aspect of tax aid in the international tax context, and then the notion of selectivity and its justification.

§3.03 TAX AID AND INTERNATIONAL TAXATION

International taxation was never the focus of the State aid prohibition. However, the CJ has considered that the expression "*in any form whatsoever*" naturally attracted potentially all tax preferences to the scope of State aid review. The CJ has accordingly provided for a large interpretation for the application of Article 107(1) TFEU to national tax measures, with a view to capturing all preferences, which could be justified from internal or intra-State tax logic.

More specifically, in *Italy v. Commission*,[4] the CJ set the scene for the distinction between intra-State tax preferences being relevant for Article 107(1) TFEU and inter-state preferences covered by Articles 116 and 117 TFEU. The case concerned a reduction in social security charges applicable for the sole textile sector in Italy on grounds that because of the dominant presence of women in the sector the charges resulted more elevated that in the average. The Commission concluded that the tax

4. ECJ, *Italy v. Commission*, Case No. 173/73 [1974] ECR 709.

reduction was State aid and directed Italy to eliminate the advantage. Italy challenged the Commission's ruling but the CJ rejected the application. It held that:

> The aim of Article 92 of the EEC Treaty is to prevent trade between Member States from being affected by benefits grated by the public authorities which in various forms distort or threaten to distort competition by favouring certain undertakings or the production of certain goods. Article 92 does not therefore distinguishes between the measures of State intervention concerned by reference to their causes or their aims but defines them in relation to their effects, so that the alleged fiscal nature or social aim of a measure taken by a Member State cannot suffice to exclude it from the ambit of Article 92.

Moreover, the CJ ruled that since Member States are free to decide their tax systems, State aid may only consist of derogations within the same national tax system, which are not justified by the nature or scheme of the same system. Many tax exceptions within a given tax system may have the effect of favoring certain undertakings. However, only the tax measures that derogate from the normal application of the tax system "*of which they form part*" may be characterized as State aid. In the case at hand, the CJ noted that "*the family allowance scheme payable out of the profits of an undertaking applies, on the same basis, to ... different branches of industry*" and therefore a reduction limited to one sector, the textile one, resulted in an unjustified intra-State differentiation.[5] On the argument of cross-border tax competition, the CJ accordingly held that:[6]

> As of the argument that the social charges devolving upon employers in the textile sector are higher in Italy than in other Member States, it should be observed that, in the application of Article 92(1), the point of departure must necessarily be the competitive position existing within the Common Market before the adoption of the measure at issue.
>
> On the other hand, the unilateral modification of a particular factor of the cost production in a given sector of the economy of a Member State may have the effect of disturbing the existing equilibrium.
>
> The Italian textile industry is in competition with textile undertakings in other Member States ... The modification of production costs in the Italian textile sector by reduction of the social charges in question necessarily affects trade between Member States.

On the other hand, the inter-State tax discrepancies or preferences may only be eliminated by the harmonization of the relevant national legislations, including the Union law scheme provided for by Articles 116-117 TFEU. In this respect, the Advocate General Darmon[7] has opined that:

> If the level of fiscal and social obligations incumbent on undertakings in one Member State is appreciably lower than it is in other States, a situation of that kind, which undoubtedly affects competition, may be resolved by applying Articles 99 to

5. *Ibid.*, para. 15.
6. *Ibid.*, paras. 18–19.
7. Opinion of AG Darmon in Joined Cases ECJ, *Sloman Neptun*, Cases No. C-71/91 and C-72/91 [1992] para. 62.

> 102 of the EEC Treaty. In other words, a general advantage conferred by national legislation of one sort or another cannot be caught by means of Article 92(1).

In essence, the CJ considered that the aim of Article 107(1) TFEU is to prevent trade between Member States from being affected by public benefits, which in various form distort competition by favoring only certain undertakings, without distinguishing between measures of State intervention by reference to their causes or aims but to their effects. A partial reduction of the social charges pertaining to family allowances devolving upon employers in the textile sector was accordingly viewed as a tax preference intended to partially exempt the Italian textile sector from the financial charges arising from the normal application of the general social security system, without there being any justification for this exemption on the basis of the nature or general scheme of this system.

§3.04 TAX AID AND TAX COMPETITION

As postulated above, the application of State aid in the area of business taxation is not at all impeded by the fiscal nature of the measure to be reviewed. Early in 1998, the Commission stepped on its pace on its practice to review international tax arrangements, by adopting a Notice on the application of State aid rules to measures relating to direct taxation (the fiscal aid Communication).[8] With it, the Commission committed to a strict application of State aid rules in the area of taxation and, in particular, the granting of tax subsidies aimed at attracting the location of multinational undertakings (MNEs), as necessary to limit the proliferation of tax distortions refraining the internal market from functioning effectively.

On December 1, 1997, following a wide-ranging discussion on the need for coordinated action at Community level to tackle harmful tax competition, the Council (Ecofin) adopted a series of conclusions and agreed on a Code of Conduct for Business Taxation (the Code of Conduct).[9] Within the Code, a Group made of the representatives of Member States assisted by the Commission was created to establish a list of tax measures providing for a significantly lower effective taxation, including zero taxation, than those levels which are generally applied. Letter B. of the Code established that its Group had to take into account the following factors in order to establish whether a tax measure had to be considered harmful and committed the Member States to agree on *rolling back* such measures:

B.1. Whether advantages were accorded only to non-residents or in respect of transactions carried out with non-residents.

B.2. Whether advantages are ring fenced from the domestic market, so they do not affect the national tax base.

B.3. Whether advantages are granted even without any real economic activity and substantive economic presence within the State granting such advantages.

8. Commission Notice on the application of State aid rules to measures relating to direct taxation, Nov. 11, 1998, OJ C 384, Dec. 10, 1988, p. 3. The Notice is largely based on the dicta of the ECJ, *Italy v. Commission*, Case No. 173/73 [1974].
9. OJ C 2, Jan. 6, 1998, 1.

B.4. Whether the rules for profit determination in respect of activities within a MNE departs from international standards, notably those agreed upon within the OECD.

B.5. Whether tax measures lack transparency and involve administrative discretion.

On that occasion, the Commission felt the need to clarify the boundaries between, on the one hand, general tax measures and, on the other hand, tax aid, based on an extensive scope of Article 107 TFEU based on the effects of the measures. This was a reason of particular concern for both national administrations and taxpayers in the area of tax preferences for MNEs "*in view of the procedural requirements that stem from designation as aid*" *of such measures and of the* "*consequences where the Member States fail to comply with such requirements*",[10] since most of the international tax arrangements concerned involved international investors.

The Commission stated at Point 30 of its Notice that the qualification of a tax measure as harmful under the Code of conduct did not affect its possible qualification as a State aid. However, the assessment of the compatibility of fiscal aid with the internal market has to be made, taking into account, *inter alia*, the effects of aid that are brought to light in the application of the Code. In general, when tax aid is granted in order to provide an incentive for firms to embark on certain specific projects (investment in particular) and its intensity is limited with respect to the costs of carrying out the project, it is no different from a subsidy. This means that such an aid may be accorded the same treatment as a subsidy because sufficiently transparent to enable the benefit conferred to be quantified. Hence, it is possible to consider such an aid compatible under one of the exceptions foreseen in Article 107(2) and (3), TFEU. On the contrary, certain forms of tax relief, such as those for the localization of MNEs or promoting certain corporate forms or regimes, provide for benefits that are not linked to the carrying-out of specific projects. Such tax aids reduce a firm's current expenditure without it being possible to assess the precise amounts involved when the Commission carries out its ex-ante examination. Such measures constitute operating aid, which are in principle prohibited. More importantly, tax aid consisting in preferential tax arrangements or regimes falling within the scope of application of the Code of conduct is considered incompatible with the internal market because of its predatory effects. Such types of aid are incompatible on their own right according to Point 30 of the Notice.

Against this background, the Commission, acting in accordance with the State aid rules, has examined a number of measures identified by the Code as harmful. The initiative, also known under the name of 'Fiscal Aid Package', concerned about two dozens preferential tax regimes of different Member States, which were all found to be incompatible with State aid rules, after individual review procedures had been carried out.[11]

10. Commission Notice on the application of State aid rules to measures relating to direct taxation, Nov. 11, 1998, OJ C 384, Dec. 10, 1988, para. 2.
11. For a comprehensive illustration of the main fiscal aid cases of the package, see P. Rossi-Maccanico, *Commentary of State Aid Review of Multinational Tax Regimes*, EStAL, I-25 (2007).

While generally the measures classed as harmless tend to be incompatible State aid because of the broad interpretation provided to the selectivity notion, in one instance a harmful measure under the Code was found not to be State aid. In 2006, following the review of the Maltese International Trading Companies and the Companies with Foreign Income Schemes (the ICT and CFI regimes),[12] Malta accepted the appropriate measures proposed by the Commission. In particular, it was proposed that the two schemes were replaced by a general measure providing the refund of Maltese company tax to all shareholders of companies in Malta irrespective of the latter companies' legal forms and the activities pursued. The Code of Conduct Group discussed the general refund scheme and concluded that it was still harmful as it could unfairly attract foreign shareholders, formally taxable but essentially exempt, to create holdings there, but the Commission concluded that the generalized refund did not constitute State aid; thus stigmatizing the difference between State aid and harmful taxation. The outcome of State aid review was eventually implemented by Malta in 2007, with the adoption of a general refund system at source to the local companies of all underlying taxes borne on any distributed dividend. Under the new general refund scheme, foreign shareholders were still preferred over national shareholders, the latter being taxed on their received dividends while the former being exempt. The resulting advantage for the foreign shareholders was not however imputable to Malta but derived from the shareholders' exemption given by the country of the beneficiary shareholder, and accordingly no State aid was involved.

On the other hand, few measures declared not harmful were found to be tax aid. One prominent example is the Luxembourg's *1929 and Billionaire Holding Companies* exemption scheme. Although initially considered harmful by the Code of conduct group, after Luxembourg limited the exemption to holdings with subsidiaries not based in low-tax countries, the scheme was decided to be no longer harmful. The Commission then initiated a separate State aid review and concluded that the exemption for the holding companies in Luxembourg exercising certain financing, reinsurance and managerial functions for their subsidiaries and affiliates in the group was a tax aid, without there being any justification for such exemptions under the nature or scheme of the Luxembourgish tax system.

One can say that the Fiscal Aid Package has been instrumental for the Council to oblige Member States to roll back the harmful measures listed by the Code's Group. However, State aid review of tax aid extends far beyond the limit of harmful taxation. It encompasses all possible forms of tax differentiations as brought into light by the effect-based doctrine on the interpretation of the State aid notion relating to tax preferences. The application of State aid discipline is based on legal criteria, however, which the recent case law of the CJ has contributed to clarify, the most important of which is the justification of the selectivity of a tax measure by the nature of tax system.

12. Commission Decision, Malta—Tax incentives in favor of "International Trading Companies" and "Companies with Foreign In- come" (Mar. 22, 2006) E 6/05, NN 26/2005, E 11/2005 and NN 35/2005,OJ C 240/2005.

The CJ has clarified that State aid control only concerns specific tax preferences granted to certain undertakings and that the specificity of a measure can be justified. However, the mere need to adjust for disadvantages resulting from international tax disparities does not justify the grant of specific tax preferences because that justification does not relate to the logic of the tax system in question.

One should note that most tax distortions derive from the cross-border disparities and lack of coordination between the tax systems of different Member States. It is true that international tax neutrality is not possible to achieve without substantive harmonization of tax rules between Member States.[13] The resulting tax disparities are not however the object of State aid control. This does not mean however that certain tax distortions, those that are specific or selective, are immune from State aid control. The difficulty of distinguishing between national tax measures aimed at achieving tax neutrality which are therefore justified or genuine tax measures, and those aimed at unbalancing the tax neutrality and are therefore fiscally predatory or unjustified is the main logical issue in the application of State aid rules in the areas of direct business taxation. State aid review of direct tax measures accordingly operates in a context of tax competition between Member States.

One shall start from describing what tax neutrality is, and how it is difficult to achieve it, especially at an international level where each States is sovereign in choosing its connecting elements to impose its tax jurisdiction which leads to unavoidable tax differences and distortions. Globalization has led public powers responsible for defining and administering direct taxation on businesses to align their tax systems to international standards dictated by tax competition combined by neutrality requirements. These standards are the ones generally applied by the Member States within the Union, as well as by the other market economies, ensuring the exercise of economic freedoms to invest and do business internationally. Union law provides pre-eminence to economic freedoms within the Internal Market. Fiscal neutrality is a consequence of this and there are two main examples of fiscal neutrality categories that Member States aim at providing with their respective tax systems. The neutrality in investing (capital import/export neutrality) embodies a first type of neutrality based on the distinction between residence and source, which are the two connecting factors of direct taxation. Capital export neutrality is neutrality of taxation from the point of view of residence. Capital import neutrality is neutrality from the viewpoint of the source State. Under the capital export neutrality principle, resident companies should be treated alike irrespective of whether income is earned in the residence-State or abroad. The fact is that absolute capital export neutrality is out of the control of the taxing country because companies may easily relocate by creating subsidiaries abroad and avoid residence taxation altogether in the State of emigration and elect to pay tax in the State of immigration. Controlled company legislations can be enacted to avoid abuse, however Union law limits the use of such legislations to purely artificial emigrations. For this reason, Member States maintain taxation relatively low for resident businesses to limit emigration. Capital import neutrality postulates that taxation at source should be the same irrespective of whether the business

13. See Opinion of AG Jääskinen in Joined Cases *Commission and Spain v. Gibraltar*, Cases No. C-106/09 P and C-107/09 P [2011], not yet reported in ECR, para. 144.

taxpayer is a resident or a foreigner. Generally, this kind of neutrality is required by Union law, which prohibits discriminatory taxation of foreign undertakings irrespective of its forms. On the other hand reverse discrimination, being more favorable taxation of foreign undertakings vis-à-vis residents, is not prohibited but it is incompatible with the principle of neutrality, which requires same effective taxation for undertakings operating locally, also to ensure a levelled playing field for undertakings competing locally in the same market.[14] Hence, capital import neutrality is also problematic because international tax competition drives sovereign States to keep the level of taxation above the one applicable to resident undertakings.

The second category of neutrality concerns the way in which business activities are financed. It is common knowledge that debt vis-à-vis equity is the most tax-efficient way of financing business ventures by a controlling undertaking, because interest on financing is deductible from the income of the leveraged undertaking and taxable once for the financing undertaking when paid. In group structures this tax disparity can give rise to arbitrage, which effectively allows transformation of active (business) income into passive (interest) income. Anti-abuse rules, such as thin-capitalization legislations, are used by sovereign jurisdictions to limit arbitrage especially internationally. However, tax competition drives sovereign States to maintain low source taxation on passive income earned by non-residents to ensure adequate capital supply to local companies and stimulate their growth. Also in this case, neutrality is difficult to preserve. Tax competition accordingly is the model influencing the way sovereign States organize their tax systems.

I have mentioned how Member States react to the competitive international tax environment. The reaction can be of two types. Member States can aim at addressing distortions by seeking to restore neutrality (for example by adopting anti-abuse measures). Their tax measures are adapting to the inevitable disparities between different tax systems and are justified. On the other hand, States can increase their attractiveness by adopting measures targeted at favoring the localization of certain undertakings only, which however further distort the level playing field, predating on neutrality of other Member States. The former reactions increase tax competition in a healthy way as genuine attempts to return to neutrality. Even if they create distortions they are justified by the territoriality of taxation and can only be cured by harmonization, or actions under Articles 116, 117 TFEU. The latter reactions are instead unjustified and unnecessary under the logic of the tax system. They belong to the genus of harmful tax competition to which the coordinated action at Union level to tackle predation under a Code of Conduct on business taxation, adopted on December 1, 1997 applies.[15]

As already mentioned, with the Code of Conduct resulting the Council established a Group entrusted to examine the existing tax preferences provided by Member States providing for a significant lower effective level of taxation than those levels generally applicable in each Member State of reference, and furthermore fulfilling criteria such as (a) granting tax advantages only to non-residents or in respect to transactions carried out to non-residents, (b) ring-fencing the advantages, (c) granting

14. This is one of the main flaws of the CCCTB proposed scheme.
15. OJ C 2, Jan. 6, 1998, 1.

advantages without any real economic substance, (d) departing from OECD international tax standards, and (e) administering taxation in non transparent or arbitrary ways. Member States committed voluntarily not only to stand still from introducing such harmful measures, but also to roll back the existing ones. Such commitments could prove elusive, and the Member States agreed early-on that the Commission would have intervened with the application of State aid rules, whenever such harmful measures were having economic impact on undertakings and being selective within the meaning of Article 107(1) TFEU, as preferences not justified by the nature or scheme of the respective systems of reference. The possible characterization of certain preferential tax measures as State aid needs therefore to be examined.

§3.05 EFFECT-BASED VERSUS PURPOSIVE INTERPRETATIONS FOR FISCAL AIDS

The case law of the CJ has consistently held that the notion of State aid, as applied to tax preferences, is effect-based and not limited by the aim of the measure. The nature and scheme of the system must nonetheless be considered when reviewing the effects of the measures to establish if it is susceptible of justification. The CJ has strived to clarify this approach in a series of controversial judgments in which the GC had justified the provision of exceptions or derogations from national systems of general charges or preferential measures, eventually quashed by the CJ.

One prominent illustration of the judicial uncertainty can be found in a State aid review concerning the exemption provided by the British finance Act of 2001 imposing a levy on the extraction and importation of virgin aggregates (AGL) exempting, among other things, non-virgin and exported aggregates. The AGL scheme was notified and, on April 24, 2002, the Commission adopted a Decision, without even opening the (so-called "phase-II") investigation procedure, stating that only the regional measure consisting in the deferred introduction of AGL for Northern Ireland was State aid, but that it was compatible with the its guidelines on State aid for environmental protection. The British Aggregate Association (BAA) challenged the Commission Decision on the part that it did not considered the AGL exemptions to be State aid and the GC ruled in favor of the Commission.[16] On appeal, the CJ reversed the GC. It held that the Commission had erred in considering the AGL exemption not to be selective, considering its specific aim of objectively differentiating between virgin and non-virgin aggregates, and that the exemptions in question were in fact State aid because the objective pursued by State measures was not sufficient to exclude those measures outright from classification as "aid" for the purposes of Article 107 TFEU under the effect-based doctrine.[17]

16. ECJ, *British Aggregates and others v. Commission*, Case No. T-359/04 [2010] not reported in ECR.
17. ECJ, *British Aggregates v. Commission*, Case No. C-487/06 P [2008] ECR I-10515, see in particular para. 82 and the case law cited.

Another illustration of the difficulties in grasping the notion of selectivity is the *Dutch Nitrogen Oxides* (NOx)[18] case relating to the justification of a regulatory preference. The CJ again quashed a prior GC judgment that annulled[19] the Commission's decision, which had found the Netherlands emission trading scheme State aid compatible with the internal market. The GC had held that the scheme did not constitute State aid in the absence of its selective nature. The Netherlands legislation at issue used a quantitative criterion of 20 Megawatts (MW) thermal installation capacity to differentiate between undertakings which fall within and those which fall outside the scope of the emission trading scheme. Only industrial facilities superseding this amount would be subject to the emission trading scheme, which foresaw the grant of emission credits valuable to recipients. In its judgment, the CJ confirmed the GC's finding that having regard to the conditions of the scheme, the Netherlands had foregone the collection of public resources in terms of prospective emission trading charges, because offset by credits, as it did not sell or auction these credits to the companies. The CJ held the measure to be selective, as only large industrial undertakings meeting the quantitative criterion could enjoy the potential benefits of the scheme. Granting emission allowances free of charge while authorizing and facilitating their tradability resulted in a financial advantage for those companies being in a position to sell their surplus allowances and still avoid fines when they exceed their own emission ceilings. According to the CJ, the 20 MW distinction was not inherent to a system aimed at reducing industrial pollution and could thus not be justified by reference to environmental objectives only having regard to the fact that smaller companies, which did not meet the 20 MW threshold, would also have been subject to certain NOx emission requirements without being able to enjoy the benefits of the trading scheme. Further, the CJ considered that it was for the Member State concerned to justify any differentiation between undertakings based on their production capacity in light of the nature or general scheme of the tax system.

A third significant case concerns a preliminary ruling of the CJ requested by the Italian Corte di Cassazione on the compatibility of certain tax exemptions and reductions in favor of the Italian cooperative companies with State aid rules in the *Paint Graphos* case.[20] On September 8, 2011, the Court of Justice (CJ) rendered a judgment remanding most of the analysis to the referring national court. The CJ gave however some general guidelines on the issue. Remarkably enough, it did not rule out the possibility that tax preferences including exemptions could escape State aid review, either because favoring certain undertakings being in a non-comparable legal and factual situation of the other undertakings, or because justified by the nature and scheme of the tax system of reference, the corporate tax system. The CJ observed that a regime for cooperatives could, in principle, amount to State aid if selective. The latter would only be the case where a cooperative is comparable to other commercial entities.

18. ECJ, *Commission v. Netherlands,* Case No. C-279/08 P [2011] ECR I-0000, see in particular para. 51.
19. ECJ, *Netherlands v. Commission,* Case No. T-233/04 [2008] ECR II-59, see in particular paras. 88–96.
20. See Joined Cases ECJ, *Paint Graphos and Others,* Cases No. C-78/08 to C-80/08 [2011] ECR I-0000, para. 45 and the case law cited.

To the extent cooperatives use a different method of operation for the sole benefit of their members based on mutuality, they are in a factually and legally distinct situation that might justify special tax benefits to the extent necessary. The CJ held that granting benefits to a cooperative that effectively acts as any other regular commercial entity may amount to selective aid, unless this benefit would both follow from the general scheme of the tax system and be proportionate.

§3.06 THE *GIBRALTAR* CASE

A final clarification with respect to determining which preferential tax regimes can be qualified as State aid arrived with the Commission review of the Gibraltar tax reform. At issue was whether the regime notified by the UK government to the Commission for State aid clearance in 2002 was selective or not, in other words whether it afforded lower rates of taxation to certain companies vis-à-vis others in a comparable fiscal situation.

The Gibraltar tax reform foresaw the abolition of the classical corporate tax system, and its replacement by a hybrid system, under which all companies domiciled in Gibraltar would be subject to a yearly payroll tax of £ 3,000 per employee and to a business property occupation tax (BPOT). The total tax liability under such taxes would however be capped at 15% of profit. In addition to the payroll and property taxes, financial services companies would be charged a top-up tax fixed at a rate between 4% and 6% of profits from their financial service activities. The total taxation of financial services companies (payroll + BPOT + top-up) would also be capped at 15% of profit. The corporate tax had not completely disappeared, but provided a cap on ordinary tax liability based on the profitable use of certain factors or production (real estate and labor).

In 2004, the Commission took a decision[21] concluding that the regime would provide companies domiciled in Gibraltar an unfair tax advantage amounting to regional aid. Moreover, the Commission ruled that the tax reform conferred materially selective advantages, namely, the requirement to make a profit seemed to confer advantages on companies that made no profit, the profit tax cap conferred advantages on those companies to which they apply, and finally the scheme favored the facto certain undertakings based in Gibraltar but with scarce labor and real estates, like the offshore companies. The GC annulled the Commission's decision in 2008 arguing, *inter alia*, that the Commission had failed to identify what was the system of reference for its assessment.[22] On appeal ledged by the Commission and Spain against the judgment about material selectivity, Advocate General Jäaskinen[23] was very supportive of the GC and critical of the Commission. He opined that the Commission had exceeded its boundaries in reviewing tax measures, which amounted to harmful tax competition

21. OJ L 85, Apr. 2, 2005, p. 1.
22. Joined Cases ECJ, *Government of Gibraltar and United Kingdom v. Commission*, Cases No. T-211/04 and T-215/04 [2008] ECR II-3745.
23. Opinion of AG Jaäskinen in ECJ, *European Commission and Kingdom of Spain v. Government of Gibraltar and United Kingdom*, Cases No. C-106/09P and C-107/09P [2011] not yet reported.

but not to State aid. The AG in particular criticized the Commission for a grave error in the assessment of the criterion of selectivity. Most notably, the Commission would have incorrectly abandoned its Notice relating to the application of Article 107(1) TFEU to tax preferences liable to constitute State aid, by failing to identify an advantage by reference to the system generally applicable to companies domiciled in Gibraltar, and having concluded that the distortions created by the rightful exercise of the sovereign tax prerogatives of Gibraltar could be classified as State aid.

The CJ reversed the GC judgment and confirmed the Commission's Decision of 2004.[24] For the CJ, the State aid assessment of tax measures is substantive and cumulative rather than formal and divisible into rigid steps. In sum, any assessment of tax preferences involves a comparison between, on the one hand, the situation of the undertakings concerned in the event of application of those advantageous measures and, on the other, a reference system, that is to say an objective standard such as the tax regime applicable under the general law. Moreover, the assessment of selectivity of fiscal preferences is based on the definition of the pool of beneficiary undertakings from a preference. Finally, a comparison between the legal and factual situations of those who benefit from the mechanisms adopted by the Member States in the exercise of their fiscal powers and those being excluded, shall take place with a view to establishing if the selective grant of a tax preference is justified by the nature and scheme of the system of reference. The justification constitutes the quintessential criterion in determining the selectivity of a tax preference. The proportionality principle governs the criterion.

The above pattern for distinguishing which preferential tax regimes are State aid does not change even if applied to harmful tax measures having cross-border effect. It is known that globalization of economic activities, trade and investments and the proliferation of MNEs operating beyond national borders are phenomena presenting serious challenges for tax jurisdictions. Activities established in certain jurisdictions cross borders in order to establish themselves in other jurisdictions which offer better overall conditions (a phenomenon also known as 'the Delaware effect'). Among such conditions, taxation plays a very important role, even though it is difficult in practice to determine its real impact precisely. This is part of a competitive process to which open market economies, such as the Union Member States, are exposed. It is a physiological process that relates to competition between States rather than competition between undertakings. The development of predatory forms of taxation on the other hand is not physiological at all. Distortion caused by the latter forms of tax measures may influence competition between undertakings in the private market for corporate charters and corporate services by altering the level playing field between providers of financial services, or asset management, holdings services, etc. Against this background, there is no reason to exclude from State aid review the harmful tax regimes considered under the Code of Conduct, in so far as these are selective under an

24. Joined Cases ECJ, *European Commission and Kingdom of Spain v. Government of Gibraltar and United Kingdom*, Cases No. C-106/09P and C-107/09P [2011] not yet reported.

effect-based analysis. Even before the *Gibraltar* judgment, the CJ[25] had expressly confirmed the superposition between the categories of fiscal aids and harmful tax measures, with reference to the preferential tax regime for Belgian Coordination Centers, a harmful tax regime within the meaning of the Code.

In that case, the CJ had followed the traditional three-step analysis for the selectivity criterion. The CJ held that, as to the condition of advantage, this is fulfilled when a preferential treatment is granted by derogation from the ordinary system of reference. Indeed, the concept of aid may cover not only positive benefits, such as subsidies, but also negative interventions which, in various forms, mitigate the charges which are normally included in the budget of an undertaking and which, without therefore being subsidies in the strict meaning of the word, are similar in character and have the same effect.[26] Furthermore, the CJ held that a measure by which the public authorities grant to certain undertakings a tax exemption which, although not involving a transfer of State resources, places the persons to whom it applies in a more favorable financial situation than other taxpayers constitutes State aid.[27] Accordingly, in examining a tax preference the Commission has to ascertain whether the preferential method of determining taxable income constitutes advantages for the beneficiaries of such a preference by reference to the normal or ordinary taxation. Under this analysis, a tax exemption is by definition an advantage unless it corresponds to a situation excluded from taxation because outside of the scope, because of territoriality, timing or accrual conditions imposed by the tax system.

As to the condition of selectivity, under the settled case law it must be appraised by comparing the pool of beneficiaries with other undertakings being in comparable legal and factual situations without there being any justification by the nature or scheme of the tax system of reference. According to settled case law, Article 107(1) TFEU requires that it be determined whether, under a particular statutory scheme, a State measure is such as to favor "certain undertakings or the production of certain goods" in comparison with others which, in the light of the objective pursued by the system in question, are in a comparable legal and factual situation. If so, the measure concerned fulfils the condition of selectivity which is a defining characteristic of the concept of State aid as set out by that provision.[28] For certain tax preferences it may be further necessary to determine whether they constitute specific tax regimes applicable to certain situations having the aim of providing resolution, for example, to the imposition of double taxation for intra-group services rendered within a MNE as it was invoked in the case of the Belgian Coordination Centres. In such situations, the Commission shall further carry out an analysis to verify whether the specific factual and legal conditions in which the preferential tax regime is intended to apply justify the preference granted, that is whether the favorable tax treatment is proportionate to its aim, both in terms of its sufficient scope (all the undertakings in comparable legal and

25. Joined cases ECJ, *Belgium and Forum 187 v. Commission*, Cases No. C-182/03 and C-217/03 [2006] ECR I-5479, points 80–83.
26. ECJ, *Gemo*, Case No. C-126/01 [2003] ECR I-13769, para. 28 and the case law cited there.
27. ECJ, *Banco Exterior de España*, Case No. 387/92 [1994] ECR I-877, point 14.
28. ECJ, *Heiser*, Case No. C-172/03 [2005] ECR I-1627, point 40 and the case law cited there.

factual conditions have access to the preference) and necessity (the preference granted addresses for the sake of tax neutrality the specific conditions in which such undertakings operate).

As to the possibility of justifying the selective nature of a tax preference, the CJ[29] considered that the selectivity of a tax preference:

> is not called into question by Forum 187's argument that the regime in question does not constitute a derogation from the ordinary tax regime which applies to undertakings, but a different type of regime, dictated by fiscal logic and the need to provide a solution to the problem of double taxation of services provided within an international group of companies. ... Forum 187 has not shown in what way the aim of providing a resolution for the problem of double taxation of intra-group services justifies restricting the benefit of the regime in question to centres established by groups of a particular size, nor in what way such an aim made each of the various advantages comprised in that regime necessary. ... Forum 187 has thus not established that the regime in question is justified by the nature or the general scheme of the Belgian tax system of which it forms part and it must therefore be held that the selective nature of the scheme has been established.

As to the condition of the distortion of cross-border competition between businesses,[30] it derives from the selective nature of the tax preference granted which puts certain undertakings in more favorable conditions than their actual or potential competitors of other Member States. Indeed, it descends from the case law of the CJ that competition is distorted where a measure mitigates the burden imposed on a beneficiary undertaking and thereby strengthens its position as regards competing undertakings.[31] In the case of MNEs providing intra-group services such as the Coordination Centres, the advantages conferred "*have the effect of distorting competition between them and service providers in the financial, trust, information technology and recruitment sectors by encouraging group companies to make use of the services provided by those centres*". Moreover, the wide-ranging nature of the activities carried on by MNEs means that a preferential tax regime inevitably impacts competition. Lastly, such a preferential scheme necessarily affects trade between Member States, since MNEs are or may be established in several Member States.

I consider that the essential question in the fiscal aid analysis is not only that of determining whether a particular scheme is imputable to the legitimate exercise of (autonomous) tax prerogatives, but also to establish whether a tax preference is selective, without there being a justification for this which might derive from a configuration created within the domestic tax system. The praetorian notion of justification of a selective tax preference is the key to resolve the conflict between State aid review and tax sovereignty. It is in fact possible, besides being mandatory, for a Member State to devise the tax preferences it wishes, provided however that it ensures

29. See Joined cases ECJ, *Belgium and Forum 187 v. Commission*, Cases No. C-182/03 and C-217/03 [2006] ECR I-5479, paras 124–126.
30. See Joined cases ECJ, *Belgium and Forum 187 v. Commission*, Cases No. C-182/03 and C-217/03 [2006] ECR I-5479, paras 130–135.
31. See, to that effect, ECJ, *Philip Morris v. Commission*, Case No. 730/79 [1980] ECR 2671 para. 11; ECJ, *France v. Commission*, Case No. 259/85 [1987] ECR 4393 para. 24.

neutrality between taxpayers. Indeed the tax preferences or other forms of indirect support granted on a sectoral basis constitute state aid. But a measure that does apply to all operators can in principle be regarded as a tax preference whose selectivity is justified by the logic or scheme of the tax system.

This holds true irrespective of the relatively large or narrow scopes of the tax preference considered. Indeed, what matters in the selectivity assessment is its possible justification. The case law is quite clear on the fact that its effect-basis doctrine on fiscal aids only finds its limit where the selectivity of a tax preference can be objectively justified by the nature or scheme of the national tax system of reference. This is expressly to avoid any discretion by the Commission in appraising the aims or objectives of a tax system. The case law is summarized below.

§3.07 CONCLUSIONS

In conclusion, one can consider that the application of State aid rules to tax preferences follows first and foremost the traditional principle of conferral, effectiveness and loyal cooperation as further integrated by the rule of reason as to the possible tax justification for a tax preference. As the CJ has consistently held, even if direct taxation is a matter of exclusive national competence, Member States are bound to exercise their discretion in compliance with Union law. Secondly, the fiscal form of a measure does not exclude it from State aid review. Moreover the selectivity of tax preferences is assessed on the basis of their effects, not their forms. Finally, the justification of selectivity is the quintessential criterion in distinguishing between general or justified tax preferences and State aid.

With respect to selectivity, it is settled case law that the fact that the number of undertakings able to claim entitlement under a measure is very large, or that they belong to different sectors of activity, is not sufficient to call into question the selective nature of that measure and, therefore, to rule out its classification as State aid.[32] Where the measure in question is governed by objective criteria of horizontal application, that fact too does not call into question its selective character, since it can serve only to show that the aid at issue falls within an aid scheme and is not individual aid.[33] Indeed, Article 107(1) TFEU defines State interventions on the basis of their effects, and thus independently of the techniques used by the Member States to implement their interventions.[34]

Indeed, under the case law of the CJ,[35] a State measure constitutes aid if it is such as to favor certain undertakings or the production of certain goods in comparison with other undertakings which are in a legal and factual situation that is comparable in the light of the objective pursued by the measure in question.

---

32. ECJ, *Belgium v. Commission*, Case No. C-75/97 [1999] ECR I-3671 para 32; ECJ, *Adria-Wien Pipeline and Wietersdorfer & Peggauer Zementwerke*, Case No. C-143/99 [2011] ECR I-8365 point 48; and ECJ, *Spain v. Commission*, Case No. C-409/00 [2003] ECR I-1487 para 48.
33. See, to that effect, ECJ, *Spain v. Commission*, Case No. C-409/00 [2003] ECR I-1487 para 49.
34. See ECJ, *British Aggregates v. Commission*, Case No. C-487/06 P [2008] ECR I-10505, para 89.
35. See, to that effect, ECJ, *Adria-Wien Pipeline and Wietersdorfer & Peggauer Zementwerke*, Case No. C-143/99 [2011] ECR I-8365 paras 34 and 41.

Therefore, the aid character of a tax preference is appraised on the basis of its effects, not its objectives. The effect of the doctrine developed by the CJ on the selectivity criterion is objective and should not leave much discretion to the Commission. If this holds true, the Commission has no ability to assess or decide whether a tax preference is justified by reference to its aim. However, to the extent that a tax preference is aimed at certain undertakings, it shall be ascertain whether that criterion of differentiation is objective and is both in conformity with the internal logic of the system (appropriate) and consistently applied (necessary). The Commission's assessment then focuses on the selectivity criterion, or the justification of the sectorial scope of the tax preference with respect to its nature and objectives, on the basis of the elements provided by the national authorites.

> As to the justification, the Commission[36], supported by the case law of the CJ, considers that "The differential nature of some measures does not necessarily mean that they must be considered to be State aid. This is the case with measures whose economic rationale makes them necessary to the functioning and effectiveness of the tax system. However, it is up to the Member State to provide such justification."

The fact that the Member States hold the primary burden of justifying the exercise of their sovereign prerogatives in setting up their direct tax system, is consistent with the idea for which the Member State is best placed to estimate the logic and effects of its planned tax measures. This principle should also be mitigated by what the CJ has affirmed with respect to direct taxation being left to the exclusive competence of Member States under the *principle of conferral* pursuant to Article 5(2) TEU. It is true that Member States have to exercise their sovereign competence consistently with Union law, which implies, for State aid review purposes, that as soon as State aid is involved a Member State should abstain to put it into effect, pursuant to Article 108(3) TFEU, and notify it to the Commission for the exclusive compatibility review procedure under Article 108(2) TFEU. However, the burden of proof in proving the compatibility of a State measure with the internal market may be in fact shared between the Commission and the Member State. Being the Commission entrusted with the exclusive power to examine the compatibility of an aid with the internal market, it bears the burden of providing evidence that a (new) aid has been granted. The Commission's burden of proof is associated with the mutual duty of loyal cooperation under Article 4(3) TEU, which is imposed on both the Commission and the Member States. Accordingly, it is for the Member State Concerned to provide the Commission with all the information in order to enable it to take a decision regarding the qualification of a measure as aid and its compatibility with the internal market. To this effect, if the Commission considers it has incomplete information, it must request all necessary additional information and if the Member State fails to comply with the request of the Commission within a specified time limit, the latter is empowered to close the procedure and adopt its decision on the basis of the information available.

36. Para. 23 of the Fiscal Aid Notice.

With the recent clarifications provided by the CJ by the *Gibraltar* judgment, the system of State aid review of tax measures disposes of accrued legal certainty, which the legal practitioners should not discard. One expects that the application of State aid discipline to national tax preferences could evolve into a system of advance rulings by the Commission to national tax administrations and taxpayers to ex-ante notify and report preferential tax measures to the Commission with a view to obtaining legal certainty as to the possibility of implementation. The Commission's examination would apply at two subordinate levels, including the examination of selectivity and justification of the measure by the nature of the tax system, followed by a compatibility assessment.

Member States' exclusive prerogatives in the area of business taxation are not pre-empted by the Union system of review of fiscal aids as the one pictured in this article, which resembles to an advanced ruling system for the review of possible tax aid. National tax authorities remain free to put their planned tax measures into effect without previously consulting the Commission. Of course, the consequence is that if an undisclosed tax preference is later found to be tax aid, the unlawful nature of the aid granted would entail the effective and complete recovery of any aid already granted, increased by interest to be applied retroactively. Recovery can be waived by the Commission only in case it had contributed to create the legitimate expectation that the tax preference was not aid, or was compatible aid.

CHAPTER 4
Recovery of Fiscal Aid

Margarida Afonso*

§4.01 INTRODUCTION

Recovery of State aid granted in the form of tax exemptions or other tax benefits poses particular challenges, essentially linked to the usually large number of beneficiaries of such aid measures and to the obligation for national authorities to take account of the individual circumstances of each actual beneficiary. This chapter reviews the general rules governing the recovery of aid, which also apply fully to fiscal aid, and discusses some specific questions arising in that particular context. In order to ensure legal certainty, it is crucial to raise the awareness of both national authorities and potential beneficiaries to the implications of the EU rules on State aid control. These rules require Member States to notify to the Commission any tax measures which may constitute State aid before putting them into effect. Beneficiaries of a selective fiscal measure that has not been duly notified may be required to forfeit the advantage they have received. Only if Member States respect their obligations, and potential beneficiaries of tax measures entailing State aid exert appropriate caution, is it possible to avoid the complex and costly litigation often associated with the recovery of unlawful fiscal aid which has been found incompatible with the internal market.

§4.02 RULES GOVERNING THE RECOVERY OF FISCAL AID

The basic rules on the recovery of unlawful and incompatible aid are set out in Article 14 of Council Regulation (EC) No 659/1999 (hereinafter: "the procedural regulation").[1]

* Any opinion expressed by the author is personal and does not necessarily reflect the views of any institution.

1. Council Regulation (EC) 659/1999 of March 22, 1999 laying down detailed rules for the application of Article 93 of the EC Treaty, OJ No. L 83, Mar. 27, 1999, 1 (hereinafter Regulation 659/1999).

These are general rules, which apply to the recovery of State aid granted in whatever form, and they confirm and restate a consistent Commission practice and the case-law of the EU courts.[2] In accordance with Article 14(1), where a negative decision is adopted in respect of a tax measure already put into effect, in violation of the prohibition laid down in Article 108(3) TFEU, "the Commission shall decide that the Member State shall take all necessary measures to recover the aid from the beneficiary". A "negative decision" is a decision by which the Commission closes the formal investigation procedure with a finding that the aid in question is not compatible with the internal market.[3]

Article 14(2) of the procedural regulation provides that the aid to be recovered shall include interest at an appropriate rate fixed by the Commission, payable from the date the aid was put at the disposal of the beneficiary until the date of effective recovery. Chapter V of Commission Regulation (EC) No 794/2004, also known as the implementing regulation,[4] sets out the method for fixing the interest rate, which shall be applied on a compound basis.[5] In this respect, it can be noted that the last sentence in paragraph 35 of the Commission's notice on fiscal aid,[6] which refers to the reference rate used to calculate the grant equivalent of regional aid, must be held as being superseded.

Pursuant to Article 14(3) of the procedural regulation, recovery shall be effected without delay and in accordance with the procedures under the national law of the Member State concerned, provided that they allow the immediate and effective execution of the Commission's decision.

In principle, only an order of the EU courts can suspend the execution of a recovery decision, in accordance with Article 279 TFEU.[7] The Member State may no longer challenge the validity of a decision addressed to it on the basis of Article 108(2) TFEU once the time-limit laid down in the sixth paragraph of Article 263 TFEU has expired. It follows from the same requirements of legal certainty that it is not possible for a recipient of aid, who could have challenged that decision and who allowed the mandatory time-limit to expire, to call into question the lawfulness of that decision before the national courts in an action brought against the measures taken by the national authorities for implementing that decision. To accept that in such circumstances the person concerned could challenge the implementation of the decision in proceedings before the national court on the ground that the decision was unlawful would in effect enable the person concerned to overcome the definitive nature which

2. See recital (2) of Regulation 659/1999.
3. See Arts. 13 and 7(5) of Regulation 659/1999.
4. Commission Regulation (EC) 794/2004 of April 21, 2004 implementing Council Regulation (EC) 659/1999 laying down detailed rules for the application of Article 93 of the EC Treaty, OJ No. L 140, Apr. 30, 2004, 1).
5. A summary of these rules is also provided in the Commission Notice towards an effective implementation of Commission decisions ordering Member States to recover unlawful and incompatible State aid, OJ No. C 272, Nov. 15, 2007, p. 4 (hereinafter The Notice on recovery). See, in particular, paras. 11 and 39.
6. Commission Notice on the application of the State aid rules to measures relating to direct business taxation, OJ No. C 384, Dec. 10, 1998, 3 (hereinafter The Notice on fiscal aid).
7. See The Notice on recovery, para. 25.

the decision assumes as against that person once the time-limit for bringing an action has expired.[8]

However, where it is not clear that the addressee of a recovery order would have standing to challenge the Commission's recovery decision before the General Court, it is settled case-law[9] that national courts may grant interim suspension measures, provided that certain conditions are met, namely:

- Where the national court entertains serious doubts as to the validity of the EU measure and the validity of the contested measure is not already in issue before the Court of Justice, that court itself refers the question to the Court.
- There is urgency, in that the interim relief is necessary to avoid serious and irreparable damage being caused to the party seeking the relief.
- The national court takes due account of the interests of the European Union.
- In its assessment of all those conditions, the national court complies with any decisions of the Court of Justice or the General Court ruling on the lawfulness of the EU measure or on an application for provisional measures seeking similar interim relief at EU level.[10]

In two recent judgments rendered in infringement actions brought by the Commission against Italy for failure to implement decisions which required it to recover fiscal aid from its beneficiaries,[11] the ECJ found that the Italian courts had made several suspension orders in recovery proceedings which did not fulfill the strict conditions of the case-law.[12]

The ECJ recalled that a national court cannot restrict itself to referring the question on validity to the Court for a preliminary ruling, but must, when making the interim order, set out the reasons for which it considers that the Court should find the EU measure to be invalid.[13] Also, a decision of a national court staying the proceedings

8. ECJ, *TWD Textilwerke Deggendorf GmbH v. Germany*, Case No. C-188/92 [1994] ECR I-833 paras. 15–18.
9. See, *inter alia*, Joined Cases ECJ, *Zuckerfabrik Süderdithmarschen and Zuckerfabrik Soest*, Cases No. C-143/88 and C-92/89 [1991] ECR I-415; ECJ, *Atlanta Fruchthandelsgesellschaft and Others (I)*, Case No. C-465/93 [1995] ECR I-3761; ECJ, *Commission v. Italy*, Case No. C-304/09 not yet reported in ECR para. 45.
10. See The Notice on recovery, paras. 58 and 59.
11. ECJ, *Commission v. Italy*, Case No. C-304/09 not yet reported in ECR, concerned recovery of aid granted in the form of tax incentives for companies admitted to listing on a regulated European market. ECJ, *Commission v. Italy*, Case No. C-302/09 not yet reported in ECR, concerned recovery of aid granted to firms in Venice and Chioggia by way of relief from social security contributions.
12. For a discussion of the implications of these cases, see J. Derenne, *La récupération des aides illégales et incompatibles: un tour d'horizon sélectif de la jurisprudence européenne depuis la communication "récupération" de 2007 de la Commission européenne*, 1 Concurrences: revue des droits de la concurrence 73–86 (2012). See also J. Derenne, *Modalités de récupération: La CJUE rappelle que les juridictions nationales ne peuvent ordonner des mesures provisoires suspendant la récupération que dans le strict respect des conditions prévues à cet effet par le droit communautaire (Commission c/ Italie)*, 2 Concurrences: revue des droits de la concurrence, 168–170 (2011).
13. ECJ, *Atlanta Fruchthandelsgesellschaft and Others (I)*, Case No. C-465/93 [1995] ECR I-3761 para. 36.

necessary to ensure the effective implementation of a Commission decision requiring the Member State to recover unlawful aid, on the ground that the legality of that decision is under challenge before the General Court, must set out the arguments showing that the decision at issue is invalid. The ECJ noted that an action brought before the General Court for annulment of a decision ordering recovery of aid does not have suspensory effect on the obligation to implement that decision. The same applies when the judgment of the General Court in such an action is under appeal before the Court of Justice. Therefore, a national court's decision to stay proceedings on the sole ground that the Commission's decision is under challenge before the EU courts constitutes a clear breach of EU law on the recovery of State aid.[14]

Article 14(3) of the procedural regulation also requires the Member State concerned to take all necessary steps available within its legal system to achieve immediate and effective execution of the recovery decision. Complying with this obligation may include litigation before the national courts, namely fending off annulment actions and requests for interim or provisional measures introduced by the beneficiaries. Where the enforcement of a repayment order has been suspended by a national court, the Member State must apply for the review and the revocation of that judicial decision, if this possibility exists within its legal system.[15]

According to the ECJ, the national courts themselves are required, under Article 14(3) of the procedural regulation, to ensure that the decision ordering recovery of the unlawful aid is fully effective and achieves an outcome consistent with the objective pursued by that decision.[16]

The purpose of the recovery is to re-establish the situation that existed on the market prior to the granting of the aid, ensuring that a level-playing field in the internal market is maintained.[17]

Since repayment of the aid is only meant to restore the prior legal situation, it cannot be regarded as a sanction.[18] Even in the case of aid granted in the form of a tax measure of an apparently general nature, the recovery of unlawful State aid for the purpose of restoring the situation existing previously cannot, in principle, be regarded as disproportionate to the objectives of the provisions of the Treaty on State aid.[19]

The ECJ has also made clear that recovery of unlawful and incompatible State aid granted in the form of a tax exemption does not amount to the retroactive application of a higher tax burden.[20] The authorities of the Member State concerned merely have

14. See ECJ, *Commission v. Italy*, Case No. C-304/09 not yet reported in ECR paras. 45–55; ECJ, *Commission v. Italy*, Case No. C-302/09 not yet reported in ECR paras. 45–50.
15. See to that effect ECJ, *Commission v. Italy*, Case No. C-304/09 not yet reported in ECR para. 43.
16. ECJ, *Scott and Kimberley Clark*, Case No. C-210/09 [2010] ECR I-4613 para. 29; ECJ, *Commission v. Italy*, Case No. C-304/09 not yet reported in ECR para. 44.
17. See paras. 13–15 of the Notice on recovery summarizing the relevant case-law.
18. ECJ, *Belgium v. Commission ("Maribel bis/ter" scheme)*, Case No. C-75/97 [1991] ECR I-3671 para. 65.
19. ECJ, *Belgium v. Commission*, Case No. C-142/87 [1990] ECR I-959 para. 66; Joined cases ECJ, *Spain v. Commission*, Cases No. C-278/92 to C-280/92 [1994] ECR I-4103 para. 75; ECJ, *Belgium v. Commission*, Case No. C-75/97 [1991] ECR I-3671para. 68.
20. See V. Di Bucci, *Direct Taxation—State Aid in Form of Fiscal Measures, The EC State Aid Regime: Distortive Effects of State Aid on Competition and Trade*, 73–90, at 87 (Cameron 2006).

to take measures ordering the undertakings which have received the aid to pay sums corresponding to the amount of the tax exemption or other benefit unlawfully granted to them.[21]

Thus, by repaying the aid, including interest, the recipients will forfeit the advantage which they enjoyed over their competitors on the market, and the situation prior to payment of the aid is restored.

§4.03 SPECIFIC QUESTIONS RAISED IN THE CONTEXT OF RECOVERY OF FISCAL AID

Because fiscal aid is almost always granted in the form of a scheme, the Commission will usually not be in a position to identify each individual beneficiary from whom the Member State must require reimbursement of the aid, nor to quantify the precise amount to be recovered from each recipient. This is the responsibility of the Member State concerned. However, it is incumbent upon the Commission to verify that the Member State has correctly implemented the recovery decision. For that purpose, the recovery decision will specify a time-limit within which the Member State will be required to provide complete information on the identity of the beneficiaries, on the amounts of aid involved and on the national procedure applied to obtain recovery. The Member State will also be required to provide documentation showing that the beneficiaries have been notified their obligation to repay the aid.[22]

[A] Determination of the Advantage that Actually Accrued to Each Beneficiary

As a prerequisite for adopting a decision ordering the recovery of fiscal aid, the Commission must have established that the fiscal measure at hand, which has been put into effect by the Member State, conferred a selective advantage on certain economic operators or on certain economic sectors ("favoring certain undertakings or the production of certain goods" according to the terminology in Article 107(1) TFEU). In this context, it is common ground that the tax advantages covered by the prohibition of State aid may take very different forms.[23] These include permanent or temporary tax exemptions, tax credits, reduced tax rates or the taking into account of a reduced taxable base. They also cover special rules allowing the accelerated depreciation of certain assets or concerning the carry-over of losses. Similarly, fiscal amnesties, negligence in the collection of taxes and measures granting discretionary facilities for the payment of fiscal debt may constitute State aid, to the extent that they do not apply in a general and objective manner.[24]

21. ECJ, *Commission v. Greece*, Case No. C-183/91 [1993] ECR I-3131 para. 17.
22. The Notice on recovery, paras. 38 (44, 47–49).
23. See The Notice on fiscal aid, paras. 9 (12–14).
24. See V. Di Bucci, *Direct Taxation—State Aid in Form of Fiscal Measures, The EC State Aid Regime: Distortive Effects of State Aid on Competition and Trade*, 76 (Cameron 2006).

Nonetheless, only an undertaking which has actually benefited from the tax measure entailing a selective advantage will be required to reimburse the aid.[25] At the stage of recovery of the aid it is therefore necessary to look at the individual situation of each undertaking concerned.[26]

Thus, although an undertaking may be eligible to apply for a particular tax exemption or another type of fiscal benefit, it should only be subject to recovery if it has indeed availed itself of that possibility and fulfilled the necessary conditions for that purpose. If no aid has been put at its disposal, then it enjoyed no advantage that it should forfeit.

For instance, in the case of aid granted in the form of a reduction in the rate of tax levied on profits, the advantage only accrues to those undertakings that have indeed made profits during the relevant period. A tax credit conditional on carrying out a particular activity or investment[27] will only benefit the undertakings which meet those conditions and which are in a position to offset the tax credit against a tax liability.

On the other hand, it is settled case-law that an undertaking cannot, in principle, bring an action for annulment of a Commission decision prohibiting a sectoral aid scheme if it is concerned by that decision solely by virtue of belonging to the sector in question and being a potential beneficiary of the scheme. Such a decision is, vis-à-vis such an undertaking, a measure of general application covering situations which are determined objectively and entails legal effects for a class of persons envisaged in a general and abstract manner.[28] In order to establish that the decision is of individual concern to it, the undertaking must, in addition, provide evidence that it is an actual beneficiary of individual aid granted under that scheme, the recovery of which has been ordered by the Commission.[29] A reference by the undertaking to a mere intention to apply the aid scheme is not sufficient for its application for annulment to be deemed admissible.[30]

In certain cases, however, the effects of a temporary tax benefit may extend beyond the fiscal years during which the unlawful measure was in force. Where the beneficiary is allowed to carry forward losses incurred during the years that the measure was in force, or to benefit from a tax reduction on profits made within a specified number of years thereafter, then the effects of the aid are simply spread over a longer period of time. The advantage procured in this manner must of course be forfeited, but for the purpose of recovery account will be taken of the dates on which

25. The Notice on recovery, paras. 32 (35 and 38). See also V. Di Bucci, *Aiuti di Stato e misure fiscali nella recente prassi della Commissione Ce e nella giurisprudenza delle giurisdizioni communitarie*, 6bis *Rassegna Tributaria* 2315–2337, at 2334–2335 (2003).
26. ECJ, *Italy v. Commission*, Case No. C-310/99 [2002] ECR I-2289 para. 91.
27. This of course only applies in cases where the tax credit linked to an investment could not be regarded as compatible with the internal market. See the Notice on fiscal aid, para. 31.
28. See ECJ, *Acegas v. Commission*, Case No. T-309/02 [2009] ECR II-1809 para. 47; ECJ, *Iberdrola SA v. Commission*, Case No. T-221/10 not yet reported in ECR para. 25.
29. Joined cases ECJ, *Italy and Sardegna Lines v. Commission*, Cases No. C-15/98 and C-105/99 [2000] ECR I-8855 paras. 34 and 35; ECJ, *Banco Comercial dos Açores v. Commission*, Case No. T-75/03 not yet reported in ECR para. 44; ECJ, *Iberdrola SA v. Commission*, Case No. T-221/10 not yet reported in ECR para. 26.
30. ECJ, *Iberdrola SA v. Commission*, Case No. T-221/10 not yet reported in ECR para. 29.

the aid, in whole or in installments, was put at the disposal of each beneficiary. In respect of any sum to be reimbursed interest is added, at an annual compound rate, from the date it was granted to the date of its effective recovery.

As noted above, rules on the accelerated depreciation of certain assets (for instance, vessels or other means of transport) may confer an advantage on the undertakings which own those assets. They will be able to offset the corresponding acquisition costs against income at a rate faster than it is generally accepted for other equipment goods or, in any event, at a rate that allows the acquisition costs to be entirely deducted well before the end of the useful life-cycle of the goods concerned. As a result, their tax liability during the initial years after the investment will be suppressed or significantly reduced.[31]

However, in order to reap that benefit, the owner of the depreciated asset should not wait too long to sell or replace that asset. Otherwise, the tax advantage which it enjoyed in the initial years after the acquisition of the asset will be progressively eliminated over time. In fact, if the undertaking concerned keeps ownership of a fully depreciated asset, it will face higher tax bills in subsequent years, as it will no longer be able to deduct any costs related to the acquisition of that asset. The individual circumstances of each undertaking may therefore lead to different conclusions as regards the existence and the extent of its obligation to repay aid granted in the form of accelerated depreciation of certain assets.

Since rules on accelerated depreciation arguably create an incentive for regular replacement of the equipment goods concerned, these rules may also be regarded as indirect aid to manufacturers of such goods. The Commission's recovery decision may require Member States to identify the undertakings which have indirectly benefitted from the special depreciation rules and to obtain from them appropriate reimbursement of the aid.

Aid can also be granted in the form of exemptions or reductions in the rate of indirect taxes, i.e., taxes which are collected at the level of the suppliers of certain goods or services but which are usually passed on in the prices of such goods and services and ultimately levied on their consumption. Despite the fact that indirect tax exemptions and reductions will primarily benefit the final consumers which normally bear the burden of the tax, they will also render the products or services concerned more attractive in the market and, consequently, favor the undertakings that supply them.[32]

The determination of the precise economic advantage granted to indirect beneficiaries of the aid gives rise to difficulties, since it may be argued that the elasticity of demand for the products or services concerned should be taken into account. In order

31. For an example of a Commission's decision discussing the operation of early and accelerated depreciation, see the opening Commission Decision in State aid SA.21233—Tax regime applicable to certain finance lease agreements also known as the Spanish Tax lease System, OJ No. C 276, Sept. 21, 2011, p. 5).

32. V. Di Bucci, *Aiuti di Stato e misure fiscali nella recente prassi della Commissione Ce e nella giurisprudenza delle giurisdizioni communitarie*, 6bis Rassegna Tributaria, 2331–2332 (2003); V. Di Bucci, *Direct Taxation—State Aid in Form of Fiscal Measures, The EC State Aid Regime: Distortive Effects of State Aid on Competition and Trade*, 76–77 (Cameron 2006).

to overcome this obstacle and assist the national authorities, it is the Commission's practice to work out in advance, in its recovery decision, a pragmatic methodology for calculating the amounts of aid to be recovered from indirect beneficiaries.[33]

[B] Quantification of the Amount to Be Reimbursed by the Beneficiary

The calculation of the amount to be recovered from each beneficiary of a scheme may give rise to difficulties, in particular where undertakings have benefited indirectly from fiscal measures directed at consumers or investors.

In accordance with Paragraph 35 of the Notice on fiscal aid, the amount to be recovered is to be calculated on the basis of a comparison between the tax actually paid and the amount which should have been paid if the generally applicable rule had been applied.

No provision of EU law requires the Commission, when ordering the recovery of aid declared incompatible with the internal market, to fix the exact amount of the aid to be recovered. It is sufficient for the Commission's decision to include information enabling the addressee of the decision to work out itself, without overmuch difficulty, that amount.[34] The obligation on a Member State to calculate the exact amount of aid to be recovered forms part of the more general reciprocal obligation incumbent upon the Commission and the Member States of sincere cooperation in the implementation of Treaty rules concerning State aid.[35]

Paragraph 49 of the Notice on recovery requires the Member State concerned to quantify the precise amount of aid to be recovered from each individual beneficiary. To that end, account will be taken of the possibility that, at the time of granting, the aid fulfilled all the conditions of any relevant block exemption regulation or of another aid scheme approved by the Commission. In those cases, the beneficiary will not be required to reimburse the aid.

The application of the so-called *de minimis* rules[36] may also allow some beneficiaries of fiscal aid to escape recovery, provided that the Member State concerned presents to the Commission sufficient evidence that all the conditions laid down in the relevant *de minimis* regulation are met. In particular, the Member State must show that during the reference period the total amount of aid received by the

33. See ECJ, *Associazione italiana del risparmio gestito et Fineco Asset Management SpA v. Commission*, Case No. T-445/05 [2009] ECR II-289 paras. 194–205.
34. See, *inter alia*, ECJ, *Spain v. Commission*, Case No. C-480/98 [2000] ECR I-8717 para. 25; ECJ, *Commission v. France*, Case C-441/06 [2007] ECR I-8887 para. 29; ECJ, *Mediaset SpA v. Commission*, Case No. C-403/10 P not yet reported in ECR para. 126.
35. ECJ, *Netherlands v. Commission*, Case No. C-382/99 [2002] ECR I-5163 para. 91 and the case-law cited.
36. Commission Regulation (EC) 1998/2006 of 15 December 2006 on the application of Articles 87 and 88 of the Treaty to *de minimis* aid, OJ No. L 379, Dec. 28, 2006, 5; Commission Regulation (EC) 1535/2007 of December 20, 2007 on the application of Articles 87 and 88 of the EC Treaty to *de minimis* aid in the sector of agricultural production, OJ No. L 337, Dec. 21, 2007, 35; Commission Regulation (EC) 875/2007 of July 24, 2007 on the application of Articles 87 and 88 of the EC Treaty to *de minimis* aid in the fisheries sector and amending Regulation (EC) 1860/2004, OJ No. L 193, Jul. 25, 2007, 6.

beneficiary has not exceeded the ceilings set out in the regulation. This excludes that the *de minimis* rules could give rise to a sort of standardized deduction to the amount of aid to be recovered from each beneficiary. If the unlawful and incompatible aid received by an undertaking exceeds the de minimis ceiling, it must be repaid in its entirety.

Paragraph 50 of the Notice on recovery also allows national authorities to take into account the incidence of the tax system in order to determine the amount to be reimbursed. In short, this means that in case the beneficiary has paid higher taxes because of the aid received, it will be required to repay only the net amount which corresponds to the economic advantage it retained.

It is clear from the case-law that a beneficiary of fiscal aid cannot escape recovery by referring to hypothetical choices that it could have made if it had not sought the tax benefit in question. In order to avoid the risk of recovery of unlawful aid, i.e., aid which was put into effect before approval by the Commission, a diligent undertaking could have structured its operations differently. At the recovery stage, national authorities may only take account of the tax treatment which corresponds to the operations actually carried out. In certain cases, such operations may still attract a favorable tax treatment under domestic rules which are compatible with EU law, thus reducing or eliminating the amounts to be recovered.[37]

It has been suggested that, in the context of the quantification of the aid to be recovered, account should also be taken of any higher taxes which the beneficiary has paid in its State of residence as a result of the tax advantage that it received in the State of the source of the income. This suggestion draws its inspiration from the ECJ's ruling in *Amurta*,[38] which envisages taking account of a convention for the avoidance of double taxation (DTC) concluded with another State in order to consider neutralized the effects of a restriction on the free movement of capital maintained by a Member State. According to this line of argument, the economic advantage granted by a Member State through fiscal aid could be deemed neutralized, or reduced, by the operation of a DTC which forms part of the wider legal and tax framework applicable to the activities of the beneficiary.

In practice, if the Member State which grants unlawful and incompatible aid were to take account, at the stage of recovery, of the higher amount of taxes paid by some beneficiaries in other States by virtue of the DTCs concluded with those States, this would imply that it accepts foregoing financial resources which instead would increase the tax revenues of other States. While for the undertaking concerned it may be indifferent how the tax burden that it bears is divided among different States, the Member State granting fiscal aid has no interest in transferring its own tax resources to the treasury of other States. The fact that Member States will prefer recovering themselves the amount of aid that they have unlawfully granted, rather than simply taking account of higher taxes paid in other States, may explain why this defense has not so far been invoked in proceedings concerning the implementation of recovery decisions. Moreover, it can be pointed out that the obligation to recover unlawful and

37. See ECJ, *Unicredito Italiano*, Case No. C-184/04 [2005] ECR I-11137 paras. 114–119.
38. ECJ, *Amurta*, Case No. C-379/05 [2007] ECR I-9569 paras. 80–84.

incompatible aid from its beneficiaries lies with the Member State that has granted it and should not be "delegated" to another State.

Usually, the amounts of aid to be recovered tend to be higher than those actually forgone by the State, because compounded interest must be added. However, this may not be the case where fiscal incentives directly benefit consumers or investors and only indirectly grant an advantage to the undertakings supplying the favored goods or services. Since recovery only seeks to eliminate the economic advantage accruing to undertakings, the amounts to be recovered may turn out to be lower that the tax revenue forfeited by the Member State.[39]

A particular problem arises in situations where the State aid has been granted in the form of an exemption from a tax imposed on a narrow sector of the economy (exceptional tax burden).[40] In order to eliminate the advantage that, within the relevant sector, was unlawfully granted to undertakings which were exempted from the tax in question, it may be appropriate to have recourse to an "inverse remedy".[41] This means that the level-playing field will be restored by allowing the Member State to reimburse with interest the tax to those undertakings which have paid it and were therefore previously put at a disadvantage, instead of requiring all exempted undertakings within the relevant sector to forfeit their advantage. It should be noted that a tax that is indistinctly applicable to domestic and imported products may nonetheless provide for exemptions that are designed to cover essentially domestic companies and their products or services, while the brunt of the tax is borne by imported products or services. In that case, if the fiscal measure constitutes State aid within the meaning of Article 107(1) of the TFEU, it may also contravene the prohibition of discriminatory taxes laid down in Article 110 of the TFEU.[42]

[C] Legitimate Expectations

A final issue worth mentioning is the extent to which the principle of legitimate expectations may help the beneficiaries escape recovery of fiscal aid.

39. See E. Righini, *EC State Aid Law/Le droit des aides d'Etat dans la CE: Liber Amicorum Francisco Santaolalla Gadea*, 265–288, at 282 (Kluwer Law International 2008).
40. Subject to certain constraints imposed by EU law, Member States are free to introduce national, non-harmonized taxes to be levied on specific sectors or activities. The sectors concerned are often those considered harmful or those that appear particularly apt to bear a higher tax burden (for instance, gambling). The levy on aggregates imposed by the Finance Act 2001 in the United Kingdom constitutes an example of a national tax imposed on a specific activity, the extraction and use of virgin aggregates, considered harmful for the environment (see ECJ, *British Aggregates v. Commission*, Case No. C-487/06 P [2008]; ECR I-10505; ECJ, *RENV*, Case No. T-210/02 not yet reported in ECR). The Danish Gaming Duties Act constitutes an example of a tax imposed on an admittedly profitable sector. See Commission Decision 2012/140/EU of September 20, 2011, OJ No. L 68, Mar. 7, 2012, 3.
41. For a discussion of the concept of "inverse remedy" and its compatibility with Art. 14(1) of the procedural regulation see J. Flett & K. Walkerova, *EC State Aid Law/Le droit des aides d'Etat dans la CE: Liber Amicorum Francisco Santaolalla Gadea*, 223–237, at 229–230 (Kluwer Law International 2008).
42. See ECJ, *Outokumpu Oy*, Case No. C-213/96 [1998] ECR I-1777.

According to the ECJ, in view of the mandatory nature of the supervision of State aid by the Commission under Article 108 of the TFEU, undertakings to which an aid has been granted may not, in principle, entertain a legitimate expectation that the aid is lawful unless it has been granted in compliance with the procedure laid down in that article. A diligent businessman should normally be able to determine whether that procedure has been followed.[43]

Further, while the ECJ admitted that a recipient of unlawfully granted aid is not precluded from relying on exceptional circumstances which may legitimately have caused it to assume the aid to be lawful, it stressed that a Member State, on the other hand, whose authorities have granted the aid contrary to the procedural rules laid down in Article 108(3) TFEU may not rely on the legitimate expectations of recipients in order to justify a failure to comply with the obligation to take the steps necessary to implement a Commission decision ordering it to recover the aid. If it could do so, Articles 107 and 108 TFEU would be set at naught, since national authorities would thus be able to rely on their own unlawful conduct in order to deprive decisions taken by the Commission under those provisions of the Treaty of their effectiveness.[44]

In later cases, the ECJ has made clear that the beneficiary of fiscal aid would only be able to rely on the principle of the protection of legitimate expectations if it had received precise assurances from the Commission (or other EU institutions) justifying such expectations. This is rarely the case if the fiscal measure concerned has not been notified to the Commission. But even if precise assurances had been given, an overriding public interest could justify that the Commission modifies the rules without even adopting transitional measures for the protection of the expectations which a beneficiary of aid might legitimately entertain. In the absence of such an overriding public interest, the Commission is required by a superior rule of law to adopt appropriate transitional measures.[45]

Although neither the Member State nor the recipient can usually rely on the principle of legal certainty or invoke legitimate expectations in respect of unlawful aid, in a number of decisions the Commission has nonetheless recognized that previous decisions in which it approved tax schemes similar to the one declared incompatible with the internal market may have created legitimate expectations for the beneficiaries of the prohibited scheme.[46]

43. ECJ, *Commission v. Germany*, Case No. C-5/89 [1990] ECR I-3473 para. 14.
44. ECJ, *Commission v. Germany*, Case No. C-5/89 [1990] ECR I-3473 paras. 16 and 17; ECJ, *Commission v. Greece*, Case No. C-183/91 [2003] I-03131 para. 18.
45. See Joined cases ECJ, *Belgium and Forum 187 v. Commission*, Cases No. C-182/03 and C-217/03 [2006] ECR I-5479 paras. 147–149; ECJ, *Commission v. Koninklijke Friesland Campina*, Case No. C-519/07 P paras. 84–87.
46. See for instance, Decision C54/2001 on aid scheme, Ireland, Foreign Income, OJ No. L 204, Aug. 13, 2003, 51, recitals 54–57. See also the Commission Decision 2011/5/EC on the tax amortisation of financial goodwill for foreign shareholding acquisitions implemented by Spain, OJ No. L 7, Jan. 11, 2011, 48, recitals 158–169.

§4.04 CONCLUDING REMARKS

What conclusions can be drawn from the recovery issues highlighted above?

Recovery of fiscal aid, because it usually concerns a large number of beneficiaries and needs to take account of the individual circumstances of each one of them, can be a cumbersome and daunting task. Difficulties arise both for the Member States and for the Commission, which must supervise the implementation of its recovery decisions. Beneficiaries will be tempted to contest every aspect of recovery orders addressed to them, in the hope of avoiding or reducing the amounts of aid they must reimburse. The only effective tool to avoid the risk of recovery, and the litigation associated with it, is for Member States to comply strictly with their obligation under Article 108(3) of the TFEU and to refrain from putting into effect any fiscal aid unless it has been authorized by the Commission.

CHAPTER 5

State Aid and Indirect Taxation

Joachim Englisch

§5.01 INTRODUCTION

Value added tax (VAT), excise duties, stamp duties and transaction taxes are commonly conceived as indirect taxes: As a general rule, the taxable person—usually a business entity—is not supposed to bear the tax for which he is liable, but instead it is assumed that the tax burden is shifted forward to his customers by a corresponding increase in the price of the goods or services whose supply gives rise to taxation. The incidence of the tax is legally presumed and intended to rest with the "consumer" who is therefore regarded as the final taxpayer, although admittedly, this statutory incidence need not coincide with the effective division of the tax burden between business and its customers[1]. Such indirect taxes account for more than half of the tax revenue in many Member States of the European Union (EU). It is therefore prima facie surprising that the scholarly discussion regarding the application of the State aid regime laid down in Articles 107 et seq. TFEU[2] on fiscal aid focuses almost exclusively on direct or "personal" taxes, and on the field of direct business taxation in particular.

The reason for the lack of research in the indirect tax area can probably be explained by the fact that the Commission itself as the "guardian" of Member States' compliance with the Treaty's State aid provisions has been—and to a certain degree still is—reluctant to assess indirect tax measures under Article 107 TFEU. Prior to the

1. As regards VAT in particular, see R.F.W. van Brederode, *Systems of General Sales Taxation*, 29 et seq. (Alphen aan den Rijn 2009).
2. Treaty on the Functioning of the European Union, consolidated version of March 30, 2010, OJ C 83/47.

1997 ECOFIN resolution on harmful tax competition,[3] the Commission did not systematically control national tax systems regarding potential fiscal aid, and only sporadically dealt with this issue. This changed in 1998, when in reaction to the aforementioned resolution, the Commission published a notice on the application of State aid rules to measures relating to *direct* business taxation in 1998[4]. Clearly, the Commission's priority was to invigorate the Code of Conduct on Business Taxation—which formed an integral part of the ECOFIN resolution[5]—through State aid control. Accordingly, in 2000 only one Commission decision on fiscal aid was concerned with indirect taxes,[6] whereas all the remaining ones dealt with direct taxes.

However, this original focus on fiscal aid in the field of direct taxation has been modified by the Commission in subsequent years. In this context, the 2004 Commission report on fiscal aid[7] is particularly relevant. Here, the Commission stated:

> Although the [1998] Commission notice in principle covers only direct taxation, it has provided a basis for analysing certain cases in the field of indirect taxation. The Commission has referred to the notice in a number of decisions relating to indirect taxation measures... Obviously, *indirect taxation measures have specific features* which are not caught by the notice in its present form.
>
> To be caught by the concept of state aid, measures must favour certain undertakings by reducing the charges normally borne by them. In this connection, VAT reductions are subject to strict Community rules and conform to the principle of equality of taxation for similar products. Such reductions are therefore not usually caught by Article 87 (1) [now Article 107 (1) TFEU]. As a general rule, the same is not true of excise duties, which directly affect businesses. A reduction in such duties which favours certain undertakings may constitute aid.[8]

As a consequence, the Commission increasingly assessed fiscal aid in the field of indirect taxation. In the years 2004/05, approximately one quarter of all Commission decisions concerning fiscal aid were related to indirect tax measures, and that portion increased further to approximately one third in 2010/11[9]. Predominantly, the Commission examined energy and other environmental excise tax measures as to their compatibility with the Treaty's State aid rules. By contrast, there are still virtually no VAT cases that have been decided by the Commission, or by the ECJ[10]. Interestingly, excise duties other than so-called "green taxes"—whether harmonized or non-harmonized—have not been scrutinized much, either.

---

3. Conclusions of the ECOFIN Council Meeting on December 1, 1997 concerning taxation policy (98 C 2/01), OJ C 2/1.
4. Commission Notice on the application of the State aid rules to measures relating to direct business taxation, OJ C 384, Dec. 10, 1998.
5. See Conclusions of the ECOFIN Council Meeting (*supra* note 3), OJ C 2/3.
6. Commission decision SG(2001) D/285038 of December 21, 2000 on the Swedish tax rate reduction for the manufacture of basic iron and steel and of ferro-alloys.
7. Report on the implementation of the Commission notice on the application of the State aid rules to measures relating to direct business taxation (COM(2004)434), Feb. 9, 2004.
8. Commission report (*supra* note 7), paras. 71 et seq. (emphasis added).
9. While there do not exist official statistics, the above portion of indirect tax cases can be inferred from the Commission database on State aid cases that have been the object of a Commission decision.
10. For an overview of relevant case law, see B. Terra, *Value Added Tax and State Aid Law in the EU*, Intertax 101 (2012).

This study intents to shed some light on the "specific features" of indirect taxes with a view towards the criteria and consequences of State aid control. In particular, I will try to show that there is still potential for a more significant role of State aid control in the ambit of indirect taxes, and concerning VAT relief measures in particular.

§5.02 THE CONCEPT OF FISCAL AID IN THE FIELD OF INDIRECT TAXATION

[A] Overview

According to settled case law of the ECJ, the notion of aid within the meaning of Article 107 TFEU is more general than that of a subsidy. "It embraces not only positive benefits, but also measures which, in various forms, mitigate the charges which are normally included in the budget of an undertaking and which, without therefore being subsidies in the strict meaning of the word, are similar in character and have the same effect."[11] And in principle, the ensuing concept of fiscal aid that has been established in the case law of the ECJ for the purposes of assessing tax concessions in direct business taxation is also relevant with regard to indirect tax measures. In the singular case that found a national VAT provision to constitute State aid, the Court itself has referred to its settled case law on direct tax measures when it laid out the substantive conditions for the indirect tax measure to be classified as State aid: "First, there must be an intervention by the State or through State resources. Second, the intervention must be liable to affect trade between Member States. Third, it must confer a [selective] advantage on the recipient. Fourth, it must distort or threaten to distort competition."[12]

As is well known, the Court has elaborated on all four of those criteria in a series of judgments, which must therefore be assumed to be relevant also in the field of indirect taxation. As regards the assessment of selectivity in particular, the Court analyzes whether the disputed measure is such as to "favor certain undertakings or the production of certain goods" in comparison with other undertakings which are in a legal and factual situation that is comparable in the light of the objective pursued by the measure in question. The determination of the reference or framework has a particular importance in the case of tax measures, since the very existence of an advantage may

11. ECJ, *De Gezamenlijke Steenkolenmijnen in Limburg v. High Authority*, Case No. C-30/59 [1961] ECR 1 para. 19; ECJ, *Banco Exterior de España*, Case No. C-387/92 [1994] ECR I-877 para. 13; ECJ, *Ecotrade*, Case No. C-200/97 [1998] ECR I-7907 para. 34; ECJ, *Adria-Wien*, Case No. C-143/99 [2001] ECR I-8365 para. 38; ECJ, *Regione Sardegna*, Case No. C-169/08 [2009] I-10821 para. 56; Joined Cases ECJ, *Paint Graphos et al.*, Cases No. C-78/08 to C-80/08 not yet reported in ECR para. 45; ECJ, *Commission and Spain v. Gibraltar*, Cases No. C-106/09 P and C-107/09 P not yet reported in ECR para. 71.
12. ECJ, *Heiser*, Case No. C-172/03 [2005] ECR I-1627 para. 27; Joined Cases ECJ, *Air Liquide*, Cases No. C-393/04 and C-41/05 [2006] ECR I-5293 para. 28; ECJ, *Altmark Trans und Regierungspräsidium Magdeburg*, Case No. C-280/00 [2003] ECR I-7747 para. 75. A more structured set of the same criteria can be found in the Commission Notice on the application of the State aid rules to measures relating to direct business taxation (*supra* note 4), paras. 9–12.

be established only when compared with "normal" or "benchmark" taxation[13]. However, according to the jurisprudence of the ECJ the concept of State aid does not refer to State measures which differentiate between undertakings and which are, therefore, prima facie selective, where that differentiation is justified by the nature or the overall structure of the system of charges of which they are part[14]. This may be assumed if the Member State concerned can show that the disputed measure results directly from the basic or guiding principles of its tax system[15]. In that connection, the ECJ makes a distinction between, on the one hand, the objectives attributed to a particular tax scheme which are extrinsic to it and, on the other, the mechanisms inherent in the tax system itself which are necessary for the achievement of such objectives; only the latter may serve as a valid justification[16].

It is respectfully submitted the crucial notion of selective fiscal aid established by the Court is not entirely convincing. First, an advantage that is liable to constitute aid should be assumed only if the disputed tax relief cannot be qualified as a corollary of the fundamental principles underlying the respective tax system[17]. Otherwise, the entire national system of direct and indirect business taxation would potentially constitute State aid, since no tax (except a head tax or other lump-sum taxes) is wholly neutral and free from distortive—i.e., for some: advantageous—effects[18]; however,

---

13. See, to that effect, ECJ, *Adria-Wien*, Case No. C-143/99 [2001] ECR I-8365 para. 41; ECJ, *GIL Insurance*, Case No. C-308/01 [2004] ECR I-4777 para. 68; ECJ, *Heiser*, Case No. C-172/03 [2005] ECR I-1627 para. 40; ECJ, *Portugal v. Commission*, Case No. C-88/03 [2006] ECR I-7115 paras. 54 and 56; ECJ, *British Aggregates v. Commission*, Case No. C-487/06 P [2008] ECR I-10515 para. 82; Joined Cases ECJ, *Commission and Spain v. Gibraltar*, Cases No. C-106/09 P and C-107/09 P not yet reported in ECR para. 75. See also Commission Notice on the application of the State aid rules to measures relating to direct business taxation (*supra* note 4), paras. 9 and 16. As the Court has clarified in Joined Cases ECJ, *Commission and Spain v. Gibraltar*, Cases No. C-106/09 P and C-107/09 P not yet reported in ECR paras. 90 et seq., the deviation from the benchmark need not take the technical form of an exception or "derogating provision" in order to be qualified as selective.
14. Cf. ECJ, *Italy v. Commission*, Case No. 173/73 [1974] ECR 709 para. 33; ECJ, *Adria-Wien*, Case No. C-143/99 [2001] ECR I-8365 para. 42; ECJ, *Unicredito Italiano*, Case No. C-148/04 [2005] ECR I-11137 para. 51; ECJ, *Portugal v. Commission*, Case No. C-88/03 [2006] ECR I-7115 para. 52. As the Court has specified in it is judgments ECJ, *Netherlands v. Commission*, Case No. C-159/01 [2004] ECR I-4461 para. 43; ECJ, *Portugal v. Commission*, Case No. C-88/03 [2006] ECR I-7115 para. 80 and Joined Cases ECJ, *Commission and Spain v. Gibraltar*, Cases No. C-106/09 P and C-107/09 P not yet reported in ECR para. 146, the Member State must show that the disputed measure is actually justified by the nature and general scheme of the system in question, whereas the Commission need not address this aspect on its own motion (ex officio).
15. Cf. ECJ, *Belgium v. Commission*, Case No. C-75/97 [1999] ECR I-3671 para. 33; ECJ, *Italy v, Commission*, Case No. 173/73 [1974] ECR I-709; W. Schön, *Taxation and State Aid Law in the European Union*, CMLRev 911 (930) (1999); regarding Pigouvian taxes see ECJ, *Adria-Wien*, Case No. C-143/99 [2001] ECR I-8365 para. 52.
16. Cf. ECJ, *Portugal v. Commission*, Case No. C-88/03 [2006] ECR I-7115 paras. 81 et seq.
17. See, for instance, ECJ, *Stadtwerke Schwäbisch Hall et al.*, Case No. T-92/02 [2006] ECR II-11 paras. 67 et seq.; W. Schön and M. Lang, *Verhandlungen des Siebzehnten Österreichischen Juristentages*, 28 et seq. (vol. IV/2 (2009). In a similar vein, see also F.P. Sutter, *Das EG-Beihilfenverbot und sein Durchführungsverbot in Steuersachen*, 104 et seq. (Linde 2005).
18. J.E. Stiglitz, *Economics of the Public Sector* (3d ed., 2000), 462 et seq.; H. Zimmermann, K. Henke & M. Broer, *Finanzwissenschaft*, 266 et seq. (10th ed.); D. Wellisch, *Finanzwissenschaft II* (2000), 95. See also Joined Cases ECJ, *Commission and Spain v. Gibraltar*, Cases No. C-106/09 P and C-107/09 P not yet reported in ECR para. 83.

Article 107 TFEU has not been devised as a general instrument to control Member States' systems of business taxation. Hence, if the disputed measure results directly from the basic or guiding principles of the national tax system,[19] this is not a question of justification (as assumed by the ECJ) but this rather rules out any need for justification under Article 107 TFEU.

Second, a fiscal advantage that could be qualified as aid within the meaning of Article 107 TFEU because the corresponding tax relief cannot be traced back to the basic principles of the respective tax system should be qualified as selective if it exclusively or predominantly benefits certain undertakings or industry sectors[20]. This may be determined either by a legal analysis based on the statutory prerequisites for the tax concession, or by a factual analysis if the measure is facially neutral but effectively reduces the tax burden of some businesses or industries more than the burden of others by a significant margin. In the latter case, the extension of State aid control beyond a concept of discrimination in a strictly legal sense should be accompanied by a parallel admission of unwritten justifications,[21] similar to the Court's case law on fundamental freedoms where the rule of reason was established in *Cassis de Dijon*[22] to counterbalance the broad *Dassonville*-formula[23].

Finally, a measure should not escape State aid review merely because the advantages that it entails for certain undertakings are a consequence of its underlying objective. Comparability of privileged undertakings and of non-privileged or less advantaged undertakings must only be determined in the light of the guiding principles of the tax system and of their statutory substantiation. By contrast, the Court's (and the Commission's) assessment of comparability by referring to the purpose of the distortive measure is equivalent to introducing additional justifications for fiscal aid without proper legal basis and without a proportionality test. For instance, special deductions for R&D investments which reduce the CIT base and which effectively benefit the car industry or the pharmaceutical industry much more than the retail sector should be regarded as State aid to the extent that they exceed the standard depreciation rates, rather than declaring the respective business sectors as incomparable relative to their R&D intensity[24]. There is no good reason why such tax expenditure should be assessed

19. In case of a Pigouvian tax, the guiding principle may also be a policy objective that is unrelated to considerations of tax fairness, and that might be considered as an "extrinsic" principle in the context of a tax that only serves to raise revenue; see also P. Rossi-Maccanico, *State Aid Review of Member States' Measures Relating to Direct Business Taxation*, EStAL 229 at 243 et seq. (2004).
20. For a similar understanding of selectivity *strictu sensu*, see Commission Notice on the application of the State aid rules to measures relating to direct business taxation (*supra* note 4), paras. 17–20.
21. Likewise C. Micheau, *Tax Selectivity in State Aid Review: A Debatable Case Practice*, EC Tax Review 276 (282) (2008).
22. ECJ, *Cassis de Dijon*, Case No. 120/78 [1979] ECR I-649 para. 8.
23. ECJ, *Dassonville*, Case No. 8/74 [1974] ECR I-837; see also J. Englisch, *Wettbewerbsgleichheit im grenzüberschreitenden Handel*, 335, 340 et seq. (2008).
24. For a different opinion, see Commission Notice on the application of the State aid rules to measures relating to direct business taxation (*supra* note 4), para. 14; confirmed by Commission Staff Working Paper, Mid-Term Review of the R&D&I Framework of Aug. 10, 2011, 2. See also Schön, *State Aid in the Area of Taxation*, 321, at 346 (Hancher et al. eds., EU State Aids

differently from direct R&D subsidies, which are normally caught by Article 107 TFEU (unless covered by a block exemption regulation)[25].

Notwithstanding the above criticism, this study will focus on the elements of the State aid concept that raise specific issues in the context of indirect taxation. In order to avoid distractions from this objective, the Court's settled case law on the concept of selective aid will form the basis of the analysis. Against this background, three questions will be discussed: Can an indirect tax relief be assumed to benefit the business entity that is acting as taxable person, even if the tax is supposed to be borne by the customer? Under which conditions can a tax relief be qualified as State aid rather than as Union aid in areas of harmonized indirect taxation, which are far more relevant than in a direct tax context? And finally, does the assessment of distortive effects of an aid scheme require some special considerations in the light of the destination principle that characterizes the allocation of taxing powers under most indirect tax systems?

[B] Indirect Tax Relief: Who Benefits?

In the context of an indirect tax, two beneficiaries of the relief resulting from a reduction or elimination of the regular tax burden are prima facie conceivable: The taxable person (business acting as "tax collector"), and—alternatively or cumulatively—the final taxpayer (the customer as the one who is supposed to bear the regular tax burden). The identification of the correct recipient matters in the context of Article 107 TFEU, because tax expenditure may be examined as possible aid under this provision only if it benefits "undertakings". If one had to presume that the tax concession is passed on to customers rather than lowering the tax burden "normally" borne by producers or suppliers, it could be argued that the advantage can be qualified as aid only to the extent that these customers are undertakings rather than private individuals or other non-business entities. Moreover, an assessment of the selective or general nature of aid[26] will also depend on the determination of its potential beneficiaries.

The Court's case law does provide for some guidance in this regard, but it is not entirely clear. To the author's knowledge, there is only one judgment that explicitly addressed the issue: In the case *Heiser*,[27] the ECJ had to deal with the failure to adjust input VAT deductions for goods and services that were initially acquired for the purpose of taxed transactions but ultimately used in order to carry out exempt

2012): State aid conferring an advantage, but not selective (because the author does not want to apply de facto selectivity standards in this context).

25. See, in this regard, the Communication of the Commission, Community framework for state aid for research and development and innovation (2006/C 323/01). See also, in more general terms (same standards for direct subsidies and tax expenditure) R. Luja, *Assessment and Recovery of Tax Incentives in the EC and the WTO: A View on State Aids, Trade Subsidies and Direct Taxation*, 22 et seq. (2002).
26. See, in this regard, ECJ, *Adria-Wien*, Case No. C-143/99 [2001] ECR I-8365 paras. 34 et seq.; Joined Cases ECJ, *Commission and Spain v. Gibraltar*, Cases No. C-106/09 P and C-107/09 P not yet reported in ECR paras. 72 et seq.; Commission Notice on the application of the State aid rules to measures relating to direct business taxation (*supra* note 4), para. 13.
27. ECJ, *Heiser*, Case No. C-172/03 [2005] ECR I-1627.

supplies[28]. Such a waiver of adjustment was available to operators in the medical field after Austria acceded to the EU and introduced an exemption for medical services that had been taxed under its preceding, non-harmonized VAT system. The Court, in examining the compatibility of the transitional regime with Article 107 (1) TFEU, ruled as follows: "... with regard to the effects of a measure such as that at issue in the main proceedings, it must be observed that, *in law*, medical practitioners are the only beneficiaries. There is *no indication* in the case-file put before the Court by the referring court *that the benefit of that measure was systematically passed on* by them to the sickness insurance bodies so that the advantage was, in the end, cancelled out for medical practitioners."[29]

At first sight, one might conclude that the Court has thereby established a general rule pursuant to which indirect tax exemptions or relief measures must be deemed to benefit the taxable person, unless evidence is put forward to the contrary. Upon a closer look, the judgment is less clear than it seems in this regard, though: In the specific context of the denial of input VAT deductions that corresponds to most VAT exemptions, the Court has repeatedly—albeit unconvincingly—held that taxable persons who avail themselves of an exemption are unable to pass any VAT charge (including non-deductible input VAT) to the person following them in the chain of supply and therefore have a VAT status largely similar to a final consumer[30]. Since the Court thus considers the taxable person to be the legally intended final taxpayer with regard to any non-deductible input tax burden, it would seem logical to presume that it is also the taxable person rather than his customer who benefits, *in law*, from the permission to refrain from making an adjustment that entails the non-deductability of input VAT. The Court's decision therefore does not preclude the assumption that in general, it is the customer upon whom the regular tax burden is supposed to be shifted who receives, *in law*, the advantage ensuing from a indirect tax concession. Hence, the only unequivocal conclusion that can be drawn from the *Heiser* judgment is that evidence as to the real economic incidence of an indirect tax must be admitted in order to determine who is the typical[31] *effective* recipient of the aid[32], and that the latter finding has precedence over the legally intended recipient for the purposes of the State aid analysis.

It would indeed seem defensible to presume by default that exemptions, special low rates and other forms of reductions of indirect tax burdens will *primarily* benefit the intended final taxpayer. This is not only consistent with the decision practice of the

28. As a general rule, under the harmonized EU system of VAT an input VAT credit may be claimed only to the extent that input goods and services are used for the purposes of taxed transactions, pursuant to Art. 168 of the VAT Directive 2006/112/EC.
29. ECJ, *Heiser*, Case No. C-172/03 [2005] ECR I-1627 para. 47.
30. Cf. ECJ, *Becker*, Case No. 8/81 [1982] ECR 53 para. 44; ECJ, *Puffer*, Case No. C-460/07 [2009] ECR I-3251 para. 59.
31. The need for generalization is expressed in the Court's formulation of the benefit being "systematically" passed on to the customer.
32. Likewise, see Schön, *State Aid in the Area of Taxation*, 321, at 352 et seq. (Hancher et al. eds., EU State Aids 2012).

Commission[33]. It also corresponds to the very notion of an indirect tax. While obviously, statutory incidence need not necessarily coincide with effective incidence, a legalistic—and therefore possibly only provisional—assessment of tax incidence can be based on the reasonable legal conception of a tax as a charge to be passed on to the customer of the taxable person. However, a contrary presumption applies if the tax expenditure measure is linked to certain production processes or to certain producer categories *in order to compensate* for competitive (cost) disadvantages of such processes or producers. Such an advantage is legally designed not to decrease the price for the consumer, but rather to increase income of the producer. Unless proven otherwise, it is thus the taxable person who is to be regarded as the recipient of the aid. The Commission practice also provides for examples of this kind of benefits[34].

If the customers to whom the tax concession at issue is supposedly or verifiably passed on are not "undertakings" within the meaning of Article 107 (1) TFEU, the question arises whether the measure could nevertheless be selective, because it *also* confers some form of (indirect) competitive advantage on the suppliers who are taxable persons. There is no directly relevant ECJ case law on this matter; and the Commission has dealt with it only in a very peculiar case[35]. However, the ECJ has clarified (with respect to non-fiscal aid) that one and the same aid measure may have two beneficiaries: the person who is receiving the advantage in the form that it has been granted by the State, *and* another person who will reap some economic benefits that do not exactly correspond to the original advantage but which are nevertheless a reflection of the aid and its effect on market mechanisms[36].

Moreover, there is consistent ECJ case law on the repayment of unlawfully *charged* indirect taxes: In this context, the Court has held that even if an indirect tax is

33. See, for instance, Commission decision COM(2009)9972 of December 15, 2009 on the Dutch exemption from environmental taxes for ceramic producers, para. 31; Commission Decision COM(2010)5769 of September 3, 2010 on the Latvian tax exemptions for primary producers, para. 21; Commission decision COM(2011)2613 of April 8, 2011 on the British exemption from the climate change levy for electrified rail, para. 15.
34. See, for instance, Commission decision COM(2009)8497 of October 30, 2009 on the Finnish excise duty exemption for biofuel, para. 18; Commission decision COM(2010)2219 of April 9, 2010 on the Bulgarian tax reduction for biofuels, para. 29; Commission decision COM(2010)2557 of April 19, 2010 on the German tax rebates for biofuels, para. 4.
35. See the Commission decision COM(2011)3504 final concerning the taxation of Greek casinos: All Greek casinos were in principle subject to a uniform fee equivalent to 80% of the admission ticket value; however, the calculation of the fee was based at least on certain minimum values regardless of the ticket price—if any—actually charged to customers. The minimum value—and thus the minimum tax liability—per customer was set differently for different types of casinos. Against this background, the Commission decided that the measure benefitted the privileged casinos rather than their customers, because the minimum levy was obviously not conceived as an indirect charge to be passed on to customers through a corresponding increase of ticket prices. See Commission decision COM(2011)3504 final concerning the taxation of Greek casinos of May 24, 2011, paras. 70 and 73.
36. Cf. ECJ, *Residex Capital*, Case No. C-275/10 not yet reported in ECR para. 43. See also ECJ, *Germany v. Commission*, Case C-156/98 [2000] ECR I-6857 paras. 26 et seq., where the Court assumed that indirect benefits to certain undertakings constituting aid within the meaning of Art. 107 (1) TFEU may result from the tax relief granted to other recipients; in the case at hands, investments in the formerly mentioned undertakings became more attractive through a special form of roll-over relief available on a general basis to all businesses. See also ECJ, *Associazione italiana del risparmio gestito*, Case No. T-445/05 [2009] ECR II-289 para. 127 (Article 87 EC

passed on to customers, it may have a negative impact on sales volume of the taxable person and may thus cause economic disadvantages that must be compensated[37]. By inverse reasoning, tax relief measures may be assumed to confer a relevant *competitive* advantage to the taxable persons who sell the privileged goods or services, by enabling them to lower their prices and thus increase their sales volume and their market share. Under the premise that turnover has a positive profit contribution effect, this constitutes a monetary advantage even though it is not equivalent to the original tax relief[38].

In some cases, the existence of a selective indirect benefit of the aforementioned kind to the advantage of the taxable person will be rather obvious. This will especially have to be assumed if the reduction of the tax burden for consumers is conditional on the use of a particular good or service from a particular undertaking[39]. In "hard cases", a thorough economic analysis of cross price elasticity between privileged and non-privileged goods or services may be required in order to ascertain whether the taxable persons are at least indirectly benefitting from tax relief measures, too, besides their customers who are (at least in law) the recipients of the proper tax advantage. For instance, if admission tickets for sporting events are exempt from VAT according to national VAT legislation[40], the degree of competition of such events with other leisure activities such as theme parks, theatres etc. needs to be assessed.

As to other forms of tax relief measures that do not consist in a reduction of the indirect tax liability of the taxable person, the identification of the beneficiary of the aid will usually be more straightforward. In particular, in a single-stage tax the customer/final taxpayer should be regarded as the beneficiary of an indirect tax rebate that can be claimed by him directly[41], whereas a deferment of the indirect tax payment granted to the taxable person will normally only benefit the latter[42].

[now Art. 107 TFEU] prohibits aid granted by a State or through State resources in any form whatsoever, without drawing a distinction as to whether the aid-related advantages are granted directly or indirectly).

37. Cf. ECJ, *Weber's Wine World*, Case No. C-147/01 [2003] ECR I-11365; ECJ, *Marks & Spencer*, Case No. C-309/06 [2008] ECR I-2283; ECJ, *Lady & Kid*, Case No. C-398/09 not yet reported in ECR.
38. For a possibly different opinion, see J. Swinkels, *State aid & VAT*, IVM 311 (at 312) (2005): "measures must be considered as taken through state resources if they entail a decrease of ... tax revenue... for the state budget and reflect in a *corresponding* advantage for certain undertakings" (emphasis added).
39. See Commission decision COM(2011)3504 final concerning the taxation of Greek casinos of May 24, 2011, para. 72.
40. As authorized by Arts. 371 et seq., read together with Annex X Part B number (1).
41. See ECJ, *Adria-Wien*, Case No. C-143/99 [2001] ECR I-8365 paras. 5 and 40(41); see also, for instance, Commission decision COM(2010)4851 of July 20, 2010 on the Czech refund of excise duties levied on motor fuels used in agricultural production, paras. 5 and 21; Commission decision COM(2011)4890 of July 13, 2011 on the German tax relaxation for agricultural diesel, para. 15; Commission decision COM(2011)5399 of July 25, 2011 on the refund of biofuel oil excise duty for agriculture and greenhouse cultivation.
42. See ECJ, *Ladbroke Racing*, Case No. T-67/94 [1998] ECR II-1 paras. 78 et seq. See also Commission decision COM(2010)2538 of May 26, 2010 (Umicore) concerning a mutually binding agreement between tax authorities and the taxable person on the facts that determine the tax liability.

[C] State Aid versus Union Aid

Pursuant to Article 107 (1) TFEU, the aid must be granted "by a Member State or through State resources" in order to fall under the substantive scope of that provision. As has already been pointed out, a measure that is resulting in a reduction of the tax liability or in a deferment of the tax payment will always have to be regarded as a form of tax expenditure; the foregone revenue or the postponed tax collection results in reduced State resources[43]. Therefore, it is only the second element of the aforementioned formula that merits further analysis: Is the imputation of the aid to the Member State an additional criterion, and if so, when can this be assumed in the field of harmonized indirect taxation?

The Commission practice seems to be inconsistent in this regard. In most cases, reference is made *only* to the financing of the aid through State resources, i.e., to the loss of revenue ensuing from the tax relief[44]. The respective decisions are obviously based on a literal interpretation of Article 107 (1) TFEU, since the provision mentions both criteria alternatively ("or"). In few decisions, the issue of imputing the aid to the State has indeed been raised. The Commission has usually "resolved" it by merely referring to the fact that the relevant national legislation providing for the aid was enacted by the Member State, rather than by the Union[45]. Only in one singular decision[46] has the Commission held that the disputed tax exemptions were "permissible, but not mandatory" under EU law and therefore imputable to the Member State. This is indeed a more convincing approach, as we shall discuss in the following.

It is actually settled case law that the use of Member State resources to finance the aid, on the one hand, and the political responsibility of the Member State for the aid measure, on the other hand, are cumulative rather than alternative criteria[47]. The Court has not explained this interpretation of Article 107 (1) TFEU in detail, but it is actually supported by several legal arguments. First, a contextual interpretation of the provision suggests that the distinction between State aid and other (especially Union or private)

43. See *supra* at note 11; see also ECJ, *Italy v. Commission*, Case No. C-6/97 [1999] ECR I-2981 para. 15; Commission Notice on the application of the State aid rules to measures relating to direct business taxation (*supra* note 4), para. 10.
44. See, for instance, Commission decision COM(2009)8093 of October 28, 2009 on the Danish NOx tax reduction, para. 45; Commission decision COM(2010)4851 of July 20, 2010 on the Czech refund of excise duties levied on motor fuels used in agricultural production, para. 21; Commission decision COM(2010)8911 of December 14, 2010 on the Finnish tax refund on certain energy products used in agriculture, para. 16; Commission decision COM(2010)9636 of December 20, 2010 on the Dutch tax reduction for the glasshouse horticulture sector, para. 14; Commission decision concerning State aid SA.26798 of September 12, 2011 on the Italian excise duty exemption for vegetal oil, para. 24.
45. See, for instance, Commission decision COM(2010)5769 of September 3, 2010 on the Latvian tax exemptions for primary producers, para. 21.
46. Commission decision COM(2009)10745 of December 23, 2009 on the Slovak tax advantages applied on electricity, coal and natural gas, para. 32.
47. Cf. ECJ, *France v. Commission*, Case No. C-482/99 [2002] ECR I-4397 para. 24; ECJ, *GEMO*, Case No. C-126/01 [2003] ECR I-13769 para. 24; ECJ, *Pearle et al.*, Case No. C-345/02 [2004] ECR I-7139 para. 35; ECJ, *Forum 187*, Case No. C-182/03 [2006] ECR I-5479 para. 127. Likewise P. Jann, *Nationale Steuern und das EG-Beihilfenverbot—ein Überblick*, Festschrift Baudenbacher 419 (at 428).

aid it is an essential feature of the State aid concept of Article 107 (1) TFEU: The provision is laid down in Part Three, Title VII, section 2 of the Treaty, with the official section heading: "Aids *granted by states*" (emphasis added). Second, and even more relevant, a purposive construction of the prohibition of State aid points in the same direction. Historically, State aid is suspicious of promoting national interests rather than Union interests, as opposed to Union aid which can normally be assumed to benefit the internal market as a whole[48]. In particular, the founding fathers of European integration feared that national subsidies could be used to undermine the abolition of tariffs in the customs Union, so as to continue protectionist policies contrary to the internal market objective[49]. Therefore, a review of selective aid under the procedure laid down in Article 108 TFEU was considered necessary only if such aid is imputable to a Member State, but not if the Union's institutions (or the private sector) are responsible for the disputed aid scheme.

The crucial question is thus how to determine, in case of harmonized indirect taxation, whether a tax relief measure that constitutes aid within the meaning of Article 107 (1) TFEU is attributable to either the Member State or to the Union. The case law of the European courts provides some guidance in this matter, too. If the granting of a selective and distortive tax advantage is compulsory under Union law (as interpreted by the ECJ), it will have to be regarded as Union aid[50]. The same applies, according to the (former) Court of First Instance, if the tax advantage forms part of the standard tax system established by a European directive, even though the directive provides Member States with the option to waive or extend the respective tax relief[51]. In the case that was decided by the CFI, the Directive on the harmonization of the structures of excise duties on mineral oils laid down a compulsory exemption for fuel that was used in commercial air traffic. By default, no exemption was available for high speed trains competing with air traffic on some routes. However, the national legislator could have granted an exemption also for train fuels based on an option granted to Member States in the Directive. In the Court's view, the element of national political discretion in the refusal to do so did not alter the qualification of the air traffic concession as Union aid.

To the author, the above-mentioned case law adequately reflects the objective of Article 107 (1) TFEU, because in those scenarios the selective and potentially distortive effect of the aid scheme has already been approved by the Union legislator. It is respectfully submitted, though, that some refinement is still required regarding non-standard but *authorized* or *optional* tax relief measures. Here, the national legislator has political discretion as to whether or not to implement certain beneficial tax regimes,

48. Cf. A. Bleckmann, *Subventionsprobleme des GATT und der EG*, 48 RabelsZ 419 (at 449) (1984); D. Wyatt & A. Dashwood, *European Union Law*, 848 (6th ed., Hart 2011). See also ECJ, *Oelmühle Hamburg*, Case No. C-298/96 [1998] I-4767 para. 37.
49. See J. Englisch, *Zur Bedeutung des gemeinschaftsrechtlichen Gleichheitssatzes im Recht der Gemeinschaftsbeihilfen*, EuR 488 (at 490) (2009), with further references. See also ECJ, *Adria-Wien*, Case No. C-143/99 [2001] ECR I-8365 para. 22.
50. Cf. ECJ, *Puffer*, Case No. C-460/07 [2009] ECR I-3251 para. 70. For a similar opinion, but based on different reasoning, see B. Terra, *Value Added Tax and State Aid Law in the EU*, Intertax 101, at 110 (2012), who considers the measure to be "justified by the nature of the general system" of Union legislation.
51. Cf.ECJ, *Deutsche Bahn*, Case No. T-351/02 [2006] ECR II-1047 para. 102.

which do not form an integral element of the harmonized system as envisaged by the Union legislator. Such options are particularly frequent in the context of the common European VAT system as well as in the common European system of energy taxation; the Commission was therefore not quite correct in generalizing that "VAT reductions are subject to strict Community rules"[52]. Traditionally, the Court will characterize these optional tax relief measures as State aid, because they result from an "autonomous decision of a Member State in pursuit of its own economic or social objectives"[53].

By analogy to a case concerned with the application of the EU fundamental freedoms to a national tax regime within the framework of Union harmonization, a more refined approach seems preferable. In the *Schmelz* case[54], the ECJ examined a personal exemption from VAT available for small undertakings. The VAT Directive allows Member to offer such an exemption provided that the small undertakings are established in the territory of the respective Member State; in the case at hands, the exemption was qualified accordingly in national VAT legislation. The Court held that the ensuing restriction of the freedom of establishment cannot be attributed to the Member States, since they do not have any discretion to implement the exemption without the qualification that privileged an establishment in the respective Member State. In a similar vein, tax relief measures based on options or authorizations in a directive should not be subject to State aid control *to the extent* that they *necessarily* entail selective and distortive effects; instead, they constitute Union aid which must be assessed in the light of the equality principle enshrined in Article 20 Charter of Fundamental Rights. Since the Commission which initiated such legislation and the Union legislator have approved the measure and, arguably, also its intrinsic effects, the measure is not susceptible any more to unilaterally promote the interests of a Member State at the expense of the internal market, even though the implementation of the measure is left to the political discretion of each Member State. The tax relief is thus not suspicious of substituting tariffs or promoting primarily national economic interests, which is however the raison d'être of the State aid control under Article 108 TFEU.

There is one explicit exception to this general rule for optional tax relief measures: According to Article 26 (2) Energy Tax Directive[55], optional measures authorized by this Directive may still constitute State aid within the meaning of Article 107 (1) TFEU. Hence, the Union legislator did not endorse all distortive effects that are inherent in the options granted in the Directive, but rather provided the Commission with the possibility to assess the compatibility of such effects with the internal market on a case-by-case basis, in the light of the justifications laid down in Article 107 (3) TFEU.

---

52. See *supra* note 7.
53. ECJ, *Denkavit italiana*, Case No. C-61/79 [1980] ECR I-1207 para. 31; ECJ, *Deutsche Bahn*, Case No. T-351/02 [2006] ECR II-1047 para. 100; ECJ, *Ireland v. Commission*, Case No. T-50/06 not yet reported in ECR para. 73.
54. ECJ, *Schmelz*, Case No. C-97/09 not yet reported in ECR paras. 51 et seq.
55. Council Directive 2003/96/EC of 27 Oct. 2003 restructuring the Community framework for the taxation of energy products and electricity. The provision of Art. 26 (2) specifies: "Measures such as tax exemptions, tax reductions, tax differentiation and tax refunds within the meaning of this Directive might constitute State aid and in those cases have to be notified to the Commission pursuant to Article 88(3) of the Treaty [now Art. 108 (3) TFEU]."

By contrast, an indirect tax aid scheme should regularly be attributed to the national legislator in case of tax relief measures that do not conform to the harmonized system of taxation, but which are admissible from the viewpoint of secondary EU law as part of a *transitional arrangement* that allows a Member State to maintain certain features of its national tax legislation that existed already prior to Union harmonization[56]. A good example is the previously mentioned VAT exemption concerning admission tickets for sporting events, which is a concession to Member States whose legislation provided for this kind of tax expenditure before they joined the harmonized system. Here, it cannot be presumed that the Union legislator endorsed any selective and distortive effects of the measure, but instead the latter was merely accepted as an interim solution. Therefore, Article 107 TFEU should apply considering its rationale.

This latter finding is not called into question by the fact that in two decisions[57], the ECJ refused to examine such transitional measures as to their compatibility with the State aid rules of the Treaty. Contrary to what has been put forward in scholarly writing[58], the Court's unwillingness to carry out a State aid review did not imply that the disputed measures were generally shielded from such review due to their authorization under the relevant EU legislation. Instead, the State aid aspect of the measures was irrelevant for the main proceedings pending before the national courts[59], because the respective claimant sought to receive an equally beneficial tax treatment, whereas the consequence of a finding of unauthorized State aid is usually the denial of the advantage to all undertakings[60].

[D] Impact on Competition and Intra-Union Trade

According to settled case law of the ECJ, it is not necessary to establish that the fiscal aid has a real effect on trade between Member States and that it actually distorts or threatens to distort competition[61]. To be caught by the prohibition of Article 107 (1) TFEU, it is sufficient that the measure is liable to have such detrimental effects[62]. Moreover, even if a measure is neutral from the point of view of the national tax system, because it is available to all domestic undertakings that compete in the relevant market, it will nevertheless have to be qualified as (in principle) unlawful aid if it

56. Likewise J. Swinkels, *State Aid & VAT*, IVM 311 (at 314) (2005).
57. ECJ, *Ideal tourisme*, Case No. C-36/99 [2000] ECR I-6049 paras. 26 et seq.; ECJ, *Evangelischer Krankenhausverein Wien*, Case No. C-437/97 [2000] ECR I-1157 paras. 51 et seq.
58. Cf. S. Rode, *Steuervergünstigungen, Beihilfen und Steuerwettbewerb*, 169 et seq. (2006).
59. See also Opinion AG Cosmas in ECJ, *Ideal tourisme*, Case No. C-36/99 [2000] ECR I-6049 paras. 26–27.
60. See ECJ, *Air Liquide Industries Belgium*, Cases No. C-393/04 and C-41/05 [2006] ECR I-5293 para. 43; ECJ, *Transalpine Ölleitung*, Case No. C-368/04 [2006] ECR I-9957 para. 49.
61. Cf. ECJ, *Italy v. Commission*, Case No. C-372/97 [2004] ECR I-3679 para. 44; ECJ, *Unicredito Italiano*, Case No. C-372/97 [2005] ECR I-11137 para. 54; ECJ, *Air Liquide Industries Belgium*, Case No. C-372/97 [2006] ECR I-5293 para. 34.
62. See, for instance, also Commission decision COM(2010)8948 of December 14, 2010 on the Danish Online Gaming Duties, para. 96.

strengthens the position of these undertakings vis-à-vis foreign undertakings competing with them in intra-Union trade[63].

However, this is somewhat less obvious in an indirect tax context: If the disputed tax advantage has selective effects only with respect to the supply side, i.e., regarding the benefits it entails for certain taxable persons, a distortion of competition may usually be assumed only if the measure is "internally distortive": If there are non-privileged substitute goods or services that compete with the privileged ones in the domestic market[64]. By contrast, a tax relief measure that is neutral with respect to competing sectors of the economy, is often not liable to distort competition *internationally* if implemented within the framework of an indirect tax on goods and services. To the extent that the territorial scope of such taxes is based on the destination principle (place of consumer principle), both local and foreign undertakings competing in the domestic market should benefit similarly from the tax relief measure[65]. This will only be different if the relevant market cannot reasonably be assumed to be confined within national boundaries, in particular because there is international consumer mobility.

Finally, a possible influence on investment (location) decisions should be disregarded. Article 107 (1) TFEU is not concerned with equality of competition as between Member States, which try to attract business investments, but with undistorted competition as between competing undertakings[66].

§5.03 RECOVERY OF INCOMPATIBLE STATE AID

Pursuant to Article 14 (1) of Council Regulation 659/1999, "where negative decisions are taken in cases of unlawful aid, the Commission shall decide that the Member State concerned shall take all necessary measures to recover the aid from the beneficiary" (recovery decision). According to settled case law, the main reason underlying the recovery obligation is the following: "The main objective pursued in requiring the repayment of unlawfully paid State aid is to eliminate the distortion of competition caused by the competitive advantage afforded by the unlawful aid... By repaying, the recipient forfeits the advantage which it had enjoyed over its competitors on the market, and the situation prior to payment of the aid is restored."[67]

---

63. ECJ, *Italy v. Commission*, Case No. C-66/02 [2005] ECR I-10901 paras. 115 and 117; Joined Cases ECJ, *Air Liquide Industries Belgium*, Cases No. C-393/04 and C-41/05 [2006] ECR I-5293 para. 35. For a different—in the author's view, less convincing—opinion see W. Schön and M. Lang, *Verhandlungen des Siebzehnten Österreichischen Juristentages*, 69 et seq. (vol. IV/2, 2009); and probably also C. Micheau, *Tax Selectivity in State Aid Review: A Debatable Case Practice*, EC Tax Rev. 276, at 281 et seq. (2008).
64. See, for instance, Commission decision COM(2010)2219 of 9 April 2010 on the Bulgarian tax reduction for biofuels, para. 29; and Commission decision concerning State aid SA.26798 of September 12, 2011 on the Italian excise duty exemption for vegetal oil, para. 24.
65. For a possibly different opinion, see Schön, *State Aid in the Area of Taxation*, 321, at 327 (Hancher et al. eds., EU State Aids 2012): State aid control should nevertheless be carried out.
66. For a different opinion, see Commission COM(2011)3504 of May 24, 2011, para. 107.
67. Joined Cases ECJ, *Associazione italiana del risparmio gestito*, Cases No. C-393/04 and C-41/05 [2009] ECR II-289 paras. 192 et seq.; ECJ, *Germany v. Commission*, Case C-277/00 [2004] ECR

Since unlawful aid may only be recovered from the *beneficiary*, it is necessary to establish the tax *benefit* incidence. In order to achieve consistency with the approach to be taken in the context of the selectivity test, the criteria developed above at § 5.02 B should be relied on for the purposes of the recovery decision, too. Hence, the standard assumption is that advantages consisting in tax base or tax rate reductions, tax exemptions, or other forms of alleviation of the tax burden will benefit the customer rather than the taxable person, aside from the second-order effects that may result from an increased market share of the taxable person.

Unless that presumption does not apply due to the nature of the aid scheme, or has been falsified by empirical evidence that the legally intended relief effects do not correspond to economic reality, the taxable person must not be required to repay a monetary equivalent to the tax relief as such. Instead, the taxable person should be burdened with a recovery of fiscal aid only to the extent that he or she has *actually* benefitted from the unlawful tax relief, i.e., in the amount equivalent to the (estimated) profit contributions arising from an increased market share[68]. This will be required, but also sufficient, in order to "restore the situation prior to payment of the aid"[69]. Instead, it is the customer who is liable to repay the tax relief *as such*, but only if the measure qualifies as selective and distortive aid also with respect to him. To the extent that the measure benefits final consumers or other non-business entities, or qualifies as a general measure from the customers' point of view, there is no room for any recovery.

Contrary to a singular decision of the Court of First Instance concerning indirect tax benefits in the context of direct taxation[70], it would not only be disproportionate to require full repayment of the entire fiscal aid from the indirect (second-order effect) beneficiary who will often not be in a legal and factual position to subsequently have recourse to his or her customers. Such a recovery claim would indeed be wholly unfounded to the extent that the aid is not selective with respect to the presumed direct beneficiaries, i.e., the customers. It is therefore a positive development that on occasion of a more recent case, the CFI has de facto reversed its position[71], and this reversal has been implicitly endorsed by the ECJ[72]. It is also noteworthy that the Court emphasized in this context that the Commission need not fix the exact amount of aid to be recovered in its recovery decision.

I-3925 para. 76; ECJ, *Residex Capital*, Case No. C-275/10 not yet reported in ECR para. 45; ECJ, *Mediaset*, Case No. C-403/10 P not yet reported in ECR para. 122. See also E. Righini, *The EC Rules Concerning Existing Aid: Substantive and Procedural Aspects*, 265, at 267 (Rodríguez Iglesias et al. eds., EC State Aid Law 2008).

68. See, by analogy, Commission decision C 52/2005 of January 24, 2007 on the Italian decoders, paras. 191–205.
69. Likewise E. Righini, *The EC Rules Concerning Existing Aid: Substantive and Procedural Aspects*, 265, at 282 (Rodríguez Iglesias et al. eds., EC State Aid Law 2008).
70. Cf. ECJ, *Associazione italiana del risparmio gestito*, Case No. T-445/05 [2009] ECR II-289 paras. 201 et seq.
71. Cf. ECJ, *Mediaset*, Case No. T-177/07 [2010] ECR II-2341 paras. 180 et seq.
72. Cf. ECJ, *Mediaset*, Case No. C-403/10 P not yet reported in ECR paras. 125 et seq. For some critical comments, see the annotation by Brevern/Grafunder, EStAL 201 (at 204 et seq.) (2012).

For instance, if the tax advantage associated with a VAT exemption concerning admissions tickets for sporting events must be presumed to have been fully passed on to the spectators in the form of lower admission fees, the taxable person need not repay the monetary equivalent to the tax concession since he or she is not the beneficiary. Instead, in the latter scenario a monetary equivalent to the second-order effects that constituted a selective advantage (increased market share etc.) must be recovered from the taxable person. The tax advantage as such cannot be reclaimed from the customers, either, since for them it is not selective within the meaning of Article 107 (1) TFEU. If it can be shown that only a portion of the tax relief was passed on to the spectators, the other portion must be recovered from the taxable persons.

The above conclusions are supported, at least to a certain degree, by the Court's case law regarding the inverse situation of repayment of indirect tax *burdens* that have been imposed contrary to Union law. Here, the ECJ has allowed Member States to take into account tax shifting and refuse the repayment of the tax to the taxable person to the extent that the tax burden has been passed on[73]. Instead, the final taxpayer will then be entitled to claim a repayment of the tax[74]. Quintessentially, this case law respects the consideration that a person should benefit from repayment to the degree that he or she has actually been burdened by the tax.

§5.04 CONCLUSION

This study has tried to show that indirect tax relief measures, while subject to the general criteria for identifying fiscal aid that have been established by the ECJ, may pose some specific challenges to the application of the State aid concept of Article 107 (1) TFEU and to the recovery of such aid. First, selectivity of an indirect tax concession can often only be assessed once the beneficiary has been correctly identified. Here, different scenarios have to be distinguished when deciding who must be presumed to be the recipient of the aid, if no unequivocal empirical analysis of the real economic effects of the disputed measure is available. Moreover, second-order effects of a tax relief that is intended to benefit the customer have to be taken into account. Second, the imputation of an aid measure to the Member State rather than to the Union, i.e., the distinction between State aid and Union aid, may become particularly relevant in the large field of harmonized indirect taxes. In this context, it is necessary to examine the legal basis for the tax relief measure in secondary Union law. To the extent that the selective and distortive features of the national tax legislation are inherent to conditions laid down in Union law, there is no room for a State aid control based on Article 108 TFEU. Third, the territorial element of indirect taxation, in particular the predominance of the destination principle, may have an impact on the analysis of the distortive effects

73. Cf. ECJ, *San Giorno*, Case No. C-199/82 [1983] ECR I-3595 para. 13; ECJ, *Dilexport*, Case No. C-343/96 [1999] ECR I-579 para. 47; ECJ, *Weber's Wine World*, Case No. C-147/01 [2003] ECR I-11365 para. 102. For a critical analysis, consult T. Capriles, *Shortcomings of the EU passing on defense*, World Journal of VAT/GST Law 47 (2012).
74. Cf. ECJ, *Danfoss*, Case No. C-94/10 not yet reported in ECR para. 70.

of the aid at issue. Finally, aid may be recovered only to the extent that it actually confers a selective advantage on its recipient. In particular, it is disproportionate to reclaim an amount corresponding to the original tax relief if the taxable person has only availed himself of indirect benefits; instead, the monetary equivalent to the positive second-order effects of the aid must then be recovered.

CHAPTER 6

The Test of Selectivity in State Aid Litigation: The Relevance of Drawing Internal and External Comparisons to Identify the Reference Framework

Humbert Drabbe*

§6.01 INTRODUCTION

The analysis of the selectivity plays a fundamental and ever-growing role in State aid assessment. In that respect, the assessment of selectivity in tax measures commands special attention. The subject, which continues to raise intricate and sensitive issues, is a topical one, as shown by the recent judgments of the *British Aggregates*[1], *Dutch NOx*[2], *Italian Cooperatives*[3] and *Gibraltar*[4] cases.

Selectivity is one of the four conditions which are enshrined in Article 107 TFEU to assess whether a measure is a State aid. It aims to establish as to whether undertakings are treated equally or whether they are subject to a different and

* The author is deeply grateful to Dr. Claire Micheau, European Commission, for her valuable and pertinent contribution to this article. Any opinion expressed by the author is personal and does not necessarily reflect the views of any institution.

1. ECJ, *British Aggregates Association v. Commission of the European Communities*, Case No. C-487/06 P [2008] ECR I-10515.
2. ECJ, *European Commission v. Kingdom of the Netherlands (NOx)*, Case No. C-279/08 P not yet reported in ECR.
3. Joined cases ECJ, *Paint Graphos and others*, Cases No. C-78/08 to C-80/08 not yet reported in ECR.
4. Joined cases ECJ, *European Commission and Kingdom of Spain v. Government of Gibraltar and United Kingdom of Great Britain and Northern*, Cases No. C-106/09 P and C-107/09 P not yet reported in ECR.

discriminatory treatment. The application of this criterion to tax measures can lead to difficult questions.

This contribution does not aim to provide concrete answers to all issues that the notion of selectivity in tax matters can raise. It should rather be regarded as an exercise in trying to clarify the picture in the light of the recent case-law. In that regard, after a short introductory comment on the notion of material selectivity, this contribution will focus on the case-law in order to comment on the test of selectivity that the Court of Justice has developed.

As a preliminary reflection, it is useful to focus on the notion of material selectivity[5]. What does the selectivity consist in within the meaning of Article 107 TFEU is a question which, as we all know, has led to much debate. Some commentators suggest that the three-step analysis developed by the Court of Justice cannot work and look for alternatives. Although the Court of Justice of the European Union (CJEU) has developed its three-step approach in a series of decisions, starting with *Italian Textiles* in 1974[6] to *Paint Graphos* in 2011[7], its application is indeed not without problems as is shown by, for example, the *British Aggregates*[8], *Dutch NOx*[9] and *Gibraltar*[10] cases. In all these cases, the Court of Justice overturned the General Court's decision. The central issue as regards material selectivity lies in the question what the appropriate reference framework was against which to assess the tax measure under examination.

The issue of material selectivity is all the more important since tax measures are an essential instrument for Member States to implement their economic policies. In matters of direct taxation, given the absence of harmonization, Member States are in principle free to design their tax measures. However, when those measures grant a selective advantage, State aid rules do apply in principle. The absence of harmonization in direct taxation effectively creates a large scope for the application of the State aid rules and thus explains the crucial importance of finding the right answer to the question when a tax measure is selective or not. It also explains the recurring discussions in this context about tax sovereignty and State aid rules.

5. This contribution will not delve into the *regional* selectivity of the tax measure, which encompasses measures only applicable to certain geographic zones. This aspect of the debate will not be addressed since it constitutes a different topic which should give rise to an entire and distinct contribution.
6. ECJ, *Italian Republic v. Commission of the European Communities*, Case No. 173/73 [1974] ECR 709.
7. Joined cases ECJ, *Paint Graphos and others*, Cases No. C-78/08 to C-80/08 not yet reported in ECR.
8. ECJ, *British Aggregates Association v. Commission of the European Communities*, Case No. C-487/06 P [2008] ECR I-10515.
9. ECJ, *European Commission v. Kingdom of the Netherlands (NOx)*, Case No. C-279/08 P not yet reported in ECR.
10. Joined Cases ECJ, *European Commission and Kingdom of Spain v. Government of Gibraltar and United Kingdom of Great Britain and Northern*, Cases No. C-106/09 P and C-107/09 P not yet reported in ECR.

§6.02 NOTION OF SELECTIVITY

A tax measure can have two major forms: (i) either a tax is imposed on undertakings so that the State can collect taxes; (ii) or an undertaking is exonerated from a tax so that its tax burden is alleviated. In both situations, the tax measure addresses either all undertakings or a defined (or "selected") group of undertakings. In any case, a tax measure always defines (and has to define) the group of companies affected by it. For this purpose, the tax measure defines its objective, such as taxing profits, property or turnover. In principle, all undertakings generating a profit, owning property or engaged in certain activities, are subject to the tax measure.

Selectivity involves determining whether a tax measure favors *certain* undertakings or productions of goods over others. In other words, it deals with the issue of assessing whether one group of undertakings receives an economic advantage that another group does not receive. Selectivity is therefore about making a comparison between groups of undertakings.

In this context, there are logically only two ways of creating different groups. The first one consists in making a de jure exception to a rule which applies to all in favor of some. The new tax measure creates a new and smaller group, which receives an economic advantage in comparison the group of which it originally formed part, i.e. the reference group.

Second, such separate groups can be identified where the tax measure does not apply *in effect* to all undertakings in the same way, although it is addressed in principle to all undertakings without distinction. In that instance, the comparison is not drawn based on a reference group outside the scope of the tax measure (external comparison), but between all undertakings which fall *within* the scope of the measure (internal comparison). In the latter situation, one could say that the reference framework is the measure itself.

The conclusion must therefore be that in theory both the external and the internal comparison are based in logic and valid as such. In other words, they are not mutually exclusive in the sense that they address different situations.

In practice, the external comparison is relevant in most cases, since the major part of direct tax measures are derived from a more general rule (e.g., taxation of corporate income). The internal comparison remains nonetheless, relevant when no reference system is available.

As an additional remark, one should keep in mind that comparing apples with pears would be inconsistent and irrelevant. In other words, the groups need to be comparable, which means that one should identify the appropriate reference framework, or, as stated by the case-law, they should be in a comparable legal and factual situation in the light of the objective of the 'measure' or 'system'. In order to be comparable, the measure should be part of the same tax system, i.e., they must have a common tax base (taxation of profits or taxation of property, etc.). This implies the existence of different reference systems which are determined by their respective tax bases.

In the light of these introductory comments, the following section addresses the recent case-law in order to comment on the test developed by the Court of Justice for assessing the selectivity of tax measures.

§6.03 RECENT CASE LAW ON TAX SELECTIVITY

At first sight, the approach adopted by the Court may seem complex -not to say inconsistent in certain cases- since the terminology used to describe the selectivity test in tax matters differs. For instance, in the founding *Italian Textile* case of 1974, the Court held that a measure is selective where it:

> intended partially to exempt those undertakings from the financial charges arising from the normal application of the general system of compulsory contributions imposed by law[11].

In the recent *Sardinia* case, the Court relied on another wording: accordingly, the measure should provide an:

> advantage for certain undertakings as compared with others which, within the legal framework in which that body exercises its competences, are in a comparable legal and factual situation[12].

This however does not mean that the Court of Justice relies on different tests. Since the landmark *Italian Textile* case of 1974, the Court of Justice has developed its approach for assessing the selectivity of a tax measure, leading to what can be described as a three-step approach. In that case the Court of Justice has laid down the principle that a derogation or the exemption of undertakings belonging to a certain sector from the financial charges arising from the normal application of a general social-security system constitutes a selective advantage which can only be justified on the basis of the nature or general scheme of the system.

Over the last decade, the case-law has developed its stance for defining the possible departure of the measure from the tax system by drawing *internal* and *external* comparisons. It is this approach that will be examined in the following.

[A] External Comparison: Recent Judgments

[1] The Adria-Wien Pipeline Case[13]

[a] Reference System: Energy Tax

This line was further developed by the Court in its *Adria-Wien Pipeline* judgment. Accordingly, a comparison should be drawn between undertakings in a comparable legal and factual situation in the light of the objective of the measure in question.

The case dealt with issues concerning energy taxes on the consumption of electricity and natural gas and rebates of those taxes and which had been referred to the Court for a preliminary ruling. In 1996, Austria initiated a tax reform which involved

11. ECJ, *Italian Republic v. Commission of the European Communities*, Case No. 173/73 [1974] ECR 709.
12. ECJ, *Presidente del Consiglio dei Ministri v. Regione Sardegna*, Case No. C-169/08 [2009] ECR I-10821 para. 61.
13. ECJ, *Adria-Wien Pipeline and Wietersdorfer & Peggauer*, Case No. 143/99 [2001] ECR I-8365.

provisions on the law of electricity and natural gas. Of particular concern was the introduction of a tax relief, which provided for a rebate of energy taxes on natural gas and electricity[14]. However, only undertakings whose activity was shown to consist primarily in the manufacturing of goods were entitled to apply for a rebate of energy taxes.

The issue was therefore whether the Austrian legislative measures, which provided for a rebate of energy taxes, but granted that rebate only to undertakings whose activity consisted primarily in the manufacturing of goods in contrast to services, should be regarded as State aid.

In this regard, Advocate General Mischo[15] endorsed the view that the tax system should be a regarded as being in line with Article 107 TFEU. In his view, the measure was not selective since it did not depart from the general tax system:

> From the overall context in which that legislation was introduced I rather take the view that we are dealing here with a new general system of ecology taxes which *from the moment of its conception* was based on the principle that the primary and secondary sectors of the national economy could not reasonably be taxed proportionately to the *whole* of their electricity and gas consumption.[16]

Since the measure was geared towards the whole primary and secondary sector of a national economy, the treatment applicable to primary and secondary sectors was not perceived as a derogation from the normal application of a general system.

The Court however did not follow the opinion of Advocate General Mischo. It took the view that the measure was selective since undertakings manufacturing goods and undertakings supplying services were in a comparable situation in law and in fact "in the light of the objective pursued by the *measure* in question"[17]. The objectives at hand were the environmental goals of the tax regime. Consequently, the Court concluded as follows:

> [T]he ecological considerations underlying the national legislation at issue do not justify treating the consumption of natural gas or electricity by undertakings supplying services differently than the consumption of such energy by undertakings manufacturing goods.[18]

The Court therefore did not limit its analysis to an *internal* comparison (i.e., the tax treatment of energy consumption applied to undertakings manufacturing goods). Since "energy consumption by each of those sectors is equally damaging to the environment"[19], the Court took a step further by carrying out an *external* comparison between the tax treatments on energy consumption applicable to all undertakings in

14. According to the law, energy taxes on natural gas and electricity were reimbursed on application in so far as they exceed, in total, 0.35% of the net production value. The rebate is paid after deduction of a maximum amount of ATS 5,000.
15. Opinion of AG Mischo in ECJ, *Adria-Wien Pipeline and Wietersdorfer & Peggauer*, Case No. 143/99 [2001] ECR I-8365.
16. *Ibid.*, para. 42.
17. ECJ, *Adria-Wien Pipeline and Wietersdorfer & Peggauer*, Case No. 143/99 [2001] ECR I-8365 para. 41 (emphasis added).
18. *Ibid.*, para. 52.
19. *Ibid.*

the light of the environmental objectives of the measure. On this basis, it found that there was a differential tax treatment between undertakings manufacturing goods and undertakings supplying services.

This case is of interest because it developed the earlier case-law and shed light on the comparison which should be drawn between groups of undertakings "in the light of the objective pursued by the measure in question". In addition, it offers an example of a *standalone measure* (i.e., an environmental tax not being part of a wider system of taxation, such as the corporation tax), where the Court could not draw an external comparison based on the general corporation tax system, since the measure was not part of the general- corporation-tax system. The Court carried out an internal comparison, within the confined reference framework defined by the environmental objectives of the measure itself. Interestingly, the Court's position was to draw a wider reference framework than the Advocate General had.

The *Adria-Wien Pipeline* ruling made clear that defining the appropriate reference framework is not an obvious exercise. The judgments by the General Court and, in appeal, by the Court of Justice in the *British Aggregates* case confirm this.

[2] The British Aggregates Case[20]

[a] Reference System: Levy on Aggregates

The *British Aggregate* case dealt with a levy applicable on virgin aggregate. By contrast, secondary or recycled aggregates (i.e., material arising as by-products or waste products from other processes) were exempt from this levy. The objective of this levy was environmental: it aimed at encouraging resource efficiency.

The General Court found that the measure was not selective. It held that an environmental levy "is (...) an autonomous fiscal measure which is characterized by its environmental objective and its specific tax base". It further emphasized that, in the absence of coordination at the EU level in this area, Member States remain free to introduce sector-based environmental levies and set priorities as regards the protection of the environment. It then came to the conclusion that such an environmental measure, targeting specific goods or services and not forming part of an overall system of taxation applying to similar activities with a comparable impact on the environment, was not to be considered to selectively favor the activities not subject to it.

More precisely, the General Court, referring to the Member State's freedom to set its policy priorities where no harmonization at the EU level exists considered the measure as being its own reference framework, since there was no wider tax system of which the measure formed part. The Court then found that there was no selectivity since the measure applied without distinction to all activities falling within its scope. In doing so, the General Court effectively limited its reasoning to an *internal* comparison in the light of the specific environmental objectives pursued by the measure itself. It did

20. ECJ, *British Aggregates Association v. Commission of the European Communities*, Case No. C-487/06 P [2008] ECR I-10515.

not make the comparison with a wider group which might be in a comparable legal and factual situation.

On appeal, the Court of Justice dismissed the conclusions drawn by the General Court by stating, among others, that in order to determine whether a measure is selective, one has to examine whether, within the context of a particular legal system, the measure constitutes an advantage in comparison with other undertakings which are in a comparable legal and factual situation[21]. It further confirmed that, where a measure is prima facie selective, but the differentiation arises from the nature or the overall structure of the system of which it forms part, the measure is not State aid.

As regards selectivity, the Court of Justice rejected the analysis carried out by the General Court, which was based on the absence of a wider framework and the specific environmental objectives of the measure. In support of its position, the Court relied on earlier judgments where the objective pursued by State measures was not sufficient to exclude those measures outright from classification as aid. An approach based solely on the environmental objective pursued by the measure itself a priori excludes the possibility that the exemption of that measure for operators in a comparable situation in the light of the objective being pursued could constitute a selective advantage, independently of the effects of that measure. In other words, in order to identify the appropriate reference framework, one cannot rely on the objective of the measure, but should examine its effects on other undertakings in a comparable situation with respect to the objective of that measure.

The *British Aggregates* case is about an environmental levy which is self standing in that it does not form part of a wider corporation tax system or other system of taxation. From that perspective, it is maybe not surprising that the General Court took the objective of the measure, i.e., taxing the worst polluters, as its starting point for identifying the group of undertakings affected by the measure and for assessing the selectivity question. Since the Court found that the measure explicitly applied to virgin aggregates, but not to recycled aggregates, and since it treated all virgin aggregates without distinction, it concluded to the absence of selectivity.

By contrast, the Court of Justice drew an external comparison between the undertakings producing recycled aggregates and those producing virgin aggregates. As the Court of Justice held, basing the test of selectivity solely on the objective of the measure—and therefore restricting its application to the group covered by the measure itself (*internal* comparison), and not on its effects—would erroneously exclude "a priori the possibility that the non-imposition (...) on operators in comparable situations in the light of the objective being pursued might constitute a selective advantage"[22] (*external* comparison).

It should be noted that this judgment confirms the *Adria-Wien Pipeline* judgment in that the reference system in the external comparison is not limited to a wider system of corporation tax rules, but it can be a body of legal rules outside the area of

21. ECJ, *British Aggregates Association v. Commission of the European Communities*, Case No. T-210/02 [2006] ECR II-2789 para. 82.
22. *Ibid.*, para. 82.

corporation taxation. The Court refers in this regard to "the context of a particular legal system"[23].

Interestingly, it seems that the General Court gives more weight to the freedom of Member States to design their tax measures in the absence of harmonization in the area concerned and thus to the objective of the measure itself, therefore limiting the scope of application of the State aid rules. By contrast, the Court of Justice, in giving full weight to the effects of the measure when assessing whether a measure is selective, seems to give less weight to considerations related to the freedom of Member States for designing their policies where no harmonization has taken place and thus gives more importance to the full application of the State aid rules in such situation.

[b] The Dutch NOx Case[24]

[i] Reference System: Obligation to Reduce NOx Emission

The more recent *Dutch NOx* case involved the Dutch NOx emission trading scheme. This scheme provides that, while all undertakings producing NOx emissions must comply with the emission rules, only the large facilities can monetize the economic value of their emission reductions (by selling the emission allowances or avoiding a fine by buying allowances from other undertakings). The question arose as to whether this tax advantage was selective since it applied to approximately only 250 large industrial undertakings.

In its judgment[25], the General Court pointed out that all large industrial facilities were subject to the emission standard and they can benefit from the tradable emission allowances for which it provides. Accordingly, the application of the measure was therefore based on an objective criterion, without sector-based or geographic connotation. Since the measure is addressed to the biggest polluters, the Court held that the measure was in line with the goal of the measure (protection of the environment) and the internal logic of the system. The Court then stated that only those undertakings covered by the scheme must comply, on pain of fine, with an emission standard or strict 'Performance Standard Rate' (PSR). The General Court then concluded as follows:

> Therefore, both with regard to the objective pursued and the specific obligations imposed on large industrial facilities (...), it must be held that the legal and factual situation of the undertakings subject to that NOx emission ceiling cannot be

---

23. "[I]t is appropriate to examine whether, *within the context of a particular legal system*, that measure constitutes an advantage for certain undertakings in comparison with others which are in a comparable legal and factual situation" (ECJ, *British Aggregates Association v. Commission of the European Communities*, Case No. C-487/06 P [2008] ECR I-10515 para. 82, emphasis added).
24. ECJ, *European Commission v. Kingdom of the Netherlands (NOx)*, Case No. C-279/08 P not yet reported in ECR.
25. ECJ, *Kingdom of the Netherlands v. Commission of the European Communities*, Case No. T-233/04 [2008] ECR II-591.

> regarded as comparable to that of undertakings to which that ceiling does not apply[26].

Since the Commission had not provided any clear evidence that other undertakings were subject to environmental legislation dealing with emission rules, the legal and factual situation of the large facilities was not regarded as comparable to undertakings to which the PSR did not apply. The Commission failed to establish the existence of a general scheme which would apply to both types of undertaking. Also the fact that the measure restricted the group of undertakings to 250 did not render it selective as it represented, "all undertakings in a particular legal and factual situation that is not comparable, with regard to the objective pursued, to the situation of undertakings not belonging to that group"[27].

The General Court did not start its assessment with the question whether there is a reference system of which the measure forms part. Instead, it focused its analysis first on the measure itself (internal comparison). It held that its application was based on an objective criterion, i.e., it applied to all big polluters with an installed thermal capacity of more than 20 MW which were all subject to the same specific obligations. It further stated that this criterion was in conformity with the environmental objective of the measure and the internal logic of the system. It only then considered that the Commission, by not clearly demonstrating the existence of a wider reference system and by only referring to the restricted number of undertakings subject to the measure, did not provide sufficient evidence that those not addressed by the measure were in a comparable legal and factual situation (external comparison) and, finally, that the measure was not selective. As regards the external comparison[28], in rejecting the Commission's argument that the measure was selective in view of the existence of a wider set of environmental rules in the Netherlands setting emission standards for other, the General Court stated that this argument was contradicted by the specific conditions laid down for big polluters in the measure in question.

Where the General Court had essentially argued that the measure treated all undertakings addressed by it equally and the Commission had not sufficiently demonstrated the existence of a reference system to enable the comparison with other undertakings, the Court of Justice adopted a different position. First, it recalled that it was for the Commission to prove that a measure was selective in that it created differences between undertakings which were in a comparable legal and factual situation in the light of the objective of the measure and, second, that the Member State had to prove that the differences were justified by the nature and general scheme of the system. The Court of Justice then held that the specific group of large undertakings enjoyed an advantage not available to other undertakings which, although not falling under the measure in question, must also comply with restrictions regarding NOx emissions. Since the two categories of undertakings were subject to the same kind of obligations, they were in comparable situations. The Court therefore followed the Commission in qualifying the measure as selective.

26. *Ibid.*, para. 90.
27. *Ibid.*, para. 95.
28. *Ibid.*, para. 91.

The two judgments in this case show again how crucial it is to determine correctly the reference framework in assessing whether a measure is selective. In the *Adria-Wien Pipeline* and *British Aggregates* cases the measure was part of a wider system of environmental rules, introducing a tax and explicitly granting a rebate respectively an exemption to that tax. In the *Dutch NOx* case the legislation in place created obligations as regards emissions also for other undertakings than the large undertakings subject to the measure. The existence of this legislation creating the same kind of obligation (reduction of NOx emission) was sufficient to identify the reference framework and to draw a comparison between the two groups of undertakings. The differential treatment providing an advantage to large polluters was then sufficient to conclude that the measure was *prima facie* selective.

As regards the comparison to be made, the Court of Justice refers in certain judgments, as in this case, to the legal and factual situation "with regard to the objective of the *measure in question*" rather than to "*the objective of the (legal) system*" as it did for instance in *British Aggregates* case. This has led to the question which of the two is the appropriate reference framework. In the *Adria-Wien Pipeline* case, the Court took the view that the objective of the measure encompassed a wider group of undertakings that the manufacturing sector. Although the Court referred to the objective of the *measure* in question (i.e., environmental objective applied to undertakings manufacturing goods), the general environmental objective of the energy tax (i.e., environmental objective applied to all undertakings) formed the reference framework against which the Court assessed the rebate. In the *British Aggregates* case, the Finance Act introduced a levy for virgin aggregates and explicitly exempted other types of aggregate, thus providing a reference framework against which to assess the exemption from the levy. In the *Dutch NOx* case, although the Court of Justice referred to the objective of the measure in question (environmental objective introducing an emission trading system for biggest polluters), such a framework was provided by the general legislation introducing obligations to all undertakings, from which the specific rules for large undertakings derogated.

In view of the above, it follows that, where such legal framework or system exists, the comparison has to be made in the light of its more general objective and not in view of the specific objective pursued by the measure itself. Otherwise, Member States could considerably narrow the scope of application of State aid rules by introducing specific objectives for specific groups of undertakings. In the absence of harmonization this, as a consequence, could open the door for distortive aid measures which would not be qualified as State aids.

[c] The Italian Cooperatives case (Paint Graphos)[29]

[i] Reference System: The Corporation Tax System

A recent, illustrative example of the three-step approach is the judgment in the *Italian Cooperatives* case that the Court gave last September. The case dealt with exemptions

29. Joined cases ECJ, *Paint Graphos and others*, Cases No. C-78/08 to C-80/08 not yet reported in ECR.

from various taxes for workers' and producers' cooperatives under Italian law. This tax regime, which was referred to the Court of Justice for a preliminary ruling, involved the issue as to whether the tax benefits enjoyed by cooperative undertakings should be classified as State aid.

In this case, the Court of Justice confirmed its traditional stance based on a three-step approach of the selectivity test:

> In order to classify a domestic tax measure as 'selective', it is necessary to begin by identifying (... .) the common or "normal" regime applicable in the Member State concerned. It is in relation to this common or 'normal' tax regime that it is necessary, secondly, to assess and determine whether any advantage granted by the tax measure at issue may be selective by demonstrating that the measure derogates from that common regime inasmuch as it differentiates between economic operators who, in light of the objective assigned to the tax system (... .) are in a comparable factual and legal situation[30].

In this case, which concerned the taxation of company income, the Court identified the corporation tax system as the reference framework by referring to the common basis for calculating the corporation tax .

The measure was regarded as *prima facie* selective since there was a derogation from the general rule: cooperatives benefit from tax exemptions to which profit making companies were not entitled. The Court then examined whether cooperatives and other undertakings were in a comparable factual and legal situation in the light of the objective of the corporation tax system (i.e., the taxation of profits). In this regard, the Court took the view that cooperatives conformed to certain operating principles which clearly distinguish them from the other undertakings (such as activities conducted for the mutual benefit of the members and not in the interests of outside investors, the non-distribution of reserves and assets, the existence of specific rules on memberships, low profit margins or the limited access to equity markets). Given these peculiarities, the Court came to the conclusion that producers' and workers' cooperatives could not in principle be regarded as being in a situation which was legally and factually comparable to the one of commercial undertakings.

In a final step, the Court analyzed whether the measure at issue was justified by the logic of the tax system. This third step will be addressed in a later section.

[d] *Intermediary Conclusion*

Special attention was given to the *British Aggregates* and *Dutch NOx* cases since they reflect the core issue of the selectivity test: what is the appropriate reference system or, in other words, what is the appropriate group of undertakings which is in a comparable legal and factual situation in light of the 'system'?

The question is all the more important since it defines the scope of application of the State aid rules to tax measures. However, determining a too wide scope for State aid

30. *Ibid.*, para. 49.

rules, and therefore excessively extending their application, might be perceived by the Member States as an excessive application of the State aid rules in direct taxation.

It appears that the two Courts—General Court and Court of Justice—are aware of the issue of determining the reference framework, but they tend to react differently in seeking to strike an adequate balance. The General Court would seem to adopt a more cautious stance by giving more weight to the objectives of the specific measure. The ultimate consequence of this approach in the *British Aggregates* case was that it offered the Member States the possibility to design their tax measures in such a way that no measure would be qualified as selective. This cannot be the right outcome. Hence, the position of the Court of Justice was therefore not surprising. In the *Dutch NOx* case, the debate was more subtle: the General Court drew a comparison with the wider group, but it concluded that the two groups were not in a comparable situation. However, in its analysis, the General Court focused on the objective of the measure in question, rather than on the wider legal framework. This approach was therefore duly overturned by the Court of Justice.

In the more recent *Italian Cooperatives* judgment[31], the Court of Justice has confirmed, at least with regard to corporation tax, its position that the appropriate reference system is the applicable corporation tax regime. By referring to the primary objective of corporate taxation (taxation of corporate profits), it appears that the Court of Justice has therefore firmly opted for a wide scope for the application of the State aid rules[32].

That may not be perceived unanimously as a welcome development, but in the absence of harmonization of direct corporate taxation at the EU level, it may not be any realistic other option, since the alternative of giving primacy to the objective of the measure itself risks leading to an absence of State aid control in tax matters.

[B] Internal Comparison: The *Gibraltar* Case

[a] Reference System: Gibraltar Tax System

The *Gibraltar* case, whose judgment on appeal was issued in November 2011[33], offers an interesting example of internal comparison in the context of tax selectivity. The case

31. Joined cases ECJ, *Paint Graphos and others,* Cases No. C-78/08 to C-80/08 not yet reported in ECR.
32. In that judgment, the Court of Justice makes clear that the reference system has to be drawn sufficiently widely. Where the tax measure at issue deals with a particular legal form of undertakings (such as cooperatives), the appropriate reference framework is the one that allows a comparison with other legal forms subject to corporate taxation. After reminding in para. 53 that aid may be selective even where it concerns a whole economic sector, the Court stated as follows: "[i]t is therefore necessary to determine whether tax exemptions (...) are liable to favour certain undertakings (...) by comparison with other undertakings which are in a comparable factual and legal situation in the light of the objective pursued by the corporation tax regime, namely the taxation of profits" (*ibid.*, para. 54).
33. Joined cases ECJ, *European Commission and Kingdom of Spain v. Government of Gibraltar and United Kingdom of Great Britain and Northern,* Cases No. C-106/09 P and C-107/09 P not yet reported in ECR.

dealt with the reform of the corporate tax system proposed by the Government of Gibraltar. This tax reform concerned *inter alia* the repeal of the former tax system and its replacement by three taxes applicable to all undertakings located in Gibraltar: a company registration fee, a payroll tax and a business property occupation tax (BOPT), liability to payroll tax and BOPT being limited to 15% of realized profits.

The Commission in its decision[34] took the view that that the proposed tax measures were both regionally and materially selective. It considered the measures regionally selective since undertakings in Gibraltar were in general taxed at a lower rate than those in the United Kingdom. Regarding material selectivity, the decision held that the tax liability under the payroll tax and BOPT depended on making a profit. It therefore favored undertakings which did not generate profits. In addition, the 15% cap on the payroll tax and BOPT favored undertakings with profits which were low in relation to the number of employees and occupation of business property. Therefore, these two taxes were inherently favorable to offshore undertakings which had no physical presence in Gibraltar and therefore do not incur income tax. In the Commission's view, the reform had created a hybrid system in that it introduced an element of a system based on the taxation of profits (15% cap) into a payroll tax and a business property occupation tax. It considered such a hybrid system inherently selective, at least in the situation of Gibraltar with its large offshore sector of undertakings without employees or property.

The General Court annulled the Commission's decision[35]. With regard to regional selectivity, it held that the three conditions in the Azores judgment were met. Hence, the territory of the United Kingdom could thus not constitute the appropriate reference framework. As regards material selectivity the General Court, first, described the analytical framework for assessing selectivity. It held that the Commission "must begin by identifying and examining the common or 'normal' regime under the tax system (… .) constituting the relevant reference framework"[36] and, in a second step, "assess and determine whether any advantage granted by the tax measure at issue may be selective (… .)"[37].

In analyzing the Commission's lines of reasoning and in view of the explanations provided by Gibraltar and the United Kingdom according to which the two taxes constituted a new tax system, the General Court came to the conclusion that the Commission has foregone of its duty to begin by identifying the normal regime under the notified system. In the absence of identification and examination of the common regime, the Commission could not "establish to the requisite legal standard that certain elements of the notified tax system constitute derogations and are therefore *prima facie*

34. Commission Decision on the aid scheme which the United Kingdom is planning to implement as regards the Government of Gibraltar Corporation Tax Reform (2005/261/EC) [2004], OJ L 85, Apr. 2, 2005, 1–26.
35. Joined cases ECJ, *Government of Gibraltar and United Kingdom of Great Britain and Northern Ireland v. Commission of the European Communities*, Cases No. T-211/04 and T-215/04 [2008] ECR II-3745.
36. *Ibid.*, para. 143.
37. *Ibid.*

selective (... .)"[38]. Nor was it convinced that the arguments put forward by the Commission and Spain were sufficient to call into question the definition of the common regime as notified. The General Court thus annulled the Commission's decision.

In a judgment issued in November[39], the Court of Justice however dismissed the judgment of the General Court. With regard to the requirements of making a profit and the 15% cap, the Court of Justice endorsed the view that these were *per se* general measures applying without distinction to all economic operators. The advantages stemming from these requirements could not be regarded as having selective effect since they were the consequence of the random event that the company was unprofitable or very profitable.

The Court however disagreed with the General Court concerning the third element relating to the advantages accruing to offshore companies. In this regard, it held, first, that the General Court's approach, based solely on considerations of the regulatory technique used, disregarded the possible effects of the measures and a priori excluded that no tax liability incurred by offshore companies could result in a selective advantage.

Second, the Court took the view that, although it considered in an earlier case that the very existence of an advantage in tax measures may be established only when compared with 'normal' taxation i.e. the reference system[40], there were still cases for which it is not possible to carry out such an external comparison. As the Court held, "that case-law does not make the classification of a tax system as 'selective' conditional upon that system being designed in such a way that undertakings which might enjoy a selective advantage are, in general, liable to the same tax burden as other undertakings but benefit from derogating provisions, so that the selective advantage may be identified as being the difference between the normal tax burden and that borne by those former undertakings"[41]. Otherwise, the consequence "would be that national tax rules fall from the outset outside the scope of control of State aid merely because they were adopted under a different regulatory technique although they produce the same effects in law and/or in fact."[42].

The Court further observed that the Commission's decision, contrary to the conclusion of the judgment under appeal, had identified the new regime as the reference framework. Recalling the essential features of the regime (no general tax base applying to all companies, but two tax bases in the form of a payroll tax and a BOPT, requirement to make a profit and a 15% cap), the Court observed that, by combining the two tax bases, although general in nature, the regime in practice discriminated

38. *Ibid.*, para. 70.
39. Joined cases ECJ, *European Commission and Kingdom of Spain v. Government of Gibraltar and United Kingdom of Great Britain and Northern*, Cases No. C-106/09 P and C-107/09 P not yet reported in ECR.
40. ECJ, *Portugal v. Commission*, Case No. C-88/03 [2006] ECR I-7115.
41. Joined cases ECJ, *European Commission and Kingdom of Spain v. Government of Gibraltar and United Kingdom of Great Britain and Northern*, Cases No. C-106/09 P and C-107/09 P not yet reported in ECR para. 91.
42. *Ibid.*, para. 92.

between undertakings which were in a comparable situation with regard to the objective of the proposed tax reform, namely to introduce a general system of taxation for all companies established in Gibraltar. Combining these two tax bases excluded from the outset any taxation of offshore companies.

In order to qualify a general tax system as selective, one should identify the recipient undertakings by virtue of the properties specific to them. In that respect, the Court observed that offshore undertakings by their nature had no employees and did not occupy business practices and therefore no tax base under the reform. It therefore held as follows:

> Thus the fact that offshore companies which constitute a group of undertakings with regard to the bases of assessment adopted in the proposed tax reform, avoid taxation precisely on account of the specific features characteristic of that group gives reason to conclude that those companies enjoy selective advantages[43].

From the perspective of this contribution, it is noteworthy that the Court first observed that the assessment of selectivity did not necessarily have to be carried out by making a comparison between undertakings subject to a "normal" tax burden under a reference framework. In other words, the external comparison is not the only possible comparison to be made. Second, the Court confirmed that not only external, but also internal comparisons can be used for assessing the selectivity of the measure. Where an external comparison is not possible (such as in the present *Gibraltar* case), then the analysis should be based on an internal comparison. Third, when assessing the proposed tax reform, the Court observed that "it is apparent that the regime (… .) in practice discriminates between companies which are in a comparable situation with regard to the objective of the proposed tax reform, namely to introduce a general system of taxation for all companies established in Gibraltar"[44]. The Court thus analyzed whether all undertakings addressed by the regime were in fact treated in a similar way. It applied effectively what has been described before as an internal comparison.

§6.04 JUSTIFICATION IN THE LIGHT OF THE SYSTEM

As mentioned earlier, there is a third step in the assessment of tax selectivity which can play a key role: the justification of the selectivity 'by the logic and nature of the system'.

This justification by the logic of the tax system, which was introduced by the Court in 1974 as an obiter dictum, is now firmly established as an additional step of the selectivity test. The justification must be based on the intrinsic features of the system concerned, or, in other words, on the basic or guiding principles of the identified tax system. This notion of 'justification by the logic of the tax system' is strictly interpreted. In that respect, one should draw a distinction between, on the one hand, the objectives attributed to a particular tax regime and which are extrinsic to it (i.e., social policy, environmental, international competitiveness objectives) and, on the other hand, the

43. *Ibid.*, para. 107.
44. *Ibid.*, para. 101.

mechanisms inherent in the tax system itself and which are necessary for the achievement of such objectives (e. g, the progressive nature of taxation). Only the latter can be taken into consideration for the purpose of this justification. In other words, all sorts of policy objectives may have been attributed to a specific tax measure. However, if the measure results in a selective advantage, it is not selective only if the selective advantage directly results from a feature inherent in the tax system itself without which the objective cannot be achieved.

In the *Italian Cooperatives* case[45], the Court interestingly added two elements which are required to establish that the tax measure is justified:

(i) The Member State concerned must *introduce and apply appropriate control and monitoring procedures* in order to ensure that the tax measures concerned are consistent with the logic and general scheme of the tax system and to prevent economic entities from choosing that particular legal form for the sole purpose of taking advantage of tax benefits provided for that form of undertaking.

(ii) It is also necessary to ensure that those exemptions are consistent with the *principle of proportionality* and do not go beyond what is necessary, in that the legitimate objective being pursued could not be attained by less far-reaching measures. This reference to the principle of proportionality constitutes a novelty in the ECJ case-law on selectivity.

Does this mean that procedures of control and respect of proportionality should now be systemically analyzed in order to justify the selectivity of the tax measure? If so, this could drastically limit the scope of the justification by the logic of the tax system, which is already subject to a limited interpretation.

One should, however, realize that if proportionality which implies that the tax measure should not go beyond what is necessary, this also involves that where a measure is proportional it can be justified in light of the logic of the system. According to Commission Notice on the Application of the State Aid Rules to Measures relating to Direct Business Taxation, the progressive nature of the tax is regarded as a justification by the logic of the tax system[46]. For instance, on the basis on the facts of the *British Aggregates* case, one could have envisaged the hypothesis where the tax would have been imposed proportionally to the environmental damages caused by the different types of aggregate. Such gradual and progressive tax, although introducing a differential tax treatment between bigger and lighter polluters, could be regarded as justified by the logic of the tax system.

45. Joined cases ECJ, *Paint Graphos and others*, Cases No. C-78/08 to C-80/08 not yet reported in ECR.
46. Commission Notice on the Application of the State Aid Rules to Measures relating to Direct Business Taxation, OJ C 384, Dec. 10, 1998, 24.

§6.05 CONCLUSION

In essence, selectivity in tax measures deals with the comparison between the tax treatment of different groups of undertakings, with the view to analyze whether they are treated similarly or differently. If all groups are treated de jure and de facto similarly, there is no selectivity. Hence, no State aid involved. In principle, a comparison can be 'external' by comparing a group defined by a specific tax measure with a wider group in a comparable legal and factual situation. It can also be 'internal' by drawing a comparison between undertakings subject to the same tax measure. The *external comparison* is relevant where a tax measure is part of a wider legal system, i.e., the reference system. The *internal comparison* is pertinent where no such reference system exists and the measure is self standing.

The Court of Justice has defined through a series of successive decisions a three-step approach for analyzing the selectivity in tax measures. This approach can be summarized as follows:

(i) defining the appropriate reference framework;
(ii) assessment whether the tax measure in question derogates from this reference framework in that it grants an advantage to the beneficiaries of that measure in comparison to undertakings which are in a comparable legal and factual situation in light of the objective of the "legal system" or "measure in question"; if so, the measure is prima facie selective;
(iii) determining whether the such a prima facie selectivity can be justified by the "nature or natural scheme of the system.

The first challenge in this three-step analysis is to identify the reference framework. Different reference systems exist, such as taxation of profits (corporation tax), property taxation, turnover taxation, etc. Where a tax measure explicitly refers to an existing tax rule and grants a certain group of undertakings a more favorable tax treatment as compared to the wider group of undertakings subject to the existing rule, the tax rule forms the reference framework.

It becomes however difficult where the measure does not form part of an existing tax system, such as the corporation tax system. The first question to be asked therefore is whether the measure stands on its own or it forms part of a wider legal system. In view of the multiplicity of tax measures and the relatively limited number of tax bases, standalone measures are rather the exception. One should therefore be careful not to be too quick in concluding that a measure is self standing.

As presented in this contribution, the General Court and the Court of Justice tend not to apply the same legal reasoning. While the General Court focuses its analysis on an internal comparison, the Court of Justice rather insists on an external comparison. For instance, in the *British Aggregates* case, the General Court limited its scrutiny to the tax treatment applied to virgin aggregates. Since all virgin aggregates were treated the same way, the General Court concluded that the measure was not selective. By contrast, the Court went beyond this reasoning and carried out an external comparison between the tax treatment applied to virgin aggregates and secondary and recycled aggregates. This external comparison was drawn in the light of the environmental objective of the measure. With regard to the *Dutch NOx* case, the General Court confined its reasoning to an internal comparison among the bigger polluters. However, the Court of Justice adopted another approach based on an external comparison, i.e., between all undertakings in the light of the body of environmental rules which introduced an obligation to reduce NOx emissions. It therefore concluded that there was a difference of tax treatment between the largest undertakings and the other ones. In the *Adria-Wien Pipeline* case, where there was no judgment adopted by the General Court (since it was referred to as a preliminary ruling), it is Advocate General Mischo which confined its assessment to an internal comparison: it compared only the tax treatment applicable to undertakings manufacturing goods. The Court of Justice however imposed an external comparison in the light of the environmental objective of the measure, i.e., a comparison encompassing all undertakings subject to the energy tax.

By contrast, the *Gibraltar* case is of particular interest because it constitutes a case where an external comparison was not possible, since it was the entire Gibraltar tax system which was notified to the Commission and considered as reference framework. Hence, the Court confined its assessment to an internal comparison.

These cases show that when looking for the reference framework one should not define it too narrowly, but take fully account of the wider legal framework, in order to carry out an external comparison (and not to limit oneself to an internal comparison). This reference framework can be a wider set of tax measures of which the measure in question forms part, or "obligations (regarding the limitation or reduction of emissions), whether or not it falls within the measure in question"[47]. In other words, the reference framework and the tax measure in question must share a common, underlying objective from which the measure departs. If there is no such common, underlying objective, a meaningful comparison whether the relevant groups of undertakings are in a legally or factually comparable situation is not possible.

All this makes clear that the first two steps of the three-step approach are closely intertwined. It also reflects that the proper identification of the reference framework is the essential element in assessing the selectivity of a tax measure. Any State aid analysis of tax measures should therefore start with identifying the reference framework. Where, as in the *Gibraltar* case, no reference framework can be found and an external comparison is therefore not possible, the objective of the measure itself becomes the benchmark against which to assess the possible selective nature the measure: an internal comparison should make clear whether the undertakings subject to the measure are equally treated or not.

The recent case-law of the Court of Justice has established that State aid rules are applicable where no harmonization of tax rules at EU level has taken place. The analysis is based on the effect of the measure. The effect-based approach also "looks through" regulatory techniques used to design a measure as non-selective. In principle, tax measures can only be qualified as no State aid where, in the second step, the

47. ECJ, *European Commission v. Kingdom of the Netherlands (NOx)*, Case No. C-279/08 P not yet reported para. 64.

relevant groups of undertakings are not in a comparable legal or factual situation in light of the objective of the system or where, in the third step the measure can be justified by the logic or nature of the tax system.

It appears therefore that the choice of the tax instrument (i.e., self standing measure or departure from the general tax system) should therefore be regarded as crucial to assess the reference framework of the measure. It is therefore *a matter of tax policies* for the Member State, who are free to choose the most appropriate tax vehicles to introduce their incentives.

At that stage, one should bear in mind that Member States are free to exercise their tax sovereignty, as long as this tax sovereignty is exercised consistently with European law[48]. In this capacity, the Member States are entitled to implement their own tax system in order to attain their policy objectives, such as the promotion of environment, R&D or training investment. The Member States are therefore free to define the most appropriate tax measures. In doing so they will, however, want to take into account any potential consequences in view of the State aid rules. The choice of a particular instrument implies the choice of a particular reference framework against which the measure may have to be assessed under the State aid rules. In that respect, the justification by the logic of the tax system emerges as the real margin of discretion for the Member States to escape the State aid rules in tax matters.

48. ECJ, *Finanzamt Köln-Altstadt v. Roland Schumacker*, Case No. C-279/93 [1995] ECR I-225 para. 21.

CHAPTER 7

The Selectivity Test: The Concept of Sectoral Aid

Raymond H.C. Luja

§7.01 INTRODUCTION

I have been invited to address material selectivity in State aid with a particular focus on sectoral fiscal aid.[1] In this contribution a selection of topics will be addressed, guided by a number of rather recent cases. First, I will address the question of whether being subject to tax must indeed be the starting point for benchmarking (if any) and how the *Gibraltar* judgment influenced this (section §7.02).[2] Second, investment funds will be looked in to in light of the *FINECO* judgment,[3] with a special emphasis on indirect aid (section §7.03). Third, I will address the *Paint Graphos* judgment. Although it is not necessarily related to sectoral aid, it provides some insights in regard to different tax treatment of legally and factually comparable undertakings (section §7.04).[4] Next, I briefly reflect on the new Work Package for the Code of Conduct Group in relation to *FINECO* and *Paint Graphos* (section §7.05).[5] Some concluding remarks will then follow (section §7.06).

1. This contribution is based on a presentation given at the 'State Aid & Tax Law' conference at Luxembourg University on November 17, 2011.
2. Joined cases ECJ, *Gibraltar*, Cases No. C-106/09P and C-107/09P not yet reported in ECR.
3. ECJ, *Fineco*, Case No. T-445/05[2009] ECR II-00289 para. 135.
4. Joined cases ECJ, *Paint Graphos*, Cases No. C-78/08 to C-80/08 not yet reported in ECR.
5. Annex to Council Document 17081/1/11 REV 1 FISC 144 of Dec. 13, 2011, adopted by the Council on Dec. 16, 2011.

§7.02 SUBJECT-TO-TAX: A STARTING POINT?

Once I argued that a selectivity analysis should include a benchmark test as it should not be assumed that being "subject to tax" is the natural starting point for any State aid analysis.[6] The ECJ frequently held that a large number of undertakings eligible for a particular tax benefit is not sufficient to call into question the selectivity of such a measure and to rule out its classification as State aid.[7] Even so, in all of those cases despite the (potential) large number of beneficiaries it always remained a minority that received the benefit and as such the ECJ's reasoning did not call into question the benchmark. In essence it would well be possible that a large number of companies or sectors would be excluded from a tax from the outset, resulting in a penalty tax that only aims to target one sector. It would also be possible to have a broadly defined tax that initially includes all sectors, but then excludes all but few. In both cases it would well be possible that the benchmark would shift to not being subject to tax, leaving some at a disadvantage. In the flowchart included hereafter this is reflected by "result I".[8]

6. See *Revisiting the Balance between Aid, Selectivity and Selective Aid in Respect of Taxes and Special Levies*, 1 Eur. St. Aid L. Q. 161–168 (2010).
7. See, for instance, ECJ, *Maribel bis/ter*, Case No. C-75/97 [1999] ECR I-3671 para. 32; ECJ, *Adria-Wien Pipeline*, Case No. C-143/99 [2001] ECR I-8365 para. 48; ECJ, *Spain v. Commission*, Case No. C-409/00 [2003] ECR I-1487 para. 48; ECJ, *Dutch Nox*, Case No. C-279/08P not yet reported in ECR para. 50.
8. This flowchart is an updated and simplified version of a chart that has previously been published in *Revisiting the Balance between Aid, Selectivity and Selective Aid in Respect of Taxes and Special Levies*, 1 Eur. St. Aid L. 165 (2010). It is not to be applied to compensation for services of general economic interest ex. Art. 106(2) TFEU.

Table 7.1 Analysis of Selectivity in Respect of Taxes and Special Levies and Exclusions / Exemptions Thereto

Q1. Is the scope (base) of the tax or levy broad enough? i.e. does it not (de jure or de facto) exclude undertakings (or activities or products) objectively comparable* to those included?	Yes →	Q2. Are undertakings subsequently entitled to a (de jure or de facto) exemption from the tax base?	Yes →	Q3. Does the exemption apply to most if not all undertakings subject to tax otherwise?	No →	Q4. Does the exemption extend to all undertakings that are in an objectively comparable * situation as those exempted?	Yes →	Q5. Is the criterion used for the exemption conditional upon meeting (other) selective criteria **, not justified by the nature and general structure of the tax?	Yes →	Selective benefit (may be declared compatible aid depending on the objectives pursued by the selectivity criterion used, unrelated to the tax at hand) [result III B]
No ↓	↗	No ↓		Yes ↓		No ↓		No ↓		
As for those undertakings initially included, a benefit may still arise; continue at Q2 as indicated. Q6. As for those excluded from the outset, does the exclusion apply to most if not all of those undertakings that would be subject to tax otherwise?	Yes →	No benefit at issue (only a general tax) [result 0]		No benefit (the exclusion or exemption is part of the benchmark used to determine whether taxes are normally due by comparable undertakings, quod non) [result I]		Selective benefit (does not meet the nature-and-structure test by means of failing the comparability test; it will most likely be declared to be incompatible aid, except for the presence of compatible objectives unrelated to the tax at hand) [result III A]		General benefit [result II] ** Like the usual suspects: exemptions based on region, sector of industry size of investment, size or geographical spread of undertakings and alike.		* Comparable in a legal and factual situation in the light of the nature and objective of the tax; i.e. an exclusion/ exemption warranted in respect of a tax's rationale should apply to all those in a comparable situation and be proportional as to the extent of incomparability.
No ↓										

However, from two rather recent cases it became clear that the ECJ is unlikely to consider this shift in benchmark. It started with the *Sardegna* case.[9] This case concerned an environmental tax for boats and ships transporting people to Sardegna, from which Sardegna-based operators would be exempted. In this case the ECJ rightly considered that the exemption as such would lead to selectivity, as the nature and general scheme of the environmental tax did not warrant the exemption of local operators who created the same environmental damage as other operators. In its analysis there was an underlying presumption that an environmental tax should cover all operators, without any determination to the actual scope of the tax as it was. Hypothetically, it would have been possible that 90% of all companies transporting people from and to Sardegna were local, thereby putting some non-locals at a comparative disadvantage albeit that the benchmark would then be not being subject to tax. Notwithstanding the infringements of fundamental freedoms in this case, one might wonder whether State aid should have been used here as an instrument without first establishing the actual benchmark of the tax. I do admit that operating on a presumption of subjecting all operators to tax was indeed feasible, but this was not provided for in the data available to the ECJ as provided by the referring domestic court.

In *Gibraltar* the ECJ became far more explicit when it held that it had rightly been argued that an exemption of 99% of all businesses from a general corporation tax led to de facto selectivity, also given the fact that this 99% effectively concerned offshore companies.[10] Here it was Gibraltar itself that declared that it intended to create a "new corporate tax regime for *all* companies in Gibraltar",[11] so the ECJ again assumed that the actual intention of the law was for all companies to be "subject to tax" as a starting point.

The ECJ emphasized that the method of introducing a benefit should not matter as "benchmarking" is not—at least not always—a necessity as part of State aid analysis. By doing so it created a dangerous precedent. It reasoned that:

> case-law does not make the classification of a tax system as "selective" conditional upon that system being designed in such a way that undertakings which might enjoy a selective advantage are, in general, liable to the same tax burden as other undertakings but benefit from derogating provisions, so that the selective advantage may be identified as being the difference between the normal tax burden and that borne by those former undertakings. [...] Such an interpretation of the selectivity criterion would require [...] that in order for a tax system to be classifiable as "selective" it must be designed in accordance with a certain regulatory technique; the consequence of this would be that national tax rules fall from the outset outside the scope of control of State aid merely because they were adopted under a different regulatory technique although they produce the same effects in law and/or in fact. [...] Those considerations apply particularly with regard to a tax system which, as in the present case, instead of laying down general rules applying to all undertakings from which a derogation is made for certain

9. ECJ, *Sardegna stopover tax*, Case No. C-169/08 [2009] ECR I-10821.
10. Joined cases ECJ, *Gibraltar*, Cases No. C-106/09P and C-107/09P not yet reported in ECR paras. 55 (64, 109).
11. *Ibid.*, para. 8; italics added, RL.

> undertakings, achieves the same result by adjusting and combining the tax rules in such a way that their very application results in a different tax burden for different undertakings.[12]

We must see that the ECJ now implicitly combines selectivity and advantage to a single test: the presence of a "selective advantage". From my perspective both must be treated separately, as it may well be possible to have a selective disadvantage. Financial disincentives, contrary to financial benefits, should remain outside of the scope of State aid scrutiny, notwithstanding compliance with other primary and secondary EU law. Be that as it may, the ECJ then continues:

> The features of that regime are, first, a combination of the payroll tax and BPOT as the sole bases of assessment, together with the requirement to make a profit, the tax on which is capped at 15%, and second, the absence of a generally applicable basis of assessment providing for the taxation of all companies covered by that regime. [...] [I]t is apparent that the regime at issue, by combining those bases, even though they are founded on criteria that are in themselves of a general nature, in practice discriminates between companies which are in a comparable situation with regard to the objective of the proposed tax reform, namely to introduce a general system of taxation for all companies established in Gibraltar [...] Combining those bases of assessment not only results in taxation according to the number of employees and the size of the business premises occupied, but also, *due to the absence of other bases of assessment*, excludes from the outset any taxation of offshore companies, since they have no employees and also do not occupy business property. [...] Thus, the criteria forming the basis of assessment which are adopted by a tax system must also, in order to be capable of being recognized as conferring selective advantages, be such as to characterize the recipient undertakings, by virtue of the properties which are specific to them, as a privileged category, thus permitting such a regime to be described as favoring "certain" undertakings or the production of "certain" goods within the meaning of Article [107(1) TFEU]. In that regard, it should be observed that the fact that offshore companies are not taxed is not a random consequence of the regime at issue, but the inevitable consequence of the fact that the bases of assessment are specifically designed so that offshore companies, which by their nature have no employees and do not occupy business premises, have no tax base under the bases of assessment adopted in the proposed tax reform. [...] Thus, the fact that offshore companies, which constitute a group of companies with regard to the bases of assessment adopted in the proposed tax reform, avoid taxation precisely on account of the specific features characteristic of that group gives reason to conclude that those companies enjoy selective advantages.[13]

While the objective of a tax exemption should play no part in determining whether there is State aid, the nature and general scheme of the tax does play an important role. An environmental tax as in *Sardegna* should effectively apply to all polluters who are

12. *Ibid.*, paras. 91–93. *Gibraltar* was not unique in respect of the ECJ pointing out that State aid relates to the effect of measures and is unrelated to the technique used by a Member State for implementation. For recent tax examples see ECJ, *British Aggregates*, Case No. C-487/06P [2008] ECR I-10505 para. 89 and ECJ, *Dutch Nox*, Case No. C-279/08P, not yet reported in ECR, para. 51. Even though both cases also focused on the benchmark issue they still addressed situations where a minority of comparable undertakings benefited, unlike *Sardegna* (where it remained unclear) and *Gibraltar* (where it was the vast majority).
13. *Ibid.*, paras. 100 (102, 104, 106–107), italics added RL.

in a similar situation as a starting point in the same way a general corporate income tax should apply to all companies as in *Gibraltar*.

In the case of Gibraltar we may argue that the offshore industry has been excluded from the tax base from the outset, if we assume that they have no local staff and occupy no business property. Technically there may be some to create a minimum substance, but even then the tax base would remain minimal. Either way, one could conclude that the offshore industry was effectively exempt from the outset (Q1 in the chart above), as the ECJ found that the tax base was not broad enough as to effectively subject the offshore industry to the proposed *general* tax on profits. From the purpose of a general tax on profits the offshore and onshore industry would be considered comparable in the ECJ's line of thought.

It follows from *Gibraltar* that the ECJ would then skip the benchmark test and not give any importance to the possibility that a tax may have been designed in a way that non-taxation would prevail (the aforementioned 99%) and only few companies would be subject to tax (the remaining 1%). This means that in my chart question 6 (Q6, and Q3 for that matter) is to be ignored.

Still, a tax system similar to that now proposed by Gibraltar could have survived State aid scrutiny if Gibraltar had not argued that it was introducing a general tax on profits aimed to cover all companies, but merely a payroll tax and a business property occupation tax. Despite the fact that such taxes could result in an even greater disadvantage to the onshore industry, should a profit cap be forfeited, it would have been safe from State aid scrutiny as no Member State or autonomous region is obliged to have a general tax on profits at all. Technically a normal payroll tax or property tax would not result in any benefit for State aid purposes (result 0 in the chart), despite the fact that offshore companies would have no tax liability under both taxes. Here we would (should) leave the domain of State aid and enter the political arena of harmful tax competition.

§7.03 INVESTMENT FUNDS

[A] Specialized investment

The interesting part of sectoral selectivity is that the nature and general scheme of the tax system may make or break sectoral aid. For example, the non-application of an anti-abuse measure aimed at limiting the carry forward of portfolio investment losses may be considered part of the normal scheme of the system for those sectors for whom such investments are their primary business. The peculiar nature of a certain sector may justify the introduction of specific tax rules in order to adapt the general tax system to the distinctive features of the sector.[14] But in doing so, such measures should not go beyond what is necessary for the proper functioning of the tax system. This sort of proportionality test is of particular interest to investment funds that are often subject to special tax rules. While some regimes may have the intention of creating transparency

14. Compare Commission Decision (December 11, 2001), OJ L 184, Jul. 13, 2002, 27, para. 32.

for investment funds in order to have their profit taxed at the level of its members, it may well be possible that Member States have a variety of regimes each with their own characteristics.

In the *FINECO* case the CFI (now: the General Court) pointed out that incorporated specialized investment vehicles may themselves constitute undertakings.[15] Thereby it raised the question what the proper benchmark should be for tax regimes aimed at specialized investments. Should we compare the tax benefits for risk capital funds, green funds or real estate investment trusts (REITs) to the general tax system or to the normal regime for investment funds? In *FINECO* the CFI held:

> It should be noted that aid may be selective for the purposes of Article [107(1) TFEU] even if it concerns a whole economic sector [...]. In the present case, the measure at issue applies to the financial sector. Within that sector, it benefits only the undertakings carrying out the operations covered by that measure. As it does not apply to all economic operators, it cannot be regarded as a general measure of fiscal or economic policy. It is, in fact, an exception to the general tax scheme. The beneficiary managing undertakings derive an indirect benefit from advantages not provided for under the normal rules of that scheme and to which undertakings in the financial sector which do not perform management operations for specialized investment vehicles have no right [...]. The measure at issue is thus also selective in respect of managing undertakings of specialized investment vehicles.[...] That finding is not affected by the fact that certain fund managers may benefit from the advantage afforded by the measure at issue for some of their activities but not for others. The fact nevertheless remains that the measure at issue confers an advantage on them for certain specific activities, whereas other, non-specialized fund managers will not benefit from it.[16]

In this case special tax benefits were provided to those who chose to put their money in specialized investment vehicles. These vehicles "are conferred an indirect advantage, since the tax reduction on investments in specialized vehicles prompts investors to buy shares in those vehicles, thereby providing them with additional liquidity and extra income in terms of management and entry fees."[17] While the *FINECO* case was primarily concerned with indirect aid to investment funds via their investors, the considerations of the CFI mentioned in the previous section would also apply to directly granted aid, such as preferential tax treatment of specialized investment funds within a corporation tax.

[B] Indirect Aid: Money Spent or Amount Received?

As for the indirect benefit in the *FINECO* case it should be pointed out that the CFI upheld the Commission's order to recover the full sum of the tax benefits given to the investors from the indirect recipients of aid (the funds and/or their managers). While the applicants rightly pointed out the difference between the actual benefit received by them (in particular the increase in fees) and the aforementioned sum, the CFI merely

15. ECJ, *Fineco*, Case No. T-445/05 [2009] ECR II-289 para. 135.
16. *Ibid.*, paras. 155–157.
17. *Ibid.*, para. 139.

pointed out that recovery of aid is the logical consequence of finding that aid is unlawful and that it is not disproportional.[18]

From my perspective the CFI failed to address a very important matter and, as such, it is a pity that the case was not brought before the ECJ. If we assume that the actual (indirect) financial benefit provided to the aid recipient would indeed have been less than the sum of tax benefits given to investors, the scope of the recovery order should have been reconsidered. This case could have settled the question whether Article 107(1) TFEU defines "aid" as the financial benefit received by the undertaking or as the amount spent by the government. In the case at hand the Commission and the CFI defined the unlawful advantage for the purpose of Article 107(1) TFEU (then: Article 87(1) EC)) mainly as the increase in fees, which makes the recovery of the full sum of tax benefits even more questionable. The CFI's reasoning that the restoration of the previous situation (prior to the tax benefit being granted) would only be possible by recovering the entire sum of tax benefits granted to the investors from the undertakings stems from an interpretation of the ECJ's case law primarily addressing direct aid.

In my opinion recovery of more than the actual indirect advantage might, in principle, be regarded as disproportional.[19] In indirect aid cases the amount of aid may well be different from the amount of money spent (i.e., the amount of tax forfeited in relation to the intermediary) by the government in order to have that aid transferred. Hopefully the ECJ will be called upon in future cases to settle whether the restoration of the status quo ex ante merely refers to taking away the financial advantage and hence restore the level playing field (i.e., the ex ante position of the undertaking that received the unlawful aid) or whether it would go beyond that and require the recovery of all tax benefits received by the investors/intermediaries in full. The elimination of the distortion of competition would not necessarily require the latter.[20]

[C] Transparency

While the *FINECO* decision raised a number of questions into fund regimes in general, the CFI only had to deal with the more straightforward case of specialized investment funds. The question remains whether there can even be a general regime for investment funds. A regime creating transparency for investment funds as intermediary vehicle may indeed fit within the nature and general scheme of a tax on investment income, but it does not provide for a carte blanche. If transparency is created, there should be immediate taxation at the level of the investor. This would effectively prevent any pre-tax reservation at fund level of any taxable profit for reinvestment, comparable to a situation of direct investment.[21] For practical expediency, the Commission has been willing to accept a 90% pass-through of profits in one case.[22]

18. *Ibid.*, paras. 191(193, 202).
19. For the ECJ's conclusion to the contrary, see *ibid.*, paras. 199–202.
20. The ECJ's case law is ambiguous in this respect as it is primarily concerned with direct aid; see the case law cited by the ECJ, *ibid.*, paras. 192–193.
21. Also see Commission Decision, Finland residential REIT regime (May 12, 2010) N131/2009.
22. *Ibid.*

After the *FINECO* decision it would be most welcome to get some further court guidance on dealing with investment fund regimes. The State aid compliance of a large number of investment fund regimes within the EU may now be considered uncertain not to say the least.

§7.04 *PAINT GRAPHOS*: PIERCING THE COOPERATIVE VEIL

From a harmful tax competition perspective, the *Paint Graphos* judgment has been a most welcome surprise.[23] The ECJ clearly points out that any special tax treatment of cooperatives must follow from the nature and general scheme of the tax system. Where transparency may be a logical consequence for a traditional cooperative where profits are taxed in the hand of its members instead, the ECJ clearly draws a line in respect to what I refer to as cooperative-in-name-only.

The active involvement of members (mutuality) is by far the most important characteristic of a traditional cooperative, and as such transparency may indeed be a logical part of the tax system, provided that Members are taxed instead forthwith. The very nature of the business structure of a traditional cooperative would warrant such tax benefits, in the ECJ's view.[24] A cooperative-in-name-only that merely uses the cooperative as a legal shell to be entitled to those tax benefits is not comparable to such a traditional cooperative, especially when there is only one real active member next to some passive or dummy members.

In essence, such a cooperative-in-name-only is to be treated as any other capitalized company from the perspective of a corporation tax. In most Member States those companies themselves pay corporation tax over their profits, the remainder of which may then be taxed at the level of the shareholder at some time in future (either upon distribution or upon realization by selling shares, notwithstanding possible credit mechanisms). Cooperatives used as intermediate holdings for tax planning purposes may thus become a dying breed within the EU in the near future, unless actual member involvement and plurality of members is guaranteed.

Paint Graphos may be considered as a clear reminder that there should be an "equal treatment" of economic activities from a tax perspective, where economic substance outranks legal form. That being said, there is still a fine line between economic operators as legal entities and as natural persons. What if two competitors have the exact same economic activity, but one is a legal entity and the other a natural person? We could easily consider them to be incomparable given their very nature and hence warrant a totally different tax treatment (corporate income tax v personal income tax). But maybe, just maybe, there is some limit to this after all. An example:

> Suppose the corporate income tax rate of a Member State would amount to 20%. Any post-tax profits would then be taxed at the level of the shareholder at 25%. The personal income tax rate would be 40% (an oversimplification, as a rate like this would normally be part of a progressive system). The Member State then

23. Joined cases ECJ, *Paint Graphos*, Cases No. C-78/08 to C-80/08 not yet reported in ECR.
24. *Ibid.*, paras. 55–61.

introduces a research and development (R&D) tax benefit resulting in an effective tax on royalties of just 5%, but only within the corporate income tax. A Ltd. now receives € 100,000 in royalties. It would effectively pay € 5,000 in tax. Upon distribution of post-tax profit its shareholders pay an additional € 23,750. An entrepreneur/natural person would still pay € 40,000 under the personal income tax over royalties received from similar activities, disregarding any personal allowances and other sources of income.

Should we actually make any such comparison for State aid purposes? If so, how? Should we compare the Ltd to the entrepreneur and disregard the shareholder altogether? Or should we compare the cumulative tax burden of the Ltd. and the shareholder to that of the entrepreneur? Or should we do neither? From a State aid perspective the relevant comparison to be made is the following: does the difference in the nature and general schemes of a corporate income tax and a personal income tax justify that a special tax treatment for royalties is restricted to the first? If so, is the difference in treatment proportional in light thereof? The latter is rather important as it might well have been possible to provide for some other kind of tax relief for royalties in the hand of the entrepreneur that is more suitable for a personal income tax than the method chosen for the corporate income tax.[25]

For now, this is still an academic matter as the ECJ's comparison in *Paint Graphos* remained within the limits of the corporate income tax. But the very nature of its economic substance test makes me wonder whether tax neutrality in respect of economic activities goes beyond the corporate shell.

Be advised that the *Paint Graphos* case was triggered by an ex officio reference of the Italian Supreme Court, an example recently followed by the Finish Supreme Administrative Court as well.[26] National courts must be careful not to become an intermediary in the granting of illegal aid when they are called upon by tax payers to settle tax disputes; when settling such disputes they should take into consideration whether doing so would by itself lead to an outcome that would result in unlawfully granted State aid.

§7.05 INVESTMENT FUNDS × *PAINT GRAPHOS* = HARMFUL TAX PLANNING?

On 16 December 2011 the Council approved the Work Package 2011 of the Code of Conduct Group, providing the Group's priorities for 2012–2013.[27] The examination of policy responses in respect to the use of investment fund regimes by multinationals for "harmful tax planning" has been put in the top-5 list of priorities. It would be possible that a harmful tax competition investigation cycle would trigger a parallel State aid investigation as it did in the "first round" of investigations from 1998 to 2003. Having

25. This line of reasoning effectively applies to all analytical taxation of certain types of income. Royalties have been chosen here just as an example.
26. Reference for preliminary ruling of December 30, 2011 not yet listed (see KHO:2011:118 at www.kho.fi/paatokset/57170.htm).
27. Annex to Council Document 17081/1/11 REV 1 FISC 144 of December 13, 2011, adopted by the Council on Dec. 16, 2011, para. 5.

an EU-wide investigation will make any action more acceptable from a political perspective contrary to having one or two Member States singled out.

In light of *FINECO* special attention should be given to those Member States with different investment fund regimes for different investment vehicles, in particular for specialized investment. To be clear on this, doing so may help to take away the uncertainty caused by the CFI and should not necessarily end in a finding of incompatibility.

In light of *Paint Graphos* the abuse of collective investment fund regimes might deserve some attention as well, in particular in regard to those funds that de facto do not concern themselves with collective investment and depend on one investor/holding only (next to dummy members needed to qualify for such special regime). The ECJ's line of thought in regard to cooperatives-in-name-only might well be applied to collective-investment-vehicles-in-name-only. These vehicles may be considered comparable to other undertakings involved in (non-collective) investment subject to regular taxation. With or without State aid, investment fund regimes can be assured of increased EU attention in the years to come.

§7.06 CONCLUDING REMARKS

Member States are obviously not in a habit of notifying existing legislation for legal certainty after a Court judgment or Commission decision provides for a change in perspective. Once a tax benefit is being used by numerous tax subjects it is difficult to do so for obvious reasons, which makes it even more important for Member States to play an active role in State aid procedures of their fellow Members. Also domestic judges may become more aware of the possible active role they could play, or better should play, in preventing the granting of unlawful State aid.

Even though sectoral aid seems to be one of the clearest kinds of selectivity at first sight, the modalities of tax regimes adapting to peculiar characteristics of certain sectors are not by definition selective. To the contrary, I would say. In regard to sectoral aid, indirect tax benefits may be considered a rather useful instrument for those governments that would like to provide benefits to a certain sector in a somewhat less visible manner. In this respect many issues are still to be settled in future ECJ judgments, in particular the question of whether the amount of recoverable aid should be the financial advantage indirectly enjoyed by the undertaking or the amount of money actually spent (or not collected) by the government vis-à-vis the intermediary. In my view, the first would best fit the purpose of recovery but, admittedly, it would be far harder to calculate.

In regard to investment funds and their use in tax planning, recent developments in regard to harmful tax competition (the 2011 Work Package of the Code of Conduct Group) may be a trigger for future State aid investigations into their compliance with State aid provisions as well. Particular attention should be paid to regimes for specialized investment and to the accessibility of regimes for collective investment by entities whose investments are de facto of a non-collective nature. If, for tax planning purposes, these latter entities make use of dummy members to qualify as a collective investment vehicle they are at risk of getting themselves in a *Paint Graphos* situation, which provided for a substance-over-form approach in State aid.

CHAPTER 8

The Selectivity Test: The Concept of "Regional Aid"

Edoardo Traversa

§8.01 INTRODUCTION

The present contribution addresses some questions related to the application of State aid regime in the area of taxation, in particular in relation to the territorial restrictions contained in favorable tax measures adopted by Member States.

In a first part, the definition of Regional aid is precised, since this notion can have different meanings. In a second part, the issue of the compatibility of favorable tax measures limited to a part of a territory of one Member State is addressed. Finally, some comments are made on the coherence between the treatment in EU law (European Commission's practice and case- law of the European Court of Justice) of territorial tax advantages in the area of fiscal State aid and of fundamental freedoms to tax measures.

§8.02 WHAT IS "REGIONAL AID" IN THE AREA OF TAXATION?

The notion of regional aid is commonly used in the area of State aid. The control on State aid exercised by the Commission, based on Articles 107 to 109 TFEU (former Articles 87 to 89 EC), covers all measures, financed by public resources and attributable to a public authority, which grants a selective advantage to certain undertakings and whose effect is to affect trade in the internal market and to distort competition. Such measures are generally prohibited, unless they can benefit from one of the exemptions listed in the Treaty. The control of the compatibility of an aid is the sole responsibility of the Commission and is subject to strict procedural rules. The overall regime also applies to tax measures[1], including measures adopted by regional authorities[2], provided they meet the four cumulative criteria of the concept of aid as interpreted by the Court of justice[3]. Among these criteria, the decisive criterion is undoubtedly the selectivity, as opposed to measures of general application, which are not prohibited by EU law, even when they are very favorable to the taxpayers. The aid can be territorially selective, when the measure applies only to a part of the territory taken as a framework of reference, usually the territory of a Member State, but also materially selective, in the case where the measure provides benefits only to a particular economic sector or to specific undertakings. As the Commission's practice shows, the reductions of the general tax burden which can be seen as prohibited aid may take extremely various forms[4].

A tax measure will be considered territorially selective if it grants a tax advantage only to undertakings situated in a part of a geographical area constituting the reference framework. However, the application of the concept of regional State aid in relation to tax measures covers two distinct realities, whether it limits the exercise of sovereign or autonomous taxing powers of the central authority of a Member State or of their subdivisions.

Tax advantages may indeed be granted by the central or national authority to undertakings under a territorial condition which is linked to a "region". It is usually the case, in order to encourage investments in some (poor) regions or parts of the country, of tax advantages which are granted only if the concerned undertakings or the concerned investors do have a place of establishment and/or economic activity on the territory of the concerned region[5].

The notion of regional aid may also refer to regional measures in the sense of measures that are adopted by sub-national entities enjoying sufficient tax autonomy under the constitutional arrangements in force in a country (fiscal federalism). There is indeed in Europe, or at least in some Member States, a movement towards greater

1. ECJ, *Italy v. Commission*, Case No. 173/73 [1974] ECR 709.
2. ECJ, *Germany v. Commission*, Case No. C-248/84 [1987] ECR 4013 para. 17.
3. On the concept of (fiscal) State aid, see M. Dony, *La notion d'aide d'État*, 29 Cahiers de Droit européen 344–399 (1993); M. Slotboom, *State Aid in Community Law: A Broad or Narrow Definition?*, 20 Eur. L. Rev. 289–301 (1995); J. Wouters & B. Van Hees, *Les règles communautaires en matière d'aides d'État et la fiscalité directe: quelques observations critiques*, 5–6 CDE, 652 et seq. (2001); A.M. Jiménez, *El concepto de ayuda de Estado las normas tributarias: problemas de delimitación del ámbito de aplicacion del article 87.1 TCE.*, 196/2001 Noticias de la UE 81 et seq. (2001); C. Pinto, *Tax Competition and EU Law*, 107 et seq. (Kluwer 2003); J. Winter, *Redefining the Notion of State Aid in Article 87(1) of EC Treaty*, 41 CMLR 47–504 (2004); F.P. Sutter, *Das EG-Beihilfenverbot und sein Durchführungsverbot in Steuersachen*, 39–72 (Linde Verlag 2005); D. Triantafyllou, *EC State Aid Law/Le droit des aides d'État dans la CE—Liber Amicorum Francisco Santaolalla Gadea*, 409–424 (Kluwer Law International 2008).
4. Report of February 9, 2004 on the implementation of the Commission notice on the application of the State aid rules to measures relating to direct business taxation (2004) COM, 434. See also P. Rossi-Maccanico, *State Aid Review of Business Tax Measures*, 6 Eur. St. Aid L. Q. 215–230 (2007); P. Rossi-Maccanico, *The Specificity Criterion in Fiscal Aid Review: Proposals for State Aid Control of Direct Business Tax Measures*, 16 EC Tax Rev. 90–103 (2007); P. Werner, *Fiscal State Aid: On Tax Exemptions and Reimbursement of Taxes*, 9 (2006/2007) Cambridge Y.B. Eur. Leg. Stud. 481–505 (2007).
5. See, e.g., ECJ, *Federal Republic of Germany v. Commission of European Communities*, Case No. C-156/98 [2000] ECR I-06857.

autonomy of sub-national entities, mostly regions, which is accompanied by the transfer of sometimes rather significant taxing powers. In this case, almost naturally, tax measures adopted by regional authorities are limited to the area where they are territorially competent, which under the State aid rule could be considered as territorially selective.

Although these two types of measures could at the end have the same effects on the taxpayers, i.e., that taxpayers located in one region could benefit from a tax advantage not available for taxpayers located in other areas, they are nevertheless treated differently by the European Court of Justice. The Court tends indeed to consider that the relevant reference framework may vary depending of institutional factors. According to the ECJ, this reference framework is usually the territory of the Member State as a whole[6], but in some cases be restricted to the territory of a region, which enjoys sufficient constitutional, procedural and economic autonomy to adopt its own tax measures and to bear the consequences of its policies[7].

This shows a clear intention of the Court to try to find a compromise between European interests of achieving the internal market and the taking into account of the freedom of the Member States to allocate taxing power to sub-national entities.

In our contribution, we will focus on regional tax measures of the second type, as the first type of regional tax measures does not raise the same problem, especially in the light of the compatibility clauses contained in the Treaty. There are indeed procedures established in order to determine, after having considered that measures adopted by the national authority and applied in one particular area of a Member State could be considered compatible, according to the guidelines of the European Commission.

§8.03 WHICH REGIONAL FAVORABLE TAX REGIMES FALL OUTSIDE THE SCOPE OF STATE AID PROHIBITION?

As the ECJ case-law states, regional tax autonomy can have an impact on the qualification of the measure, and therefore on the compatibility of a regional tax measure with State aid rules. The Court case-law has developed in several directions in order to distinguish selective measures from measures adopted by regional authorities which were to be considered general, insofar as applicable to all undertakings located on the territory of the regions having adopted the tax measures, and therefore not constituting State aid.

6. On territorial selectivity in the area of taxation, see EFTA Court, *Norway v. EFTA Surveillance Authority*, Case No. E-6/98 [1999] available on www.eftacourt, which deals with Regional differentiation in the rates applicable to employees and employers payment for social security contributions in Norway.
7. On the definition of the reference framework in the case of regions enjoying tax autonomy, see ECJ, *Portugal v. Commission*, Case No. C-88/03 [2006] ECR I-07115 (Azores Case); Joined cases ECJ, *Unión General de Trabajadores de La Rioja (UGT-Rioja) and Others v. Juntas Generales del Territorio Histórico de Vizcaya and Others*, Cases No. C-428/06 to C-434/06 [2008] ECR I-06747 and Joined cases ECJ, *Commission and Kingdom of Spain v. United Kingdom and Government of Gibraltar*, Cases No. C-106/09 and 107/09 not yet reported in ECR, commented *infra*.

In this prospective, it is important, before analyzing the criteria set up by the Court of Justice, to establish a classification between regional tax measures, according to the level of autonomy granted to regions in the area of taxation. Not all regions in the EU Member States enjoy the same tax autonomy. The analysis of the compatibility of the tax measures they adopt with the State aid regime should therefore take into account the peculiarities of each constitutional system, and in particular the level of imbrications of the relations between the central and the regional authority in the area of taxation.

Three different hypotheses can be considered:

The first hypothesis is also the simplest. It is the case of fully centralized taxes which apply differently according to the region where they are levied. Even if the region has some administrative or spending powers as regards those taxes, like the power to collect the tax revenues, or to use them to fund sending polices-, it is clear that such an hypothesis has to be treated as if it concerned a central tax, and therefore has to be considered selective in so far it grants an advantage to undertakings located in the region where lower taxation applies.

Second, tax measures can be adopted by regions in the framework of their exclusive tax competence, without any interference or connection with the taxing powers of the central authority. In this case, the measures adopted concern taxes that have been levied by the region of a Member State by virtue of an autonomous constitutional power, including both the right to determine all the constitutive elements of the levy as well as the right to use the tax revenues generated by the tax for the implementation of own regional policies. In this case, the position of the European Court of Justice is relatively straight forward. If a region adopts a tax which results from a totally independent decision of the region (independent from the central authority), not only this measure cannot be considered as prohibited State aid but even more radically cannot be considered as aid. The mere fact that the levy applies to the territory of a region alone cannot indeed be an element to assess the territorial selectivity of the measure.

There are—at least—two strong arguments to support this position.

First, such measure may not grant an advantage. In order to be considered an advantage, undertakings established on the territory of the region should be favored compared to other undertakings not established on the territory of the region. The fact that the region applies a tax could hardly be considered as an advantage. There is however a situation where an "advantage" could be observed at first glance. It is the case of the simultaneous application by several regions of a Member State of similar or identical levies, which could differ according to constitutional tax autonomy as to the tax rates or the tax base. In this case, it could be advantageous to locate this activity in one region instead of another one. However in this case, it is rightly considered by the Court that such a situation could not be seen as territorially selective[8]. The reason is to be found in the cause of the difference of treatment between undertakings. The concept of aid indeed is based on the assumption that the public authority granting the

8. See K. Lenaerts, *Fiscal Federalism in the European Union—EU Presidency Seminar* (Flemish Department of Finance and Budget eds., Larcier 2012) (forthcoming).

advantage is the same as the public authority which applies rules to other undertakings that are considered the so-called normal regime or at least the regime without the advantage. In the hypothesis considered, the differences in treatment are not caused by a different application of a tax regime by the same authority but rather by the simultaneous application of similar tax regimes although not identical by different authorities. This lack of coordination between regions of the same Member State can be seen as similar to the absence of coordination between Member States in the exercise of their sovereign taxing powers, which has been recognized by the Court of Justice as a cause of justification of a difference in treatment between taxpayers in the application of the EU freedoms of movement[9].

There is no reason not to transpose *mutatis mutandis* this kind of justification also in the area on State aid. Therefore, the mere fact that different levies apply to different taxpayers in different areas of a country because of the constitution of tax autonomy of sub-national entities could not amount to State aid. Both the Commission and the Court of Justice acknowledge that the mere exercise by Member States' regional and local authorities of autonomous taxing powers they have been granted under constitutional arrangements does not in itself constitute a measure territorially selective[10]. A measure adopted under such autonomy cannot a priori be classified as State aid and is not contrary to EU law. Such an assertion could not however be construed as giving *carte blanche* to Member States' regional and local authorities for circumventing the EU State aid prohibition applicable to the central authorities. Regional authorities enjoying autonomous taxing powers are indeed not free from the European State aid control. Within the territory where the regional tax measures apply, the obligation arising from the State aid provision in the treaty are to be implemented. In particular a region could not adopt tax measures which are more advantage for particular undertakings within the region and which create a disadvantage for other undertakings also active in the region. The prohibition to distinguish between taxpayers concerns both territorial distinctions (tax advantages granted to undertakings of a sub-region) and material restrictions resulting in excluding from a tax advantage particular categories of taxpayers[11].

The third type of taxes that can be considered regional and that raises issues that are more difficult to solve are what we could call partly-regional taxes. Partly-regional taxes cover two distinct realities. First, there can be taxes that normally fall within the competence of the central authority but in respect to which one or more regions of the

9. See, e.g., ECJ, *Kerckhaert-Morres v. Min. of Finance*, Case No. C-513/04 [2006] ECR I-10967 para. 131; ECJ, *Jacques Damseaux v. Etat belge*, Case No. C-128/08 [2009] ECR I-06823 para. 27; or ECJ, *Margarete Block v. Finanzamt Kaufbeuren*, Case No. C-67/08 [2009] ECR I-00883 para. 54.
10. See, e.g., Commission Decision on the aid scheme which the United Kingdom is planning to implement as regards the Government of Gibraltar Corporation Tax Reform (2005/261/CE) [2004], OJ L 085, Apr. 2, 2005, 1-26, para. 115, and ECJ, *Portugal v. Commission*, Case No. C-88/03 [2006] ECR I-07115, para. 64.
11. See ECJ, *Presidente del consiglio dei Ministri v. Regione Sardegna*, Case No. C-169/08 [2009] ECR I-10821 (Sardinia tax on stopovers for tourist purposes exclusively levied on non-residents); ECJ, *Commission and Kingdom of Spain v. United Kingdom and Government of Gibraltar*, C-106/09 and 107/09 not yet reported in ECR (Gibraltar tax reform).

country have extended autonomous taxing powers. This situation is called by the Court asymmetrical federalism. It concerns mainly some Spanish (mainly Basque country and Navarra) and Portuguese regions (Azores) and also dependent territories of the United Kingdom (Gibraltar)[12], but could also apply to some Italian Regions (*regioni a statuto speciale*).

Partly-regional taxes can also be taxes which are jointly regulated by the central authorities and by the regions. In this case all the regions have more or less the same taxing powers (contrary to asymmetrical federalism) but the area of competence of the regions is limited to some elements of the tax while the federal authority keeps the power to regulate other elements of the tax. In this case, there are two possibilities: sub-national authorities could have either a power to increase or a power to reduce the national or federal tax rate (or both of them). The exercise of an increase in the tax rate, whether by one or by various sub-national entities, could hardly be constitutive of a State aid because the criterion of advantage is lacking. Even if all regions of a Member States except one decide to increase the rate of a federal tax, the only regions which would not have done it could not be considered as having granted a State aid to its taxpayers just because of the behavior of other entities. When all regional authorities in a Member States are granted the competence to reduce the level of taxation, one could be tempted to adopt the same line of reasoning. However, if it seems likely that there would be no State aid if all regions decide to lower the federal level of taxation to the same extent, an asymmetrical use of this power (by one region only, or by some of them) should be analyzed—based on the effect of the measure—as if it were the result of an asymmetrical division of powers between regions, and not only an asymmetrical exercise of taxing powers equally granted to all the regions of a Member State.

This distinction between partly regional and totally regional taxes is not to be found in the case-law of the European Court of Justice. The Court has said indeed that:

> the essential criterion for the purpose of determining whether procedural autonomy exists is not the extent of the competence which the infra-State body is recognized as having, but the possibility for that body, as a result of that competence, to adopt a decision independently, in other words, without the central government being able directly to intervene as regards its content[13].

However, this distinction appears necessary to raise some criticism against the ECJ case-law (see *infra*) while excluding the scope of this criticism to situations which are the expression of "pure" regional and local tax autonomy, i.e., what we have called fully regional(ized) taxes.

Concerning these partly regional taxes, the Court has developed a rather complex three-step test to assess whether the concerned region had autonomously adopted the

12. See ECJ, *Portugal v. Commission*, Case No. C-88/03 [2006] ECR I-07115 (*Azores*); ECJ, *UGT La Rioja*, Cases No. C-428/06 to C-434/06 [2008] ECR I-06747; ECJ, *Government of Gibraltar and United Kingdom of Great Britain and Northern Ireland v. Commission of the European Communities*, Cases No. T-211/04 and T-215/04 [2008] ECR II-03745 and Joined cases ECJ, *Commission and Kingdom of Spain v. United Kingdom and Government of Gibraltar*, Cases No. C-106/09 and 107/09 not yet reported in ECR.
13. ECJ, *UGT La Rioja* , Cases No. C-428/06 to C-434/06 [2008] ECR I-06747 para. 107.

measure. This test was adopted for the first in the *Azores* case, and subsequently confirmed in the *UGT La Rioja* case[14]. It is important to notice that until now the different cases decided by the Court only concern partly regional taxes in a context of asymmetrical federalism *sensu stricto*, i.e., asymmetry in the division and not in the exercise of taxing powers. These cases concerned indeed the situation of a region—peculiar but not unique in the European Union—which has been granted more taxing powers under the constitutional arrangements of a Member State than (most of) the other regions of the same Member State. The Court considered that in such an hypothesis it must be ascertained, in order to exclude the qualification of State aid, whether the region adopting the tax measure has "a fundamental role in defining the political and economic environment in which corporate works"[15], which implies a political and tax autonomy in the domestic system of the Member State concerned, which has to be assessed from a constitutional, a procedural and a financial perspective. According to the Court, "[...] in order that a decision taken in such circumstances can be regarded as having been adopted in the exercise of sufficiently autonomous powers, that decision must, first of all, have been taken by a regional or local authority which has, from a constitutional point of view, a political and administrative status separate from that of the central government. Next, it must have been adopted without the central government being able to directly intervene as regards its content. Finally, the financial consequences of a reduction of the national tax rate for undertakings in the region must not be offset by aid or subsidies from other regions or central government" [16]. In this case, the measure cannot be considered as territorially selective State aid because the territorial framework of reference to determine the selectivity of the measure is the territory of the region concerned and not the whole Member State. However, the measure could be considered selective from a material point of view, as it already happened in several Commission decision involving the Basque Country[17].

14. Joined cases ECJ, *Unión General de Trabajadores de La Rioja (UGT-Rioja) e.a*, Cases No. C-428/06 to C-434/06 [2008] ECR I-06747. For a comment, see D. Arnesto, *The ECJ's Judgment Regarding the Tax Autonomy of the Basque Country*', 1 Eur. Taxn. 11–20 (2009). See also Joined cases ECJ, *Gibraltar and United Kingdom v. Commission*, Cases No. 211/04 and T-215/04 [2008] ECR II-03745. For a comment, P. Rossi-Maccanico, *Gibraltar and the Unsettled Limits of Selectivity in Fiscal Aids*, 2009/1 Eur. St. Aid L. Q. 63–72 (2009).
15. ECJ, *Republic of Portugal v. Commission*, Case No. C-88/03 paras. 58 (66).
16. ECJ, *Republic of Portugal v. Commission*, Case No. C-88/03 [2006] ECR I-07115 para. 67. As the Court stated in *the UGT-Rioja case*, "[...], where an infra-State body is sufficiently autonomous, in other words, when it has autonomy from the institutional, procedural and economic points of view, it plays a fundamental role in the definition of the political and economic environment in which the undertakings operate. That fundamental role is the consequence of the autonomy and not a precondition for that autonomy" (para. 55).
17. See, e.g., the Commission Decision (2000/795/CE) [1999], OJ L 318, Dec. 16, 2000, 36; or the Commission Decision (2003/192/CE) [2001], OJ L 77, 24 Mar. 2003, p. 1; as well as Joined cases ECJ, *Diputación Foral de Álava a.o. v. Commission*, Cases No. T-103/00 and T-92/00 [2002] ECR II-1385 (confirmed on appeal Joined cases ECJ, *Ramondín a.o. v. Commission*, Cases No. C-186/02 P and C-188/02 [2004] ECR I-10653; Joined cases ECJ, *Diputación Foral de Álava a.o. v. Commission*, Cases No. T-127/99, T-129/99 and T-148/99 P [2002] ECR II-1275 (confirmed on appeal Joined cases ECJ, *Demesa and Territorio Histórico de Álava v. Commission*, Cases No. C-183/02 P and C-187/02 P [2004] ECR I-10609; Joined cases ECJ, *Diputación Foral de Álava v. Commission*, Cases No. T-346/99 to T-348/99 [2002] ECR II-4259.

These three conditions established by the European Court of Justice are not always easy to assess in practice. In particular, it is the third aspect of the autonomy of a region that raises the most difficulties. According to the Court the fact that a reduced taxation of undertakings established or active on the territory of one region is subsidized by the central government, directly or indirectly or by equalization mechanisms or by other region is constitutive of State aid. This latter condition implies for the judge to inquire into the financial relations between levels of government within Member States.

For example, one question that could come in mind is whether in order to establish the insufficient degree of financial autonomy it must be proven that a compensation is directly linked to the reduction of the tax by the region in question or if it is sufficient to establish that the region could benefit from some kind of solidarity mechanism or redistribution mechanism that could generally allow it not to bear the financial consequences of a tax measure.

The Court devoted several paragraphs of its judgment in the *UGT-Rioja* case, to the question whether the existence of financial transfers between the central authority and the autonomous regions could alone suffice to prove the absence of financial autonomy:

> 129 (...). There must be compensation, namely, a causal relationship between a tax measure adopted by the foral authorities and the amounts assumed by the Spanish State.
>
> 130 As has been stated before the Court, the attribution rate is set on the basis of economic data during political negotiations in which the Spanish State participates and in the context of which it defends the national interest and that of the other regions of the Kingdom of Spain. It is for the national court to determine whether that process of setting the rate has the aim of permitting the central government to compensate the cost of a subsidy or a tax measure adopted by the Historical Territories which is of benefit to undertakings.
>
> 131 Likewise, it is for that court to examine the effects of that process and to verify whether, because of the methodology adopted and the economic data taken into account, the setting of the attribution rate and, more generally, the calculation of the quota may have the effect of causing the Spanish State to compensate the consequences of a tax measure adopted by the foral authorities.
>
> 132 In its written observations, the Commission also contends that a number of other financial transfers which compensate for tax measures reducing taxes also exist, such as those resulting from the existence of a single social security fund, a minimum public service guaranteed by the State or the Inter-territorial Compensation Fund. Moreover, at the hearing, the Commission referred to transfers and subsidies of considerable amounts to public authorities of the Autonomous Community of the Basque Country which are not taken into account in the calculation of the quota.
>
> 133 In that regard, if financial compensation may be declared and specific, it may also be hidden and result only from the actual examination of the financial flows existing between the infra-State body concerned, the Member State which it comes under and the other regions of that Member State.
>
> 134 That examination may indicate that a tax reduction decision adopted by the infra-State body results in larger financial transfers in its favour, because of the calculation methods used in order to determine the amounts to be transferred.

> 135 However, as the Advocate General stated in point 109 of her Opinion and contrary to what the Commission appears to be claiming, the mere fact that it appears from a general examination of the financial relations between the central State and its infra-State bodies that there are financial transfers between the former and the latter, cannot, in itself, suffice to demonstrate that those bodies do not assume the financial consequences of the tax measures which they adopt and, accordingly, that they do not enjoy financial autonomy, since such transfers may take place for reasons unconnected with the tax measures[18].

Therefore, it appears that State aid implies that transfer of funds from the central government do exist and are connected—expressly or implicitly—to the adoption of a tax measure by the region that is to be considered as favorable in comparison with the tax regime applicable in other regions.

However, other questions could be raised, like the fact that sometimes a reduction of the tax rates—and therefore of the tax burden on taxpayers—does not lead to a reduction of the financial resources of the region in question. The effects of a tax measure being indeed not always easy to assess, it could happen that some taxpayers enjoy a reduction of their tax burden in a region that do not benefit from any form of compensating mechanisms. In this case, it would be almost impossible to demonstrate the existence of a selective advantage.

Although the three criteria established by the ECJ appear relatively reasonable, their application could lead to controversies and undermine the effectiveness of the general prohibition of State aid. One should also bear in mind that until now all the cases that have been brought before the European Court of Justice are situation of so-called asymmetrical federalism, from a constitutional prospective, and that it is not sure that those criteria could easily apply to the other type of partly regional taxes, i.e., taxes that are jointly regulated at the central and at the regional level, where the interaction between authorities from a financial prospective can be more blurred.

We are reluctant to abandon the tradition view adopted by the Court of Justice in other cases and supported by the Treaty that European law and institutions should be neutral towards the structure and organization of government of the Member States. In the case of regional selectivity of State aid, the Court uses the constitutional structure as a cause of justification which may "neutralize" the normal application of European law. One could argue that this position goes beyond a certain neutrality towards the institutional structure of Member States and that could have unexpected consequences.

A first consequence of the ECJ case-law is that the same factual situation (based on the effects of the measure), for example a reduced rate of corporate income tax in a region of a Member State, could be treated differently depending on purely internal constitutional arrangements[19].

A second consequence of the Azores doctrine could concern the responsibility of the central authority in the case of a possible violation of the State aid regime by a

18. Joined cases ECJ, *Unión General de Trabajadores de La Rioja (UGT-Rioja) e.a*, Cases No. C-428/06 to C-434/06 [2008] ECR I-06747 paras. 129–135.
19. See also M. Merola & L. Cappelletti, Fiscalité européenne: actualités et points sensibles, 83–120 (Bruylant 2009).

region which meets the three criteria established by the European Court of Justice. It appears incoherent on the one hand to consider that a regional authority is perfectly autonomous in the adoption of tax rules and on the other hand that the central authority should bear the consequences of hypothetical violation of the same State aid rules (although under another aspects, for example, material selectivity). One should indeed consider that these two elements are inextricably linked. Either institutional autonomy of region cannot justify a violation of the State aid rules, at least when there is the possibility to have some kind of national benchmark to establish the existence of an advantage, and in this case a central authority can and even must be considered responsible for the tax adopted by regional entity, or European law recognizes a "waterproof" division of taxing powers as provided by internal arrangements of the Member State concerned and in the case of the violation of State aid rules, or other rules of the EU law, and also recognizes the direct responsibility of the concerned region without targeting the Member State as a whole (represented by its central authority).

Moreover, another consequence of the Court's attitude of giving too much weight to constitutional arrangements within a Member State could be that richer regions within the European Union would be protected in some way when applying favorable tax regimes. Acknowledging regional tax autonomy the same way as national tax sovereignty could lead to create the condition of regional tax competition which should be at the same time an incentive for region to claim additional taxing powers. One could wonder whether this—probably undesired—effect would from a political prospective be coherent with the regional policy within the EU consisting of helping poor regions in their economic and social development.

Finally, as regards partly regional taxes, the intertwinement between the powers of the central and regional authorities within the Member States could serve as a base for EU institutions, namely the European Commission, to challenge not only the exercise of taxing powers by regions within Member States but also to challenge the transfer of taxing powers from the central authority to regions within some Member States. In is indeed important to consider the effects of a measure as such and not only consider it from a purely formal perspective. It should be desirable indeed to allow an immediate action by EU authorities when a breach of EU law appears to be inevitable. For example the transfer of the possibility to violate the EU law as such (for example the power to grant incentives only to company resident on the territory of a region) should be considered as a violation of the prohibition of State aid, before it is implemented by the concerned region. It could also be considered as a violation of EU treaty freedoms (see *infra*). Far from being an obstacle to constitutional reforms within Member States, such a "preventive" procedure would increase legal certainty, by avoiding that a long and sometimes a necessary procedure takes place when it appears that EU law has not been taken properly into consideration during the process of the constitutional reforms aiming at increasing of the tax autonomy of sub-national entities.

A good example is what happened as regards the Basque countries for corporate taxes, or what is happening for the other Spanish regions, as regard inheritance and gift taxes. In both cases the central authorities retain taxing powers as regard non-residents while the regions are competent for taxing their (regional) residents. Whenever a region would lower the tax rates applicable to its residents, this inevitably leads to difference in treatment which is some cases could be considered as State aid in the present stand of the EU tax case-law (according to the *Sardinia* case-law). The only way to disjoin the competence as regard resident and non- resident taxpayers would be to provide *ex ante* a mechanism which would automatically and not optionally[20] reduce the tax burden of non-resident taxpayer and to equalize it with the tax burden applicable to regional resident in the same factual situation.

§8.04 WHICH "REGIONAL AID" IS COMPATIBLE WITH THE INTERNAL MARKET?

One should bear in mind the fact that a measure is considered as State aid does not imply that this measure is incompatible with EU law. The EU regime on State aid is indeed also a tool of EU policy for the regional development. The compatibility of aids is assessed by the Commission, on the basis of the criteria laid down by the EU Treaty. Among these criteria, the Treaty provides some derogations for Member States' "regions" which are considered socio-economically behind the EU average, according to objective criteria established by the Commission. According to Article 107, para. 3, a. and c.) TFEU, "aid to areas where the standard of living is abnormally low or where there is serious underemployment" and "to facilitate the development (...) of certain economic areas, where such aid does not adversely affect trading conditions to an extent contrary to the common interest." The European Commission controls the application of these derogations. According to the Commission Guidelines on Regional Aid, "*regional aid should be granted under a multi-sectoral aid scheme which forms an integral part of a regional development strategy with clearly defined objectives*," which usually exclude ad hoc measures[21]. Moreover, some sectors are excluded, such as coal, fisheries, agriculture. Although these "regions" are defined according to purely geographical criteria, in some Member States, including Italy, they cover the territory of autonomous political authorities. In some exceptional cases, derogations for specific regions are authorized directly by the Treaty. It is the case of outermost regions (Madeira tax-free zone or Azores corporate tax reductions) or East German regions (see Article 107, 2, c TFEU).

Inversely, the fact that a regional tax measure is not considered as State aid does not necessarily mean that the Member State or the region having adopted it shall be allowed to apply it. Besides the issue of the application of Treaty freedoms (see *infra*), EU control over State aid is strengthened, with respect to direct business taxation, by the development of soft law instruments to fight against harmful tax competition between Member States, in particular the Code of Conduct on business taxation[22]. The

---

20. See ECJ, *F. Gielen v. Staatssecretaris van Financiën*, Case No. C-440/08 [2010] ECR I-02323.
21. On the compatibility of regional aids, see Commission Regulation (EC) 800/2008 of August 6, 2008 declaring certain categories of aid compatible with the common market in application of Articles 87 and 88 of the Treaty (General block exemption Regulation), OJ L 214, Aug. 9, 2008, 3-47, Arts. 13 and 14 and Guidelines on National Regional aid for 2007-2013, OJ C 54, Mar. 4, 2006, p. 13.
22. On tax competition within the EU in general and the Code of conduct in particular (including its relation with State aid control), see A.C. Dos Santos, *L'union européenne et la régulation de*

Code of Conduct on business taxation, despite—or perhaps thanks to—its soft law nature, proves to be a rather effective instrument in combating certain special tax regimes established by the Member States in order to attract investors from other Member States or even from third States, and considered harmful to the entire EU. These non-binding rules may concern tax measures adopted by all authorities of Member States, including regional and local authorities[23]. Indeed, some of the special tax regimes rolled back thanks to the Code of Conduct had been adopted not by central government but by local authorities with extensive fiscal autonomy. This feature has not prevented the Primarolo Group, responsible for the implementation of the Code of Conduct, to declare these regimes harmful. Concerning the application to the Code of Conduct, one could also wonder whether the fact that a harmful tax measure is adopted by regional authorities of a Member States could have an impact of its qualification. The answer is clearly negative. It is true that the Code of Conduct is meant to apply to tax schemes that derogate from the (national) common tax regime. This concept refers in principle to the tax system of the Member State, understood as a single entity. However, concerning certain tax regimes adopted by local authorities, the Primarolo group, in the cases where it was not possible to compare the regional regime with a national benchmark, took as a benchmark the tax system of the regional authority[24].

§8.05 TERRITORIALITY, STATE AID AND FUNDAMENTAL FREEDOMS: A—STILL—UNRESOLVED ISSUE?

In the same way, State aid may have a territorial dimension, treaty freedoms may also prohibit territorial limitations to the granting of tax advantages by Member States based on distinctions between taxpayers. A distinction made by a tax measure between (comparable) domestic and cross-border situations may lead to declare it—if unjustified—incompatible with EU law. There is certainly a similarity between the two systems in the fact that both constitute a form of European control of the definition made by Member States of the categories of taxpayers benefiting from a tax advantage and those that do not. To a certain extent, both systems reflect a certain idea of neutrality and of non-discrimination.

Territorial selectivity in the area of State aid seems to imply however more than a differentiation between domestic and foreign goods or undertakings. As the Court said in a 2000 decision:

> (...) as a rule aid is granted to undertakings established on the territory of the Member State granting it. Such a practice, and the consequent unequal treatment

la concurrence fiscale (Bruylant 2009); W. Schön (ed.), *Tax Competition in Europe* (IBFD 2003); C. Pinto, *Tax Competition and EU Law* (Kluwer Law international 2003).

23. In the Primarolo Report, implementing the Code of Conduct, some regional tax regimes were found to be harmful, like for example some tax measures opted by the Basque Country. See Primarolo Report of 29 November 1999, available on the European Commission (DG TAXUD) website, measure A005, 24.
24. See in the Primarolo Report, the analyses of the tax regimes of the Basque Country (Spain), Gibraltar (United Kingdom) and the Aland islands (Denmark), in particular the measures A005 and B012.

> of undertakings of other Member States is thus inherent in the concept of State aid. It does not, however, amount in itself to covert discrimination or a restriction on [fundamental freedoms] (...)[25].

In the case-law of the Court, national tax measures have in some cases be considered incompatible with EU law requirement both under the EU Treaty freedoms and the State aid regime[26]. In some of these cases, this double declaration of incompatibility concerned two different features of a national tax measure. In other cases, it was the same aspect of a national measure (i.e., the same criteria used by the national legislator to distinguish between the beneficiaries of the tax advantage and the other taxpayers) that was considered twice EU incompatible.

In this perspective, the analysis of territorial restrictions to tax incentives is particularly interesting. In the *Germany v. Commission* case, the Court upheld the Commission's decision, which considered as prohibited State aid and as a violation of the freedom of establishment a German scheme aimed at fostering investment in the *Länder* of the former East Germany. The scheme consisted in the right to set off a gain resulting from the sale of shares against the costs of purchasing new shares in capital companies, provided that the latter companies had both their registered office and their central administration in one of the new Länder or in Berlin, and that they had no more than 250 employees at the time the shares are acquired (or were holding companies whose sole object is to administer participations in companies having such characteristics). According to the Commission, "*the tax scheme confers a direct advantage on certain natural and legal persons, who are the direct beneficiaries, to encourage them to acquire certain assets from certain firms, who are the indirect beneficiaries*"[27]. The selectivity of the measure could be further established as the measure favored undertakings in a specific geographical area and of a specific size (more than 250 employees). On the compatibility with treaty freedoms, the Commission decided that "the scheme thus favors east German and Berlin companies as compared with companies with their registered offices outside Germany, and consequently infringes the ban on discrimination in [the provisions of Treaty on the freedom of establishment]."

The Court followed the Commission on both grounds. Concerning the freedom of establishment, the Court focused—contrary to the Commission which did not address this issue—on the absence of objective difference between "undertakings having their registered office on its territory," and "undertakings having their registered office in another Member State" in the light of the objectives of the measure. According to the Court, "there can, however, be no such objective difference of situation between a company established in a Member State other than the Federal Republic of Germany

25. ECJ, *ARGE*, Case No. C-94/99 [2000] ECR I-11037 para. 36.
26. In a *Commission v. France* case, the simultaneous application of State aid and treaty freedoms was acknowledged by the Court. ECJ, *Commission v. France*, Case No. C-18/84 [1985] ECR 01339. See on this case, W. Schön, *Taxation and State Aid Law in the European Union*, 36 Comm. Mkt. L. Rev. 911–939 (1999).
27. Commission Decision on tax concessions under § 52(8) of the German Income Tax Act (98/476/EC) [1998] (notified under document number C(1998) 231: Only the German text is authentic), OJ L 212, Jul. 30, 1998, 50–57.

and carrying on economic activity in the new Länder through a branch, agency or fixed establishment, a company which cannot claim the benefit of the contested measure, and a company having its registered office on German territory, which does profit from the tax concession introduced by that measure.[28]

This latter paragraph of the Court's decision allows us to distinguish between two different aspects of the German tax measure. Under a first aspect, the measure favored only undertakings which were active in a certain geographical area. Under another aspect, the measure was not applicable to undertakings that, however being materially in a comparable situation of those benefiting from the advantage as to the geographical area of activity, did not fulfill a criteria of residence because not being a legally distinct entity of a legal person having its registered office in another Member State. However, since the German legislator had used the criteria of the place of the registered office in order to consider that an undertaking was active in the new *Länder* the overlap was almost inevitable.

The same view was adopted by the Court in the more recent—and in our view, more controversial—*Sardinia* case concerning the exemption of resident undertakings from a Regional tax on stopovers for tourist purposes by aircraft used for the private transport of persons, or by recreational craft[29]. Interestingly, the Court used almost the same wording to define the comparability test in the analysis of the compatibility of the tax measure with the free movement of services and the selectivity test in assessing whether the measure constituted State aid.

About the free provision of services, the Court said, at para. 36:

> It follows that, in terms of the consequences for the environment, all natural and legal persons who receive the services in question are—contrary to the contentions of the Region of Sardinia—in an objectively comparable situation with regard to that tax, irrespective of the place where they reside or are established.

On the existence of prohibited State aid, the Court declared, at para. 63:

> Is clear from paragraphs 36 and 37 of the present judgment, it must be held that, in the light of the nature and objectives of that tax, all the natural and legal persons who receive stopover services in Sardinia are, contrary to what is argued by the defendant in the main proceedings, in an objectively comparable situation, irrespective of their place of residence or the place where they are established. It follows that the measure cannot be regarded as general, since it does not apply to all operators of aircraft or pleasure boats which make a stopover in Sardinia.

In this case however, one could legitimately question the need of assessing the compatibility of the exemption under the State aid regime. To consider the Sardinian measure as an incentive scheme designed at favoring resident undertakings not only goes much beyond what the region's probable objectives were, but most importantly

28. ECJ, *Federal Republic of Germany v. Commission of European Communities*, Case No. C-156/98 [2000] ECR I-06857 para. 86. Interestingly, the advocate general Saggio considered that the Commission, for procedural grounds, was not allowed to consider the aid scheme incompatible with the freedom of establishment. He was however not followed by the Court.
29. ECJ, *Presidente del consiglio dei Ministri v. Regione Sardegna*, Case No. C-169/08 [2009] ECR I-10821.

adds very little to the judgment both from the point of view of the taxing authority and the taxpayers[30].

Indeed, if the exemption is considered incompatible with the free provision of services, which implies necessarily its removal and a modification of the existing legislation, the qualification as State aid cannot render this exemption "more" incompatible with EU law that it is already under the Treaty freedoms. Additional support for this position can be found in the cases *Commission v. France* (aid to press undertakings) and *Germany v. Commission* (*Einkommensteurgesetz*) referred above, where the Court made clear that State aid rules do not—and cannot—have an impact on the provisions of the Treaty concerning non- discrimination and the freedoms of movement[31].

Moreover, this double statement of incompatibility—which has been made by the Court without any prior decision of the Commission on the State aid aspect[32]—bears the risk to put the taxing authority in an impossible position as to the correct implementation of the judgment. Must the tax be recovered on the resident taxpayers who have unduly benefited from the exemption, as it normally the case under the State aid regime, or on the contrary, could Sardinia reimburse the non-resident taxpayers and abolish the tax as it is for the future?

These two possibilities are incompatible with one another, but the Court's decision does not give any hint about how Sardinia should behave, leaving "the referring court to draw the appropriate inferences from that conclusion" (para. 65). The fact that the tax measure was adopted by a region in the framework of its autonomous taxing powers adds further complexity to the issue of implementation. Therefore, we think that the Court, once established the incompatibility of the tax exemption, with the free provision of services, should have refrained from answering to the preliminary question asked by the Italian *Corte di cassazione* concerning the compatibility of the measure with the State aid regime.

The issue of simultaneous application of Treaty freedoms and State aid provisions has also to take into account the European Commission's practice. As the Court repeatedly held, the Commission cannot authorize under State aid rules a Member State to apply tax measures which do not fulfill the requirements of equality of treatment imposed by the Treaty freedoms[33]. However, some decisions adopted by the Commission allow Member States to impose conditions for the granting of an aid

30. Maybe the only reasonable justification of considering the discrimination also under the State aid regime could have lied in the consequences of the decision for undertakings resident in the other parts of the Italian national territory. According to the restrictive case-law of *Communauté Francaise* case (ECJ, *Government of Communauté française and Gouvernement wallon v. Gouvernement flamand*, Case No. C-212/06 [2008] ECR I-01683), treaty freedoms do not apply to purely internal situation. However, the Court did not limit its findings on Art. 49 CE to resident undertakings of other Member States.
31. See also the opinion of the Advocate general in the *Geurts and Vogten* case concerning an exemption from inheritance duties for the transfer of family undertakings: ECJ, *Geurts and Vogten*, Case No. C-464/05 [2007] I-09325.
32. On the demarcation of competences between the Commission and the national courts in State aid law, see opinion of AG Kokott in ECJ, *Presidente del consiglio dei Ministri v. Regione Sardegna*, Case No. C-169/08 [2009] ECR I-10821 paras. 118–122.
33. See the case-law quoted above.

scheme, which entail a territorial restriction. This is the case of several decisions authorizing tax advantages in favor of film investment and /or production[34], which are linked to the obligation for the beneficiary to invest a considerable part of the aid on the territory of the Member State granting the aid scheme.

Those decisions are based on a 2002 Commission communication[35], in which the Commission considered that:

> The Commission accepted that Member States may require a certain part of the film production budget to be spent on their territory as an eligibility criterion for aid. This is based on the reasoning that a certain degree of territorialisation of the expenditure may be necessary to ensure the continued presence of the human skills and technical expertise required for cultural creation. This should be limited to the minimum degree required to promote cultural objectives.

On these grounds, the Commission accepted "as an eligibility criteria territorialisation in terms of expenditure of up to 80% of the production budget of an aided film or TV work." One could wonder—in the light of the case-law referred above—whether the Commission has not acted *ultra vires* and allowed a potential violation of the Treaty freedoms; it is indeed unclear whether such a territorial restriction to the granting of a tax advantage could be justified on the ground of the promotion of culture[36].

This communication, and the Commission decisions adopted as a result of it, as well as other decisions admitting territorial conditions for the granting of an aid scheme, show how the Commission proceeds in its analysis[37]. It is interesting to see that the Commission seems to limit the control of the respect of the fundamental freedoms requirement to differences in treatment based directly or indirectly on the nationality (i.e., residence) of the beneficiaries. The other potential restrictions, i.e., the measures which tend to restrict cross-border economic transactions by granting them a less favorable treatment than purely domestic transactions, are analyzed from a State aid perspective, in the assessment of the selectivity test, or of the grounds of compatibility listed in Article 107 TFEU. In its analysis, the Commission often strikes a balance between conflicting interests, according to the proportionality as regards the

34. See for example, Commission Decision concerning Italy (C(2009) 5512 final) [2009]: "80 pc of the aid must be spent in Italy"; Commission Decision concerning the Belgian Tax shelter (C(2009) 10668) [2009]: "150pc of the sums invested benefiting from the tax incentive has to be spent in Belgium as production costs." A similar regime also exists since 1988 in Luxembourg (Audiovisual Investment Certificate Program). Although it has been extended in 2007 to "production costs incurred in the European Union and in particular on the Luxembourg territory" (only mentioned before), it is limited to resident companies, which seems incompatible with the EU Treaty freedoms (see "Loi du 21 décembre 1998 instaurant un régime fiscal temporaire spécial pour les certificats d'investissement audiovisuel," Memorial, A-111, 24 Dec. 1998, art. 2).
35. Commission Decision on certain legal aspects relating to cinematographic and other audiovisual works (2001/0534/EC), OJ C 043, Feb. 16, 2002, 6–17.
36. On the restrictions to Treaty freedoms based on the promotion of culture, see ECJ, *Unión de Televisiones Comerciales Asociadas (UTECA) v. Administración General del Estado*, Case No. C-222/07 [2009] ECR I-01407, as well as the Commission decision cited above.
37. See for example Commission Decision concerning a French tax credit in favor of the development of videogames (C(2007) 6070) [2007], State aid C 47/2006 (ex N 648/2005), in which the Commission allows the compatibility of an aid based on criteria such as the protection of the "European cultural diversity and creation" or of the "European cultural patrimony."

objective that the proposed tax scheme pursues. This Commission's position does not directly concern a tax measure adopted by a regional authority. However, it is worth comparing it with the relatively strict attitude adopted by the Court on the compatibility with EU law of regional tax provisions, in particular in the *Geurts and Vogten* and the *Missionswerk Heukelbach* cases[38].

In conclusion, the application of the State aid regime to regional tax measures puts in evidence the—often conflicting- interactions between three levels of governments: European, national and subnational[39]. Uncertainties arise as to the relevance to be given to the concept of territoriality of taxing powers when it comes to justify differences in the application of tax advantages to situations which differ from a territorial viewpoint. The construction of a workable multi-tiered federalism in Europe will necessitate further clarification, not only as regards the possibility to justify territorial differentiation within a Member States on the grounds of the extent of the taxing powers granted to regional authorities, but also as regards the coherence between the application of the State aid regime and of the freedoms granted by the TFEU.

38. ECJ, *Geurts and Vogten,* Case No. C-464/05 [2007] I-09325; ECJ, *Missionswerk Werner Heukelbach v. Belgian State,* Case No. C-25/10 not yet reported in ECR. For a comment, see E. Traversa & B. Vintras, *Beyond Discrimination* (provisional title), (W. Schoen, I. Richelle & E. Traversa eds., Springer 2012) (forthcoming).
39. On these aspects in general, E. Traversa, *Is It Still Room Left in EU Law for Tax Autonomy of Member States' Regional and Local Authorities?,* 20 EC Tax Rev. 4–15 (2011).

CHAPTER 9

State Aid: Towards a Theoretical Assessment Framework

Frank Engelen & Anna Gunn

> Nothing is as practical as a good theory.
>
> —Kurt Lewin[1]

§9.01 INTRODUCTION

At the time of writing it is a public secret that the 1998 Commission Notice on the application of the State aid rules to measures relating to direct business taxation (98/C384/03) (hereinafter referred to as: "the 1998 Notice") is up for revision. We wholeheartedly support this initiative because unfortunately the application of the State aid rules in this field of law too often still leads to uncertainty. The overhaul of the 1998 Notice offers an excellent opportunity to remedy this.

In this Chapter we will discuss an aspect of the State aid rules which in our view will certainly have to be dealt with in any future guidance issued by the European Commission (hereinafter simply referred to as: "the Commission"). The question which we seek to answer pertains to the qualification of a direct tax measure under Article 107(1) TFEU. How should it be established whether a direct tax measure constitutes aid within the meaning of this provision? By way of an answer to this question we have composed a theoretical assessment framework which can be used to test whether a particular direct tax measure satisfies the requirements set out in Article 107(1) TFEU. This framework differs from the approach currently taken in *inter alia* the official Commission guidance, and we believe that it may offer a more workable approach for assessing direct tax measures in the light of the State aid rules.

This Chapter is constructed along the following lines. Section §9.01 starts with the requirements which must be met in order for a measure to be regarded as State aid

1. Kurt Lewin (1890–1947) is regarded as one of the founding fathers of social psychology.

under Article 107(1) TFEU. Sections §9.02, 9.03 and 9.04 then deal with three specific problems associated with the application of this provision to direct tax measures. These are: the concept of an "advantage"; the question of material selectivity; and the relationship between State aid and the fundamental freedoms. After this, the theoretical assessment framework is discussed in section 9.05.

§9.02 ARTICLE 107(1) OF THE TFEU

[A] The State Aid Criteria

Article 107(1) TFEU contains the prohibition of certain forms of aid granted by EU Member States (State aid). The text of this provision is as follows (emphasis added):

> Save as otherwise provided in the Treaties, *any aid* granted *by a Member State or through State resources* in any form whatsoever which *distorts or threatens to distort competition* by *favouring certain undertakings* or the production of certain goods shall, in so far as it *affects trade between Member States*, be incompatible with the internal market.

Article 107(1) TFEU thus contains four cumulative criteria which must be met in order for a direct tax measure to be within scope of the State aid rules. These criteria are:

(1) The measure must confer an advantage.
(2) This advantage must only be conferred to certain undertakings or the production of certain goods (selectivity).
(3) This advantage must be granted by a Member State of through State resources.
(4) The measure must distort or threaten to distort competition in the internal market, and affect trade between Member States.

The Commission has provided guidance on the application of these criteria to direct tax measures in the 1998 Notice and the Report on the implementation of the aforementioned Commission Notice[2] (hereinafter referred to as: "the 2004 Report").

[B] Applying the Criteria to Direct Tax Measures

At the beginning of this Chapter we noted that the application of Article 107(1) TFEU too often still proves troublesome. In our view, this problem can be localized to the first and second criteria listed in section 1.1 (the existence of an advantage and the requirement of selectivity). The third and fourth criteria (loss of State resources and distortion of competition) are, by contrast, easily to apply in the field of direct taxation.

2. Commission Report of February 9, 2004 on the implementation of the Commission notice C(2004)434 on the application of the State aid rules to measures relating to direct business taxation (hereinafter Commission Notice 1998).

It is settled European case law that a loss of tax revenue for a Member State should be equated with a tax expenditure.[3] The provision of State aid though the direct tax system generally would entail a loss of revenue. An exception to this rule arises where the Member State accepts for example a lower standard of documentation, which in turn reduces the compliance costs of the undertaking concerned. Although this case does not involve a loss of State resources, it clearly is an advantages granted "by a Member State", and for this reason is also potentially within scope of Article 107(1) TFEU.

The last requirement is that the measure results in a (threatened) distortion of competition and is also liable to affect intra-EU trade. Here, the 1998 Notice correctly observes:

> This criterion presupposes that the beneficiary of the measure exercises an economic activity, regardless of the beneficiary's legal status or means of financing. Under settled case law, for the purposes of this provision, the criterion of trade being affected is met if the recipient firm carries on an economic activity involving trade between Member States. The mere fact that the aid strengthens the firm's position compared with that of other firms which are competitor's in intra-Community trade is enough to allow the conclusion to be drawn that intra-Community trade is affected. Neither the fact that aid is relatively small in amount,[4] nor the fact that the recipient is moderate in size or its share of the Community market very small, nor indeed the fact that the recipient does not carry out exports or exports virtually all its products outside the Community do anything to alter this conclusion.[5]

The criterion that the aid must be liable to distort competition and affect trade between Member States is, therefore, virtually almost always met.

§9.03 ADVANTAGE

[A] The Concept of an "Advantage"

The term "aid" is not defined in the European Treaties. However, it is settled case law that this concept is wider than just aid provided in the form of subsidies, and instead also includes aid delivered through a reduction of the charges normally borne by an undertaking. In the *Ufex* judgment (C-83/01 P, C-93/01 P and C-94/01 P), the ECJ for example held that (emphasis added):

> The concept of aid (...) encompasses not only positive benefits, such as subsidies, but also *interventions which, in various forms, mitigate the charges which are normally included in the budget of an undertaking* and which, without therefore

3. Commission Notice 1998, para. 10.
4. Footnote in the original: "With the exception, however, of aid meeting the tests of the *de minimis* rule."
5. Commission Notice 1998, para. 11.

> being subsidies in the strict sense of the word, are of the same character and have the same effect.[6]

As the "charges which are normally included in the budget" of an undertaking include direct taxes, any measure which results in a reduction of taxes "normally" payable by an undertaking can be regarded as aid within the meaning of Article 107(1) TFEU.

In the 1998 Notice, the Commission illustrates this concept using a number of examples (emphasis added):

> the measure must confer on recipients an *advantage which relieves them of charges that are normally borne from their budgets.* The advantage may be provided *through a reduction in the firm's tax burden in various ways,* including:
>
> - a reduction in the tax base (such as special deductions, special or accelerated depreciation arrangements or the entering of reserves on the balance sheet),
> - a total or partial reduction in the amount of tax (such as exemption or a tax credit),
> - deferment, cancellation or even special rescheduling of tax debt.[7]

Meanwhile in relation to the quantification of fiscal State aid it is considered that:

> In the case of State aid in the form of tax measures, the amount to be recovered is calculated on the basis of a comparison between the tax actually paid and *the amount which should have been paid if the generally applicable rule had been applied.* Interest is added to this basic amount.[8]

It follows from the above that in the context of a direct tax measure the existence of an advantage must be determined with reference to the amount of tax which would normally have been levied upon the beneficiary of the tax measure under consideration (hereinafter referred to as: the "normal tax burden").

[B] How Is the Normal Tax Burden Determined?

The normal tax burden serves as a benchmark against which it can be determined whether a direct tax measure has granted an advantage to a taxpayer. Although the normal tax burden may sometimes be self-evident,[9] this is not by definition the case.

If the normal tax burden is not immediately obvious, an approach is needed through which to establish this amount. Potentially this can become a somewhat hazardous exercise. In view of the fact that the Member States have, to a great extent, maintained their fiscal sovereignty in matters of direct taxation, it is not possible to assess the existence of an advantage allegedly caused by a direct tax measure of one of

6. Joined cases ECJ, *Ufex,* Cases No. C-83/01P, C-93/01 P and C-94/01P ECR [2003] I-06993 para. 65. See for the same approach: ECJ, *Banco Exterior de España,* Case No. C-387/92 ECR [1994] I-00877 para. 13.
7. Commission Notice 1998, para. 9.
8. Commission Notice 1998, para. 35.
9. If, for example, an undertaking concludes a unique agreement with the tax authorities allowing him a special reduction in the applicable corporate income tax rate of 50%, it is clear that the advantage should be ascertained with reference to the normal corporate income tax rate.

the Member States with reference to the abstract notion of what a direct tax system ought to look like. We submit that instead, the question of what constitutes the normal tax burden must always be ascertained in the context of the tax system at hand and in the light of the objectives pursued by the measures in question. We thus reject the notion that there could exist a framework of reference for assessing the existence of an advantage *outside* the actual tax system of the Member State itself.

[C] The *Gibraltar* Case

In view of our comments in section §9.03[B], it will not come as a surprise that we concur with the position taken by Advocate General Jääskinen in his Opinion to the *Gibraltar* case (C-106/09 P and C-107/09 P) (emphasis added):

> Inasmuch as *European Union law does not have any default tax system*, the *reference framework must remain the national reference framework* or the one identified in accordance with the *Azores* case-law. Consequently, if the Court of Justice considers that Gibraltar may in itself constitute an appropriate reference framework, it is appropriate to adhere to the traditional analysis of an advantage and selectivity.[10]

The *Gibraltar* case centered on three taxes which had been proposed by Gibraltar in the context of the reform of its company taxation. The taxes at hand were a payroll tax, a tax on the use of real estate (Business Property Occupation Tax) and a company registration fee. The combined effect of these taxes was such that offshore companies effectively paid no or minimal tax in Gibraltar, due to the fact that their activities by and large did not trigger taxation under the proposed system. One of the difficulties in the *Gibraltar* case was whether it could, under these circumstances, be argued that the offshore companies had enjoyed an "advantage". The ECJ answered this question positively and on the basis of the objectives of the Gibraltar tax system itself. It was considered that:

> In view of the features of that regime, outlined in the preceding paragraph, it is apparent that the regime at issue, by combining those bases, even though they are founded on criteria that are in themselves of a general nature, in practice discriminates between companies which are in a comparable situation *with regard to the objective of the proposed tax reform, namely to introduce a general system of taxation for all companies established in Gibraltar.*[11]

We fully agree with the basic approach taken by the ECJ in the *Gibraltar* case. By assessing the existence of an advantage with reference to the objective of the proposed regime itself, the ECJ in our view avoids an outcome that would jeopardize the fiscal sovereignty of Member States.

10. Opinion of AG Jääskinen in Joined cases ECJ, *Gibraltar*, Cases No. C-106/09 P and C-107/09 P not yet reported in ECR para. 175.
11. Joined cases ECJ, *Gibraltar*, Cases No. C-106/09 P and C-107/09 P not yet reported in ECR para. 101.

§9.04 SELECTIVITY

[A] The Concept of "Selectivity"

For a measure to be within scope of Article 107(1) TFEU it must grant an advantage to *certain* undertakings or the production of *certain* goods. This is referred to as the requirement of selectivity. In the 1998 Notice the Commission provides the following principles with regard to the application of this criterion to direct tax measures (emphasis added):

> The main criterion in applying [Article 107(1)] to a tax measure is (...) that the measure provides in favour of certain undertakings in the Member State an exception to the application of the tax system. The *common system applicable* should thus first be determined. It must then be examined whether the *exception to the system or differentiations within that system are justified "by the nature or general scheme" of the tax system*, that is to say, whether they derive directly from the basic or guiding principles of the tax system of the Member State concerned. It this is not the case, then State aid is involved.[12]

Selectivity of the measure is thus assessed in two steps. First, it is assessed whether the measure constitutes an exception to the application of the tax system (common system applicable). After this it is assessed whether the exception can be justified in the light of the nature and general scheme of the tax system itself. In section §9.04[D] we refer to the second step as the justification of prima facie selective measures.

Three types of selectivity are commonly distinguished: regional (also referred to as geographic), sectoral and material selectivity. [13] From the perspective of direct taxation, it is material selectivity which is the most troublesome, and so we will focus on this in section §9.04[E].

[B] Establishing Selectivity on the Basis of the Comparability Test

To assess the selectivity of a measure the position of the recipient of the aid should be compared with that of undertakings which are in an objectively comparable factual and legal situation in light of the objective pursued by the measure (we refer to this below as the "comparability test").This follows *inter alia* from the judgment in the case of Adria-Wien (C-143/09), where the ECJ held that (emphasis added):

> For the application of (...) [Article 107] of the Treaty, it is irrelevant that the situation of the presumed beneficiary of the measure is better or worse in comparison with the situation under the law as it previously stood, or has not altered over time (see, to that effect, Case 57/86 *Greece* v *Commission* [1988] ECR 2855, paragraph 10). The *only question* to be determined is whether, under a

12. Commission Notice 1998, para. 16.
13. In our view the establishment of the Azores-criteria for regional autonomy has made the concept of regional selectivity—from a legal perspective—sufficiently clear. See ECJ, *Azores,* Case No. C-88/03 [2006] ECR I-07115.

> particular statutory scheme, a State measure is such as to favour "certain undertakings or the production of certain goods" within the meaning of (...) [Article 107(1)] of the Treaty in *comparison with other undertakings which are in a legal and factual situation that is comparable in the light of the objective pursued by the measure in question* (see, to that effect, Case C-75/97 *Belgium* v *Commission* [1999] ECR I-3671, paragraphs 28 to 31).

The ECJ continues:

> According to the case-law of the Court, a measure which, although conferring an advantage on its recipient, is justified by the nature or general scheme of the system of which it is part does not fulfil *that condition* of selectivity (see Case 173/73 *Italy v Commission* [1974] ECR 709, paragraph 33, and *Belgium v Commission*, cited above, paragraph 33).[14]

It follows that the only question which needs to be addressed in the context of determining whether a particular tax measure constitutes State aid, is whether the measure favors taxpayer A in comparison with taxpayer B, where taxpayer B is in a legal and factual situation that is comparable in the light of the objective pursued by the measure in question. If the taxpayers compared are not in a legal and factual situation that is comparable in the light of the objective pursued by the measure in question, the different treatment can be said to be justified by the nature or general scheme of the system of which it is part, and does not, therefore, constitute aid within the meaning of Article 107(1) TFEU.

The question set out above logically presupposes that taxpayer A is subject to any taxation or any requirement connected therewith, which is less burdensome than the taxation and connected requirements to which taxpayer B is subjected. For such less burdensome taxation to constitute aid, it must be considered "abnormal" in the light of the objective pursued by the measure in question, i.e., the objective pursued by the measure in question requires that taxpayer A is subjected to the same taxation and connected requirements to which taxpayer B is subjected (see also sections §9.02[B] and §9.02[C]).

This in turn implies that the measure pursues no objectives other than favoring taxpayer A. Indeed, if the measure in question would pursue another objective than favoring taxpayer A (and would also be suitable and necessary for attaining such objective), taxpayer B could not be said to not be in a legal and factual position that is comparable in the light of such objective, and the different tax treatment of taxpayer A and B would not constitute aid. The conclusion must, therefore, be that only tax measures which pursue objectives other than restricting the tax benefit in question can escape State aid control.

It follows that to apply the comparability test meaningfully, the objective of the measure *itself* ought to be compatible with the State aid prohibition (hereinafter referred to as a "legitimate objective"). If, for example, the objective of the abovementioned measure was to provide State aid to taxpayer A (an illegitimate objective), it is clear that taxpayer B would—in the light of the objective of this measure—not be in a

14. ECJ, *Adria-Wien*, Case No. C-143/99 [2001] ECR I-08365 paras. 41 and 42.

comparable position and therefore would fall outside the reference framework, which would mean that the measure would not qualify as selective. In our view it is beyond doubt that this cannot be the correct application of the comparability test. The solution lies in the requirement that when assessing selectivity, the objective of the measure under consideration must be "legitimate", i.e., compatible with the State aid rules.

[C] Significance of the Objective of the Measure

It is established European case law that the qualification of a measure as State aid is dependent on the economic effects of the measure, and not the objectives with which the Member State introduced it. This means that if a Member State introduces a measure that meets all the criteria of Article 107(1) TFEU, the reasons for doing so cannot prevent that the measure constitutes aid.

The above does not, however, mean that the objectives of the Member State are irrelevant when determining whether the measure meets the requirements of Article 107(1) TFEU. Indeed, when establishing the selectivity of the measure it is necessary to apply the comparability test discussed in section §9.03[B]. This test calls for a comparison with undertakings in a legally and factually comparable situation, in light of the *object and purpose* of the measure in question. As the ECJ held in the Azores case (C-88/03):

> (...) a distinction must be made between, on the one hand, the objectives attributed to a particular tax scheme which are extrinsic to it and, on the other, the mechanisms inherent in the tax system itself which are necessary for the achievement of such objectives.

[D] Justification of Prima Facie Selective Measures

Measures which grant an advantage to certain undertakings are, although appearing prima facie to be selective, not selective if the Member State concerned can show that these measures can be justified by the nature and general scheme of the system of which they are a part.

In the Azores case (C-88/03), the ECJ states (emphasis added):

> A measure which creates an exception to the application of the general tax system may be justified by the nature and overall structure of the tax system *if the Member State concerned can show* that that measure results *directly from the basic or guiding principles of its tax system.*[15]

Under the approach suggested by the ECJ in the Azores case a measure which deviates from the general system can—under certain circumstances—be justified. Note that it is up to the Member State to prove that a measure which is prima facie selective can be justified the in the light of the general principles of the tax system concerned.

15. ECJ, *Azores*, Case No. C-88/03 [2006] ECR I-07115 para. 81.

It is not entirely clear from this passage whether such a measure should then be regarded as: (a) having initially been selective, but then being justified; or (b) having never been selective in the first place. The Commission's comments in the 1998 Notice (cited in section §9.03[A]) in our view suggest the latter interpretation.[16] If this is indeed the correct reading of the Commission's position, we would agree with this approach: we consider that issue of the justification is an integral part of the determination of selectivity.

[E] Material Selectivity

Material selectivity refers to differentiation between undertakings on other grounds than business location or sector of activity. The 1998 Notice includes two examples of situations in which tax measures could be materially selective. The first is the case of public undertakings. The Commissions observes that:

> In several Member States, different tax rules apply depending on the status of the undertakings. Some public undertakings, for example, are exempt from local taxes or from company taxes. Such rules, which accord preferential treatment to undertakings having the legal status of public undertaking and carrying out an economic activity, may constitute State aid within the meaning of Article [107] of the Treaty.[17]

In the case of public undertakings, material selectivity is established along the dividing line of the legal status of the undertakings involved. The second example is less concrete, and in fact appears to cover both material *and* sectoral selectivity:

> Some tax benefits are on occasion restricted to certain types of undertaking, to some of their functions (intra-group services, intermediation or coordination) or to the production of certain goods. In so far as they favour certain undertakings or the production of certain goods, they may constitute State aid (...).[18]

The 2004 Report provides various examples of measures which were considered to be materially selective by the Commissions. These are outlined below:

- Rules laying down thresholds relating to turnovers.[19]
- Rules related to establishment in a specific number of countries.[20]
- Measures reserved for certain types of intra-group transactions.[21]
- The requirement to establish a company in order to benefit from an advantage linked to the performance of intra-group business (i.e., tax

16. By contrast, the 2004 Report seems to put forward the first approach when it includes the "justification of the measure by the nature of the tax system" as a separate criterion for assessing a measure alongside the question of whether a "selective advantage exists" (Commission Report 2004, para. 7).
17. Commission Notice 1998, para. 19.
18. Commission Notice 1998, para. 20.
19. Commission Report 2004, para. 27.
20. Commission Report 2004, para. 27.
21. Commission Report 2004, para. 28.

concessions only granted in the case of a "captive" insurance company; the Commission regarded this as selective because it required a certain economic strength).[22]
- Rules applicable only to companies incorporated *after* a certain date.[23]
- Measures applying only to multinational or large companies.[24]

Apart from the Commission's general comments on selectivity, the guidance specifically on *material* selectivity consists almost entirely of examples which need to be applied by analogy. The casuistic nature of the guidance on material selectivity as included in the 1998 Notice is not optimal, because it can be hard to transpose to a situation not specifically mentioned. This is unfortunate because it reduces the legal certainty both of the recipients of (potential) aid measures, and of the Member States, and for this reason we submit that a more abstract approach is called for. We will discuss our solution to this problem in section §9.06.

[F] The Principle of Proportionality

When considering whether a deviating measure can be justified by the nature or general scheme of the system, the proportionality of the deviation is relevant. This follows clearly from the ECJ's judgment in the case of Paint Graphos (joined cases C-78/80 to 80/80) (emphasis added):

> In any event, in order for tax exemptions such as those at issue in the main proceedings to be justified by the nature or general scheme of the tax system of the Member State concerned, it is *also necessary to ensure that those exemptions are consistent with the principle of proportionality and do not go beyond what is necessary*, in that the *legitimate objective* being pursued could not be attained by less far-reaching measures.[25]

The proportionality test in Paint Graphos shows more than a passing resemblance to the Rule of Reason test used in the context of the fundamental freedoms, and in our view there can be little doubt that the same approach should be taken in the context of State aid. When considering whether a prima facie restriction can be justified, the ECJ classically asks whether it is suitable, necessary and proportionate for attaining its legitimate objectives. Although the wording of the *Paint Graphos* judgment does not expressly include the question of "suitability" we hold the view that this requirement is logically included in the requirements that the measure be proportionate. After all, a measure which is entirely unsuitable for fulfilling its objectives cannot be considered to have met the proportionality requirement at all.

22. Commission Report 2004, para. 28.
23. Commission Report 2004, para. 29.
24. Commission Report 2004, Box 5.
25. Joined cases ECJ, *Paint Graphos*, Cases No. C-78/08 and C-80/08 not yet reported in ECR para. 75.

§9.05 RELATIONSHIP BETWEEN STATE AID AND THE FUNDAMENTAL FREEDOMS

[A] Is Every Discriminatory Tax Measure Also State Aid?

As selectivity means discriminatory treatment, the question could come up whether a measure which discriminates between undertakings could at the same time be regarded as State aid and a restriction on the fundamental freedoms. This question has been answered in the affirmative by the ECJ in the Sardinia case (C-169/08).[26] Does this mean that any discriminatory taxation of non-resident undertakings compared to resident undertakings should be regarded both State aid and a prohibited restriction on free movement?

[B] The *Iannelli & Volpi* Case

In light of the *Iannelli & Volpi* case (74/76),[27] we believe that the answer to this question raised above should be negative. This case shows that aid as such is outside the scope of application of the fundamental freedoms. In Iannelli & Volpi an Italian national challenged the legality of an Italian import levy on the basis of EU law. The ECJ held that it was in this case possible for the litigant to challenge the Italian rule, as the EU ban on import restrictions has direct effect and creates individual rights. The ECJ further stated that the prohibition on import restrictions does not include obstacles to free trade regulated in other parts of the Treaty, noting that the legal consequences of the infringement of other rules varies and that this implies that the respective fields should also be distinguished. To quote the ECJ (emphasis added):

> Since the legal consequences of the application or of a possible infringement of these various provisions [which had been invoked by the litigant—FE/AFG] have to be determined having regard to their particular purpose in the context of all the objectives of the treaty, they may be of a different kind and this implies that their respective fields of application must be distinguished, *except in those cases which may fall simultaneously within the field of application of two or more provisions of Community law.*[28]

According to the ECJ:

> (...) the fact that a system of aids provided by the State or by means of State resources may, simply because it benefits certain national undertakings (..), hinder (...) [intra-EU trade and investment], is not in itself sufficient to put an aid as such on the same footing as a [restriction on the fundamental freedoms].[29]

What Ianelli & Volpi shows is that where a measure could prima facie fall under more than one Treaty provision and where the legal consequences of these provisions differ,

26. ECJ, *Sardinia*, Case No. C-169/08 [2009] ECR I-10821.
27. ECJ, *Ianelli & Volpi*, Case No. 74/76 [1977] ECR I-00557.
28. ECJ, *Ianelli & Volpi*, Case No. 74/76 [1977] ECR I-00557 para. 9.
29. *Ibid.*, para. 10.

the qualification of the measure at hand will need to be established. In the example of a tax measure which discriminates against cross-border situation, we therefore need to ascertain whether the measure leads to a discriminatory treatment of non-residents (which could be within scope of the fundamental freedoms) or a granting of aid to resident (which could be within scope of State aid rules).

[C] Distinguishing Aid from Breaches of the Fundamental Freedoms

How, then, should we determine whether discriminatory taxation of non-resident undertakings compared to resident undertakings constitutes State aid?

The answer lies in the concept of an "advantage". As discussed in section §9.03, the existence of an "advantage" in the context of direct taxation essentially depends on whether the measure at hand leads to a reduction of the tax charge "normally" due. We submit that the inclusion of this requirement in Article 107(1) TFEU provides a mechanism for assessing whether a discriminatory tax measure constitutes State aid or not.

[1] Under- and Overinclusivity of the Measure

In this regard it is helpful to make a distinction between measures which are underinclusive, and measures which are overinclusive.

A measure is underinclusive if, assessed in light of the objective of the measure, taxpayers who should logically be within scope of the rules are not so. A simple example of this would be an environmental tax aimed at the reduction of CO2. In light of the objective pursued, it would be logical to subject *all* producers of CO2 to this tax; this group can be regarded as the legitimate subjects of the measure at hand. If certain producers are exempt from the tax, this would indicate that the measure is underinclusive. The reverse situation is also possible. This would be the case where the CO2 tax is also imposed on certain CO2 non-producers. In the light of the objective of the measure, these persons ought not to have been subject to this form of taxation, and so the measure should be regarded as overinclusive in relation to these persons.

In the event of an advantageous tax measures, the legitimate subject of a measure with is underinclusive cannot be regarded has having benefitted from State aid, notwithstanding the fact that there are also some taxpayers who are in an objectively comparable situation and have not enjoyed the benefit. For example, a Member State introduces a special tax deduction for R&D expenses. The objective of this measure is the general promotion of all R&D activities. However, this deduction is not available to non-resident tax payers who are carrying on R&D activities. In light of the objective of the measure, the normal tax treatment is for taxpayers engaged in R&D activities to receive the deduction and so the recipients of the deduction cannot be regarded as having enjoyed an advantage is the sense of Article 107(1) TFEU. The measure is underinclusive vis-à-vis the non-resident taxpayers, who—under certain circumstances—may be able to argue that they have suffered an infringement of their rights under the fundamental freedoms.[30]

Another way of looking at this, is to say that in the case of an underinclusive rule, enjoyment of the benefit is the norm and the withholding of that benefit from certain taxpayers the exception. The conclusion thus become that this rule has not granted any aid, but that it has discriminated against the non-recipients. In the case of an overinclusive advantageous tax measure, can be regarded as conferring a benefit upon the recipient taxpayers, which they ought not normally have received in view of the logic of the system. The receiving of the benefit must be regarded as the exception to the system, and it can therefore be concluded that this measure has resulted in an advantage for certain taxpayers.

This brings us to the conclusion that more favorable taxation of resident undertakings compared to non-resident undertakings constitutes aid *only* if the measure reduces the tax which, in the light of the objectives pursued by the tax system, should also have been imposed on resident undertakings. Notwithstanding the *Sardinia* judgment, it is therefore not the case that every discriminatory tax measure is *per se* also State aid.

§9.06 TOWARD AN ASSESSMENT FRAMEWORK FOR DIRECT TAX MEASURES

Article 107(1) TFEU contains four criteria which must be met in order for a measure to be State aid within the meaning of Article 107(1) TFEU. For obvious reasons, these criteria are frequently presented as a "check list" for establishing State aid (see section §9.02). This check list is not altogether helpful for assessing direct tax measures, as two out of the four criteria tend to be problematic in their application. This holds true for the requirement of material selectivity, and—perhaps to a lesser extent—for the question whether a measure confers an advantage. At the same time, it should be recognized that the requirement of the use of State resources and the distortion of competition can, in a direct tax context, generally be assumed to have been satisfied.

How then should it be established whether a direct tax measure constitutes aid within the meaning of the State aid rules?

By way of an answer to this question we have developed a theoretical assessment framework which takes into account the abovementioned considerations. This framework consists of a series of questions which we imagine would be applied in cases where there is a suspicion that a direct tax measure has lead to the provision on aid.

In order for a measure to constitute State aid, the first and fourth question needs to be answered affirmatively, and either the second or the third questions negatively. Although the order in which the questions are answered is not decisive, the most logical way of applying the framework is to start at the top and work downwards.

We include a number of comments on the framework below.

30. See for an example of this: ECJ, *Commission v. Austria*, Case No. C-10/10 not yet reported in ECR.

[A] Theoretical Assessment Framework

(1) Does the measure in question result in different treatment of certain taxpayers compared to others?
(2) Is the different treatment justified by a legitimate objective?
(3) Is the measure suitable to achieve the objective pursued and does it not go beyond what is necessary (principle of proportionality)?
(4) Does the measure result in a reduction or exemption of tax that should have been charged in the light of the objective pursued?

[B] Comments

- The first question is of a factual nature, and seeks to establish whether there is cause to apply the framework. In order for there to be State aid, an affirmative answer is needed. A negative answer to this question would mean that the measure in question would be generally applicable to all taxpayers and therefore not give rise to any differences of treatment between taxpayers. Under these circumstances the measure should be regarded as a general part of the tax system under consideration and therefore outside the scope of Article 107(1) TFEU. Lastly, when answering the first question, the issue of objective comparability between the taxpayers is irrelevant.
- The second question considers whether the differential treatment can be justified by a legitimate objective pursued by the measure at hand. If this is the case, no State aid would be involved. This means that the second question needs to be answered negatively for there to be State aid. The only objective which is *not* compatible with the State aid rules, is the provision of unlawful or illegal State aid. If the differentiation *cannot* be justified by the objective of the measure, this means that a distinction has been made between cases which—seen from the perspective of the objective of the measure—*ought* to have been treated in the same manner. In this way, the second question incorporates the comparability test (see section §9.03[B]).
- The third question pertains to the principle of proportionality, and seeks to ascertain whether the measure at hand is suitable and proportionate to the aim pursued. If the answer is no, there would be State aid. The inclusion of a proportionality test can be regarded as a logical component of the selectivity test. We find support for this position in the ECJ's *Paint Graphos* judgment (see section §9.03[F]).
- The fourth question establishes whether the measures gives rise to an exemption from the normal tax burden. This question is included to establish whether the measure at hand (just) gives rise to a discriminatory treatment, or whether State aid may be involved. If the answer is affirmative, the measure can fall within the purview of the State aid rules. If the answer is however negative, the measure will constitute a discriminatory treatment of some taxpayers. This does not automatically mean that there exists a

breach of the fundamental freedoms; this point needs to be assessed separately (see section §9.04).

- The framework does not include questions on the use of State resources, because fiscal State aid by definition constitutes a loss of tax revenue and in this way a loss of State resources. For the same reason, the framework does not consider whether the measure (threatens to) distort competition or intra-EU trade. This is because this requirements can effectively be assumed to have been satisfied (see section §9.01).

CHAPTER 10

Case Studies of Tax Issues on Selectivity: Analysis of the Patent Box Scheme and the Reduced Taxation of Foreign-Source Interest Income

Claire Micheau and Gauthier Charles de la Brousse*

§10.01 INTRODUCTION

The application of State aid law to the area of taxation crosses boundaries between different legal fields at EU and national levels. In that respect, EU law has evolved subtle sets of rules to adapt the provisions of State aid as laid down in Article 107 TFEU to the characteristics of taxation.

The Treaty qualifies as State aid a measure "granted by a Member State or through State resources in any form whatsoever which distorts or threatens to distort competition by favouring certain undertakings or the production of certain goods"[1]. On the basis of this provision, it is common ground that there are four major criteria which should be fulfilled: the State-originated resource, the advantage, the selectivity and the distortion of competition and trade. In taxation, the Court's case-law and the Commission's decision making-practice have adapted these criteria to provide a relevant approach which takes into account the peculiarities of tax matters.

In that respect, the criterion of tax advantage is considered to be fulfilled where it "relieves [recipients] of charges that are normally borne from their budget"[2]. Regarding the element of State-originated resource, the Court and the Commission

* Any opinion expressed by the authors is personal and does not necessarily reflect the views of any institution.

1. Article 107 TFEU.
2. Commission Notice on the Application of the State Aid Rules to Measures relating to Direct Business Taxation, OJ C 384, Dec. 10, 1998, 9.

have evolved with such a broad interpretation that it includes directly and indirectly measures granted by the State. This involves not only tax measures introduced by governments and federal tax authorities, but also those designed by infra-State entities with taxation powers, funds under State control or public funds managed by private entities. With regard to the criteria of distortion of competition and affectation of trade between Member States, they are usually analyzed together since they are regarded by the Court as "inextricably linked"[3]. It is settled case-law that the recipient is deemed to be affected by the aid where the "State financial aid strengthens the position of an undertaking compared with other undertakings competing in intra-competition trade"[4].

The last criterion to qualify a tax measure as State aid is the selectivity one. According to the wording of Article 107 TFEU, one should establish as to whether the tax measure favors certain undertakings or the production of certain goods. This criterion is key in tax matters. It has given rise to elaborate jurisprudential rules, which can raise subtle issues. The objective of this paper is not to review the case-law in tax selectivity. This aspect of the debate has already been previously addressed in other contributions[5]. Rather, this chapter aims to deal with the notion of tax selectivity in a concrete context and to confront it with the practice. It is from this perspective that some cases will be addressed in the following. Special attention will be given to the review of two relevant theoretical cases: the tax reduction from profits generated by intangible assets and the reduced taxation for interest income from foreign sources.

§10.02 THE PATENT BOX

Analyzing the application of the State aid rules to tax measures promoting research, development and innovation emerges as an interesting exercise which is at the crossroads of different issues. In that regard, one could consider analyzing a tax scheme which aims to promote, *inter alia*, the exploitation of patents (so-called "Patent Box" scheme). To this end, this section will provide a short description of a tax regime and analyze it in the light of the State aid rules applicable to tax matters.

[A] Description of the Measure

One could consider a tax regime which aims at promoting research and development activities in undertakings in order to encourage technological and scientific development. For this purpose, such a tax regime would support the production of intangible assets.

3. ECJ, *Regione Friuli Venezia Giulia v. Commission of the European Communities*, Case No. T-288/97 [1999] ECR II-1871 para. 41 (emphasis added). See also Joined cases ECJ, *Alzetta and others v. Commission of the European Communities*, Cases No. T-298/97, T-312/97, T-313/97, T-315/97, T-600/97 to T-607/97, T-1/98, T-3/98 to T-6/98 and T-23/98 [2000] ECR II-2319 para. 81.
4. ECJ, *Philip Morris Holland BV v. Commission of the European Communities*, Case No. 730/79 [1980] ECR 2671 para. 11.
5. See in particular in Chapter 6 of the present book the contribution by H. Drabbe, *The Selectivity Test in Tax Measures*.

In this context, one could envisage examining a tax regime where a Member State introduces a 30% reduction on the revenue generated by certain intangible assets. The reduction of these intangible assets would result in reducing the tax base and therefore the tax burden that the recipients are liable to.

In order to fall within the scope of this tax regime, the qualified intangible assets should be patents, designs, models and plans. Other assets, such as trademarks, artistic, literacy and scientific work or software are not eligible for this tax relief.

This tax reduction applies to any undertaking which has generated the intangible assets. The rationale behind this tax measure is to promote undertakings involved in the research and development area, which have taken on the risks and benefits attributable to the intangible assets.

In addition, regarding to the undertakings which can benefit from the tax regime, the measure does not introduce any differentiation based on objective criteria, such as the sector involved, the regional area where these undertakings are established, the legal form or the size of the undertakings.

In view of the above, the question arises as to whether this tax measure can be regarded as being in compliance with article 107 TFEU. In other words, the issue is to determine whether this tax reduction for the exploitation of certain intangible assets can be termed State aid.

[B] Legal Analysis of the Measure

[1] Criteria for State Aid

In order to qualify as a State aid within the meaning of Article 107 TFEU, a measure should satisfy the criteria which have previously been mentioned. With regard to the particular *Patent Box* case at issue, it appears that the criteria of State-originated resources, tax advantage and distortion of competition and trade do not leave room for debate.

More precisely, concerning the element of State-originated resource, a loss of tax revenue is equivalent to consumption of State resources in the form of fiscal expenditure. By allowing undertakings to have a reduced tax base, the Member State foregoes revenue which constitutes State resource. Hence, the *Patent Box* regime involves a loss of State resources and it is therefore granted through State resources.

Regarding the condition of advantage, it is settled case-law that this encompasses not only positive benefits, but also interventions which, in various forms, mitigate the charges which are normally included in the budget of an undertaking[6]. Under the *Patent Box* scheme, the tax measure provides for a reduction on the revenue from certain intangible assets which have the effect of reducing the tax base of the

6. ECJ, *De Gezamenlijke Steenkolenmijnen in Limburg v. High Authority of the European Coal and Steel Community*, Case No. 30/59 [1961] ECR 1 para. 19; Commission Notice on the Application of the State Aid Rules to Measures relating to Direct Business Taxation, OJ C 384, Dec. 10, 1998, 9.

undertakings. Hence, since the recipients benefit from a reduction of their tax burden, the condition of advantage is established.

With respect to the conditions of effects on competition and trade, undertakings benefiting from the reduction on tax revenue from certain intangible assets are exposed to trade in the EU. Consequently, the *Patent Box* regime, which provides for a favorable treatment for these undertakings established in a Member State, necessarily affect trade and distorts or threatens to distort competition.

It follows from the foregoing that the three above-mentioned criteria are not problematic. In contrast, the analysis of selectivity in the present case raises subtle issues and therefore commands attention.

[2] General Measure Open to All Economic Operators?

The key issue is to assess as to whether the *Patent Box* scheme should be regarded as general or selective. In that respect, the Commission takes the view that "measures which are open to all economic agents operating within a Member State are in principle general measures"[7]. To be termed general, the measure "must be effectively open to all firms on an equal access basis, and they may not de facto be reduced"[8].

In the present case, one could consider that the measure applies to all undertakings, regardless of their sector or their size. Hence, any undertaking dealing with innovation activities is concerned by the measure. Since the measure does not seem to introduce differentiation between undertakings, it would therefore appear to be general.

In this regard, one can argue that the activities of research and development, which fall within the scope of the *Patent Box*, are carried out in all sectors. They should not be confined to the manufacturing sector. For instance, in the service sector, there is a substantive increase of research and development, in particular with regard to business models, e-banking and mobile banking. Business methods are even patentable in some Member States.

In addition, one should bear in mind that the *Patent Box* regime applies not only to patents, but also to design and model, plan, secret formula or process. This gives some force for considering the measure to be general.

However, different legal analysis could be carried out. In this regard, different opinions have been raised during the Conference which took place in Luxembourg on 17 and 18 November 2011 on "State Aid and Tax Law." The following developments are hypothetical assessments based on the opinions expressed during this conference.

7. Commission Notice on the Application of the State Aid Rules to Measures relating to Direct Business Taxation, OJ C 384, Dec. 10, 1998, 9.
8. *Ibid.*

[3] De Facto Selectivity

One could also conduct an analysis which would consider that the *Patent Box* is not open to economic operators. Since the objective of the measure is to promote scientific and technological development by exempting profits attributable to intangible assets, it appears that the measure favors undertakings in the research and development manufacturing sector. Such reasoning involves a de facto analysis. De facto selectivity encompasses measures which apply in principle to all undertakings, but are in practice only available to a limited number of undertakings. In other words, tax regimes, which are often framed in general terms, can be designed in such a way that only certain undertakings may benefit from them. To assess whether a tax measure is de facto selective, one should go beyond the general terms of the provisions. In the present case, one could take the view that the scheme favors de facto research and development in the manufacturing sector. Hence, the measure could be perceived as being selective since it de facto favors certain undertakings.

In support of this position, one can keep in mind that the measure applies only to the use or exploit of patent, design and model, plan, secret formula or process. It however does not apply to other intangible assets, such as trademarks, literary and artistic works.

[4] Objective of the Measure

Another analysis could also be carried out on the basis of the recent three-step approach introduced in the case-law. In this regard, the Court of Justice of the European Union and the Commission have developed an approach which may be subtle in practice. In substance, according to the Commission's Fiscal Notice, one should determine whether the measure confers an advantage in favor of certain undertakings, which would constitute an exception to the application of the tax system. The notion of selectivity is interpreted by the jurisprudence in such a way that the measure is selective if it is "intended partially to exempt those undertakings from the financial charges arising from the normal application of the general system of compulsory contributions imposed by law"[9]. Hence, the measure is selective if it constitutes a departure from the application of the general tax framework. For such an analysis, the Court has consistently held that one should assess whether a given measure favors certain undertakings in comparison with other undertakings which are in a legal and factual situation that is comparable in the light of the objective pursued by the scheme[10] or the tax system[11] in question.

9. ECJ, *Italian Republic v. Commission of the European Communities*, Case No. 173/73 [1974] ECR 709 para. 33.
10. ECJ, *Portuguese Republic v. Commission of the European Communities*, Case No. C-88/03 [2006] ECR I-7115 para. 54; ECJ, *Wolfgang Heiser v. Finanzamt Innsbruck*, Case No. C-172/03 [2005] ECR I-1627 para. 40; ECJ, *Presidente del Consiglio dei Ministri v. Regione Sardegna*, Case No. C-169/08 [2009] ECR I-10821 para. 61.
11. Joined cases ECJ, *Paint Graphos and others*, Cases No. C-78/08 to C-80/08 not yet reported in ECR para. 49.

In an additional step, one should define as to whether the selectivity of the measure can be justified by the logic of the tax system. As stated in the Commission's Fiscal Notice:

> the common system applicable should thus first be determined. It must then be examined whether the exception to the system or the differentiations within that system are justified "by the nature or general scheme of the tax system, that is to say, whether they derive directly from the basic or guiding principles of the tax system in the Member State concerned." If this is not the case, then State aid is involved[12].

In the present *Patent Box* case, a possible justification, which should be based on the objectives inherent in the tax system itself, does not seem to be established. No justification deriving directly from the basic or guiding principles of the tax system emerges. This aspect of the debate will therefore not be further discussed.

The key issue is actually to assess as to whether there would be a departure from this general tax system. In other words, one should determine whether the *Patent Box* scheme derogates from the general corporation tax system by introducing a reduction on the revenue from certain intangible assets. In this regard, the Court held that:

> the only question to be determined is whether, under a particular statutory scheme, a State measure is such as to favour "certain undertakings or the production of certain goods" within the meaning of Article 92(1) of the Treaty in comparison with other undertakings which are in a legal and factual situation that is comparable in the light of the objective pursued by *the measure in question*[13].

The *Patent Box* scheme pursues the objective of promoting innovation. Therefore, the reference framework, which can be defined in the light of the objective of promoting innovation, should be limited to the tax treatment of undertakings producing intangible assets and exploiting these assets.

According to this position, the comparison would be carried out between undertakings which are involved in producing intangible assets and those exploiting these assets. On this basis, it seems that there is a differential tax treatment between undertakings exploiting patent, design and model, plan, secret formula or process which are covered by the *Patent Box* scheme and undertakings exploiting other intangible assets, such as trademarks, literary and artistic works, which cannot benefit from the *Patent Box*.

It follows from this approach that the measure could be regarded as selective since it would confer a tax advantage to undertakings in comparison with other

12. Commission Notice on the Application of the State Aid Rules to Measures relating to Direct Business Taxation, OJ C 384, Dec. 10, 1998, 16.
13. ECJ, *Adria-Wien Pipeline and Wietersdorfer & Peggauer*, Case No. 143/99 [2001] ECR I-8365 para. 41. See also the *NOX* case, where the Court stated as follows:
in order to prove that the measure in question applies selectively to certain undertakings or to the production of certain goods, it is for the Commission to prove that it creates differences between undertakings which, with regard to the objective of *the measure in question*, are in a comparable factual and legal situation (ECJ, *European Commission v. Kingdom of the Netherlands (NOX)*, Case No. C-279/08 P not yet reported in ECR para. 62).

undertakings which are in a legal and factual situation that is comparable in the light of the objective pursued by the *Patent Box* scheme.

[5] Objective of the System

Another analysis mentioned during the conference would consist in focusing on the objective of *the tax system*. In the second step of the three-stage approach, one should assess as to whether the tax regime departs from the general tax system inasmuch as it differentiates between economic operators. In that regard, the Court of Justice held that "in order to determine whether the measure at issue is selective it is appropriate to examine whether, within the context of a *particular legal system*, that measure constitutes an advantage for certain undertakings in comparison with others which are in a comparable legal and factual situation"[14].

In the same line, in the *Italian Cooperative* case, the Court stated that:

> it is in relation to this common or "normal' tax regime that it is necessary, secondly, to assess and determine whether any advantage granted by the tax measure at issue may be selective by demonstrating that the measure derogates from that common regime inasmuch as it differentiates between economic operators who, in light of the objective assigned to *the tax system of the Member State concerned*, are in a comparable factual and legal situation[15].

In light with this case-law which differs from the aforementioned one based on the objective of the measure, one could take into consideration the objective of the tax system for assessing the selectivity of the *Patent Box* scheme. More precisely, within a reference framework defined in the light of its general objective, a comparison could be drawn between (i) undertakings which have invested in the creation of patents and are exploiting these patents (ii) and any other undertakings.

The objective of the general system of taxation is to raise tax revenues. In that regard, the Court endorsed the view in the *Italian Cooperative* case that the objective pursued by the corporation tax regime is the taxation of company profits[16]. It is

14. ECJ, *Portuguese Republic v. Commission of the European Communities*, Case No. C-88/03 [2006] ECR I-7115 para. 56 (emphasis added).
15. Joined cases ECJ, *Paint Graphos and others*, Cases No. C-78/08 to C-80/08 not yet reported in ECR para. 49 (emphasis added). See also the *British Aggregates* case:
in order to determine whether a measure is selective, it is appropriate to examine whether, *within the context of a particular legal system*, that measure constitutes an advantage for certain undertakings in comparison with others which are in a comparable legal and factual situation. (ECJ, *British Aggregates Association v. Commission of the European Communities*, Case No. C-487/06 P [2008] ECR I-10515 para. 82, emphasis added).
In the same vein, see the *Gibraltar* case:
it is clear from settled case-law that Article 87(1) EC requires assessment of whether, under a particular legal regime, a national measure is such as to favour "certain undertakings or the production of certain goods" in comparison with others which, in the light of the objective pursued by that *regime*, are in a comparable factual and legal situation (Joined cases ECJ, *European Commission and Kingdom of Spain v. Government of Gibraltar and United Kingdom of Great Britain and Northern*, Cases No. C-106/09 P and C-107/09 P not yet reported in ECR para. 75, emphasis added).
16. Joined cases ECJ, *Paint Graphos and others*, Cases No. C-78/08 to C-80/08 not yet reported in ECR para. 54.

therefore in the light of this objective that one should draw a comparison between undertakings invested in the creation of certain intangible patents and other undertakings. There is a differential tax treatment between these two groups of undertakings, which are in a comparable legal and factual situation in the light of the objective of the system (i.e., of raising tax revenues). Hence, the measure should be deemed selective.

Although there is some force in the different hypothetical assessments which have been raised during the conference and which are briefly mentioned in the above, it seems that the first approach based on the generality of the measure open to all economic operators prevails. Before reviewing this Commission's decision on this case, one should however mention other elements which can be relevant to the assessment of the *Patent Box* scheme.

[6] Discretional Powers

The assessment of the *Patent Box* scheme could however differ substantially if it involves administrative discretion by the tax authorities. In that regard, one should bear in mind that discretionary practices can play a key role in the assessment of tax selectivity. If a national administration enjoys room for discretion to grant a favorable tax measure, the measure can be regarded as selective[17]. For instance, the Court found that the treatment where an authority which enjoys a certain degree of latitude in adjusting "its financial assistance having regard to a number of considerations such as, in particular, the choice of beneficiaries, the amount of the financial assistance and the conditions under which it is provided"[18] should be regarded as State aid. In essence, where the treatment of undertakings is based on a discretionary basis which goes beyond the implementation and the management of the tax scheme, the measure can be selective[19]. The Commission's practice refers to a *presumption* of selectivity[20] which depends on the room for maneuver enjoyed by the tax authorities.

In light with foregoing, the analysis of the *Patent Box* scheme would be different if the tax administration enjoys administrative discretion in the application of the measure to the undertakings. For instance, if the regime is subject to a prior authorization of the administration, the selectivity of the measure can be challenged. The scheme is most likely deemed selective if the authorization is given on subjective criteria. The outcome would be the same if the decision to grant the tax reduction from certain intangible assets were adopted by the administration in an opaque and non-transparent way.

17. In that respect, see Commission Notice on the Application of the State Aid Rules to Measures relating to Direct Business Taxation, OJ C 384, Dec. 10, 1998, 21.
18. ECJ, *French Republic v. Commission of the European Communities*, Case No. C-241/94 [1996] ECR I-4551 para. 23.
19. Commission Notice on the Application of the State Aid Rules to Measures relating to Direct Business Taxation, OJ C 384, Dec. 10, 1998, 21.
20. "Every decision of the administration that departs from the general tax rules to the benefit of individual undertakings in principle leads to *a presumption* of State aid and must be analysed in detail" (Commission Notice on the Application of the State Aid Rules to Measures relating to Direct Business Taxation, OJ C 384, Dec. 10, 1998, 22, emphasis added).

In contrast, if the application of this scheme is not subject to a discretionary administrative practice, the scheme can be found to be in line with State aid disciplines.

[7] Compatibility

Article 107 (1) TFEU is governed by the principle of State aid prohibition. In other words, any measure which falls within the scope of the conditions enshrined in this provision should be regarded as incompatible with the internal market.

This prohibition is however tempered by Article 107 (2) and (3) TFEU. While Article 107 (2) TFEU provides for aids which are de jure compatible with the internal market, Article 107 (3) TFEU lists aids which may be compatible depending on the assessment of the Commission. In this category of aid, aid for Research & Development & Innovation can be justified on the basis of Article 107(3)(b) and 107(3)(c). In this regard, the Commission has laid down rules (the "R&D&I Guidelines")[21] in order to exercise its discretion by ensuring legal certainty and transparency in its decision-making process.

In the present case, the question could arise as to whether the *Patent Box* could be regarded as compatible with the internal market according to the R&D&I Guidelines. In this regard, the Guidelines state as follows: "on the basis of evaluation studies provided by Member States in the notification, the Commission will consider that R&D&I fiscal aid schemes have an incentive effect by stimulating higher R&D&I spending by undertakings"[22].

One should however note that the requirements provided by the R&D&I Guidelines are strict and limitative. Paragraph 5.1.6. provides for a calculation based on the aid intensity of an R&D&I fiscal State aid measure with regard to the individual projects being at stake or the undertakings concerned[23]. With regard to the *Patent Box* case, it may be difficult to the Member State to define precisely whether the research project would fall within a research category provided for by the R&D&I Guidelines, including projects on fundamental research, industrial research or experimental experience. In addition, providing in advance an estimate number of beneficiaries may be complex in practice. Moreover, ensuring that the aid intensity does not exceed 25 % pursuant to the R&D&I Guidelines may be fraught with difficulties given the importance of the tax scheme. In addition, the eligible costs as provided for by the *Patent Box* scheme do not systematically fall within the scope of the R&D&I Guidelines[24]. Furthermore, the

21. European Commission, Community framework for state aid for research and development and innovation, OJ C 323, Dec. 30, 2006, 1–26.
22. *Ibid.*, para. 5.1.6.
23. "The aid intensity of an R&D&I fiscal State aid measure can be calculated either on the basis of individual R&D&I projects or, at the level of an undertaking, as the ratio between the overall tax relief and the sum of all eligible R&D&I costs incurred in a period not exceeding three consecutive fiscal years. In the latter case, the R&D&I fiscal State aid measure may apply without distinction to all eligible R&D&I activities; the applicable aid intensity for experimental development must then not be exceeded" (*ibid.*).
24. *Ibid.*, para. 5.1.4.

application of the R&D&I Guidelines would require the specific exclusion of undertakings in difficulty from the scope of the *Patent Box* scheme.

In view of the above, one can draw the conclusion that the application of the R&D&I Guidelines to the *Patent Box* scheme may be ruled out. It follows therefore that the *Patent Box* scheme would not be regarded as compatible with the internal market on the basis of Article 107(3)(b) and 107(3)(c) TFEU.

[8] The Commission Decision N 480/2007

A similar case to the *Patent Box* scheme has been referred to the Commission in 2007. This case dealt with the reduction of tax from intangible assets as introduced by a new Spanish law. This new tax regime was notified by the Spanish authorities on August 2007 and gave rise to a decision adopted in February 2008[25].

The Spanish regime provided for a 50% reduction on the revenue from certain intangible assets, which encompassed the use and exploit of patent, design and model, plan, secret formula and processes. This list was exclusive and it did not include other revenues, such as those generated by trademarks, literary, artistic or scientific works (e.g., cinematograph films, image rights, software, industrial, commercial or scientific equipment).

The 50% reduction on the revenue of the eligible intangible assets led to reduce the tax base and therefore the tax burden that undertakings were liable to. The question arises as to whether this tax scheme was regarded as State aid within the meaning of Article 107 TFEU. The scrutiny of the selectivity criteria was key in the assessment of the tax scheme.

The Commission found that the application of the tax scheme to undertakings did not entail any administrative discretion. In support of this position, the Commission noted that the application of this scheme was not subject to any prior authorization by the tax authorities. As a matter of fact, the control exercised by the tax administration was only *a posteriori*, once the taxable undertakings had already applied the reduction. Based on this absence of administrative practices, the Commission ruled out a possible presumption of selectivity.

With regard to the approach adopted for assessing the selectivity of the tax scheme, the Commission did not draw a comparison between undertakings in the light of the objective of the system or the measure. Rather, it proposed an analysis which stayed at the preliminary stage of the selectivity review.

The Commission took the view that the measure applied to all undertakings in Spain, notwithstanding of their activity, sector, geographical area, size, legal form or turnover. The Commission carried out a de facto analysis and noted that some undertakings dealing with research and development activities may benefit more from the tax scheme, since the objective of the scheme was actually to strengthen scientific and technological development in the business sector.

25. Commission Decision, Spain—The reduction of tax from intangible assets [2008] State aid N 480/20007, OJ C 80, Apr. 1, 2008, 3.

The Commission however also observed that the measure applied to all economic persons, without any distinction. In that respect, one should keep in mind that the Court[26] and the Commission[27] have consistently maintained that the mere fact that some undertakings or productions of goods would benefit more than others from a tax measure under consideration does not necessarily mean that such measure is selective. In the same vein, the Commission held with regard to the use of tax incentives in favor of Research & Development that "the majority of existing tax incentives aimed at increasing R&D activities *are general in nature* and, therefore, do not focus on specific types of firms, sectors or technologies"[28].

In support of this position, the Commission noted that an indefinite number of sectors can be potentially interested in developing and exploiting patentable inventions, designs, models, plans, secret formulas and processes. In addition, the Commission established that the Spanish preparatory legislative reports on the introduction of the tax regime did not suggest at any case that the scheme would pursue the underlying objective of favoring in practice a specific group of undertakings. Hence, the Commission came to the conclusion that the measure was not selective since it was available to all undertakings.

In essence, the position adopted in this case is relevant since the Commission found that the measure was not selective at a very early stage of its analysis: the measure was general because it applied to all economic operators. Therefore, there was no necessity of assessing as to whether there would be a departure from the general corporation tax system by carrying out a comparison between undertakings in legal and factual comparable situations in the light of the objective of the regime.

The review of the test of selectivity applied to tax matters should however not be confined to the analysis of the selectivity test with regard to the de facto selectivity and the comparability test based on the objectives of the system. The assessment of the selectivity raises other complex issues, such as the application of the justification by the system, which will now be examined in the light of another hypothetical case.

§10.03 FOREIGN-SOURCED INTEREST INCOME

The analysis of the case of reduced taxation for interest income from foreign source is of particular interest with regard to State aid rules. Such a case does not only involve issues raised by the analysis of the criterion of tax advantage, but it also entails subtle questions regarding the selectivity criterion and its justification by the logic of the tax system. In that regard, after presenting the main general rules governing the taxation of cross-border interest income in the EU, this section will examine such a tax regime in the light of State aid rules.

26. ECJ, *Stadtwerke Schwäbisch Hall GmbH*, Case No. T-92/02 [2006] ECR II-11 para. 109.
27. Commission Notice on the Application of the State Aid Rules to Measures relating to Direct Business Taxation, OJ C 384, Dec. 10, 1998, 14.
28. Commission Staff Working Document, SEC(2006) 1515 final, Towards a more effective use of tax incentives in favor of R&D, Point 3.1.2 (emphasis added).

[A] Background: Taxation of Cross-Border Interest Income in the EU

As a preliminary comment, one should bear in mind the general principle governing foreign-source interest income, according to which interest incomes deriving directly[29] from foreign sources are deductible in the source country and taxable for their net amount, i.e., after deduction of expenses, in the recipient country. Such interest may however be subject to a withholding tax in the source country. In the absence of tax relief in the destination country, this would lead to double taxation.

Against this background, Member States have designed a set of rules which allows double taxation of foreign-sourced interest to be usually prevented by the following means:

(i) Unilateral relief

Member States may provide a double taxation relief on a unilateral basis. Such reliefs apply in the absence of binding international agreements or they complement such agreements by providing higher relief.

(ii) Double Taxation Treaties

Double taxation treaties usually reduce or waive withholding taxes on cross-border interest payments[30]. They also provide a relief from double taxation in the recipient country, in the form of a tax credit[31] (credit method)[32]. The imputable tax credit is calculated on the basis of the withholding tax paid in the source country. It is usually accompanied with a limitation of the tax credit up to a maximum amount. This limitation can for instance be based on the corporation tax liable in the recipient country on the interest gross amount[33].

(iii) Interest and Royalty Directive[34]

National tax provisions, even if there are coupled with bilateral or multilateral agreements, cannot systematically ensure prevention of double taxation. To face this issue, the Interest and Royalty Directive[35] was introduced in 2003 with the aim of preventing interest payments between associated companies of different Member States to be subject to less favorable tax conditions than those applicable to the same transactions carried out by companies established in the same Member States.

In substance, the Directive provides that interest payments arising in a Member State are exempt from tax in that State, provided that the beneficial owner of the interest is a company (or permanent establishment) of another

---

29. This principle applies only to direct income, notwithstanding income of a permanent establishment abroad.
30. See Art. 11 of the OECD model convention on income and capital.
31. See Art. 23A(2) of the OECD model convention.
32. By contrast, the "exemption" method provides for the (partial or full) exemption of foreign-sourced income from the taxable basis.
33. This includes the net interest amount and the withholding tax paid in the source country.
34. Council Directive 2003/49/EC of June 3, 2003 on a common system of taxation applicable to interest and royalty payments made between associated companies of different Member States, OJ L 157, Jun. 26, 2003.
35. This Directive applies to all Member States since Jul. 1, 2005.

Member State. The paying company must be considered as an "associated company"[36] of the company which is the beneficial owner[37].

Member States are nonetheless allowed under the Interest and Royalty Directive to adopt measures to counter fraud and abuse, or to disallow the benefits of the Directive where for instance the interest payment would be treated in the source country as a distribution of profits. As a result, situations of double taxation of cross-border interest can still arise. This is for instance the case where the interest originates from a third country with whom the recipient Member State has no double taxation treaty, or where the source country requalifies the interest paid into dividends or it applies thin capitalization rules while no relief is granted in the recipient country.

[B] Description of the Measure

In view of the above, it is interesting to examine a hypothetical case which involves State aid issues in the context of the taxation of cross-border interest income in the EU. In that regard, one could consider a tax scheme where a Member State provides for a corporation tax exemption of 80% of the interest income derived from foreign sources. This measure would therefore be based on the aforementioned "exemption" method. Under the applicable tax system, foreign income other than interest remains subject to the credit method.

By contrast, interest income from a domestic source is subject to full corporate taxation, without any possibility of partial exemption.

The 80% tax exemption applies regardless of the fiscal treatment of interest income in the source country. This involves that it applies in the following situations: (i) where the interest income is received from a foreign affiliated company qualifying for the application of the Interest and Royalty Directive (0% withholding tax in the source country); and (ii) where the applicable double taxation treaty provides for a 0% withholding tax in the source State.

In other words, by contrast with a tax credit system, the application of the tax exemption is not related to the existence of an effective taxation in the source country.

Under this hypothetical case, one should assume that the statutory corporation tax rate in the given Member State is 20%.

Finally, it is worth mentioning that most double taxation treaties concluded by the Member State concerned provide for a 0% withholding tax in the source countries.

36. See the definition of associated company in Art. 3(b) of Directive 2003/49/EC.
37. For this purpose, the beneficial owner should hold a minimum capital holding of 25%.

[C] Objective of the Measure

The rationale for introducing this tax scheme lies in the prevention of double taxation of cross-border interest. More precisely, in the Member State concerned, the traditional credit method where tax credits are granted to compensate foreign withholding tax would have failed to prevent double taxation of cross-border interest in the following situations:

(i) where the interest income is treated differently in the source and destination countries, e.g., where the source State does not allow the deduction of the interest which is taxed as dividends ("requalification" of interest in dividend). In that event, the taxation of the interest income in the recipient country would lead to an economic double taxation of the same interest[38];

(ii) where the avoidance of double taxation would be problematic under the credit method. For example, if a company has generated losses, it would be unable to set off the foreign tax or even to postpone the setting off of such amount. Under such circumstances, the application of the exemption method would be more efficient[39];

(iii) other administrative practices in the source countries, e.g., where the source country administration requires for the application of the withholding tax exemption a certificate declaring that the recipient is the effective beneficiary. Such a requirement may be problematic where the tax administration of the recipient company does not deliver such certificate.

In this context, the new tax provision would aim at ensuring the prevention of double taxation by *systematically* granting a tax exemption for cross-border interest income.

In this regard, some could argue that the State which introduces this tax scheme would pursue the hidden objective of attracting or maintaining financial centers of multinational companies in its territory by granting them tax exemption on a large part of their profits. Such a position might affect the assessment of State aid with regard to the de facto selectivity. It however does not seem to be relevant for the three-steps approach applied to the selectivity assessment, which will be addressed in detail in the following.

State aid issues raise by this case may be all the more relevant since the 80% tax exemption would also apply in situations where the applicable double taxation treaty provides for the imputation of the withholding taxes paid abroad.

38. Double taxation treaties do not prevent the double taxation in situations where the source State is typically allowed to treat such types of interest as dividend. The Treaty however does not oblige the recipient State to apply the exemption on the interest treated as dividend in the source State.

39. In such a loss-making situation, the loss of the recipient company would be further increased by the exempted income, which it can carry over to a subsequent fiscal year.

[D] State Aid Assessment

In light with foregoing, the question arises as to whether the tax scheme on taxation of cross-border interest income could be regarded as State aid within the meaning of Article 107 TFEU.

As already mentioned, in order to be qualified as State aid, the following cumulative conditions have to be met: (i) the measure has to be granted by State resources; (ii) it has to confer an advantage to undertakings; (iii) the advantage has to be selective; and (iv) the measure has to affect trade between Member States and to distort or threaten to distort competition. Since the conditions of State-originated resources and affectation of trade and competition do not raise problematic issues, this contribution will focus hereunder on the assessment of the notions of advantage and selectivity.

[1] Advantage

The new scheme appears to provide an advantage for the undertakings receiving foreign interest income compared with undertakings receiving domestic interest income. While the first benefit from an 80 % exemption, the latter are subject to full taxation without any possible exemption.

In this context, in order to assess the advantage, one should draw a comparison between undertakings receiving foreign-sourced interest and those receiving domestic interest. It emerges from this comparison that the measure favors undertakings receiving foreign-sourced interest to the detriment of undertakings receiving domestic interest.

In that respect, one could also consider the hypothesis where the corporation tax rate in the Member State (which is the recipient State applying the measure) would be reduced to a lower level, such as a rate of 10%. If so, the application of the measure might, in a limited number of situations, increase the taxpayer's taxable basis and therefore its tax burden in comparison with the tax treatment of the former tax regime (tax credit). This comparison is however not relevant for the purpose of the assessment of the advantage criterion[40]. In any case, one should keep in mind that although the measure may in exceptional cases lead to a higher taxation, this would not be sufficient to exclude the existence of an advantage[41].

40. The relevant test does not lie in the comparison of a new measure with the former one, but in the comparison of undertakings subject to different tax treatments.
41. In its assessment of the tax regime for the coordination centers established in Belgium, the Court of Justice considered that the flat-rate assessment of income under the cost-plus method constitutes an economic advantage for the purposes of Article 107 TFEU and that:
"*that analysis cannot be called into question either by the fact that the inclusion of the financial charges could, in some cases, lead to a tax base that was unduly high or by the scale of the tax burden that might be imposed on the group, nor can it be called into question by the fact that a centre may be taxed when it has not made any profits.*"
The Court further considered that the exemption from property tax in favor of coordination centers conferred an economic advantage on them and that:

[2] *Selectivity*

As already mentioned, in order to determine whether a measure is selective, the Court's case-law assesses as to whether, within the context of a particular legal system, the measure constitutes an advantage for certain undertakings in comparison with others in a comparable legal and factual situation[42]. For that purpose, the following three-step approach applies: (i) identification of the reference legal system; (ii) assessment as to whether the measure derogates from that common regime inasmuch as it differentiates between economic operators who, in the light of the objective assigned to the tax system, are in a comparable factual and legal situation (so-called "comparability test"); and (iii) justification by the logic of the tax system (justification test). It is these three steps which will be examined in the following.

[a] *Reference System*

The measure in question is part of the overall corporation tax system in the Member State concerned and it cannot be dissociated from it. It is therefore the corporation tax system that should be regarded as the reference tax system for the assessment of the measure.

[b] *Comparability Test*

Under the second step, one should analyze whether undertakings receiving interest income from a domestic source are in a comparable legal and factual situation with undertakings receiving interest income from foreign sources, in the light of the objective of the corporation tax system, i.e., taxing profits.

Interest income deriving from a domestic source is subject to the following tax rules in the given tax system:

- There is no withholding tax on interest paid to resident companies.
- At the level of the receiving company, the interest income is taxable at the normal corporation tax rate.

---

the fact that only 5% of the coordination centres benefit from it in practice, as all the others hold their buildings under lease, does not affect that assessment, since the choice between owning a building and leasing it is a matter entirely at the discretion of the centres (ECJ, *Kingdom of Belgium and Forum 187 ASBL*, Case No. C-217/03 [2006] ECR I-5479 paras. 86–118).

42. See, *inter alia*, ECJ, *British Aggregates v. Commission of the European Communities*, Case No. C-487/06 P [2008] ECR I-10515 para. 82; ECJ, *Kingdom of Spain v. Commission of the European Communities*, Case No. C-409/00 [2003] ECR I-1487 para. 47; ECJ, *Portuguese Republic v. Commission of the European Communities*, Case No. C-88/03 [2006] ECR I-7115 para. 54; Joined cases ECJ, *UGT-Rioja and Others*, Cases No. C-428/06 to C-434/06 [2008] not yet reported para. 46.

- In principle, the payment of interest is deductible at the level of the paying company in the source country with the exception of possible anti-abuse adjustments (thin capitalization[43] and transfer pricing rules[44]).

By contrast, with regard to *interest income from foreign sources*, the following rules apply when the receiving company is resident for tax purposes in a given Member State:

- A withholding tax can apply to the interest paid in the source country. However, there will be no withholding tax if the Interest and Royalty Directive applies[45]. In addition, as mentioned in the description of the measure, the major part of double taxation treaties concluded by the Member State provides for a 0 % withholding tax on interest in the source country.
- In principle, the interest paid is deductible in the source country. However, thin capitalization and transfer pricing rules may apply in various forms depending on the tax legislation of the source country concerned.
- In the Member State concerned, the interest income is subject to the 80% interest deduction measure.

Table 10.1 illustrates the fiscal consequences where a company "A" established in the source State pays EUR 1,000 interest to a company "B" resident in the Member State applying the measure (i.e., the recipient State) depending on the application of the Interest and Royalty Directive or the application of a reduced withholding tax under the applicable double taxation treaty.

43. Thin capitalization rules are designed to combat thinly capitalized financing structures with excessive debt financing. In a cross-border context, thin capitalization may be part of a strategy to lower income taxes, as interest expenses are tax deductible, while dividends are not.
44. Transfer pricing rules scrutinize the terms that associate enterprises use when they conduct business with each other. Associated enterprises may agree on conditions that they would not have agreed upon between unrelated parties ("arm's length" principle, in order to shift profits from a high-tax to a low-tax jurisdiction). Due to differences in the tax base and the tax rates in different jurisdictions, the pricing of cross-border intra-group supplies and services can have serious repercussions for tax receipts in the jurisdictions concerned.
45. The Interest and Royalty Directive applies if the interest is paid by an associated company established in another Member State.

Table 10.1 *Tax Treatment of Interest Income*

Domestic / Cross-Border Transactions	*Source Country*	*Tax-Agreement (DTA) / EU Int-Royalty Dir.*	*With-holding Tax*	*Net Amount Received*	*Tax Exemp-tion*	*Taxable Basis in MS*	*Overall Tax Burden (Standard Tax Rate = 20%)*
DOMESTIC	MS	N/A (0%)	0	1000		1000	200
INTRA-EU	MS1	DTA (0%)	0	1000	800	200	40
	MS2	DTA (10%)	100	900	800	200	140
	MS3	DTA (15%)	150	850	800	200	190
	EU (intra--group)	EU Directive (0%)		1000	800	200	40
WITH THIRD COUNTRIES	Third country 1	DTA (0%)	0	1000	800	200	40
	Third country 2	DTA (10%)	100	900	800	200	140

Table 10.1 demonstrates that in the case of a corporation tax rate of 20% the application of the tax deduction systematically leads to a lower tax burden for foreign-source interest, in comparison with domestic interest. As a matter of fact, the application of this tax measure may even lead to a kind of *double non-taxation*, since it would involve the deduction of interest paid and absence of withholding tax in the source country, and 80% exemption in the given Member State.

In order to comply with the Court's case-law, one should address the following questions: are undertakings receiving interest income from a domestic source in a comparable legal and factual situation with undertakings receiving interest income from foreign sources? If the answer is positive, we must then proceed with the third step, which consists in analyzing whether the tax measure is justified by the logic of the tax system. If the answer is negative, the measure is not selective.

In that respect, one should recognize that in certain cases foreign-source interest can be subject to taxation (withholding tax) in the source country. There is therefore a risk that this interest would be subject to double taxation. However, in the large majority of cases, the interest income from foreign sources is exempted from any foreign withholding tax either on the basis of the Interest and Royalty Directive (2003/49/EC), or on the basis of the double taxation treaties in force.

It is also true that the application of thin capitalization rules in the source country may lead to the requalification of part or all of the interest in the source State. This may lead to double taxation in the recipient country if the requalification is not taken into account in the assessment of the corporation tax in the recipient State. However, the application of thin capitalization rules in the source State should be regarded as exceptional since they aim at preventing abuses. In addition, one should bear in mind that thin capitalization rules also apply to domestic transactions.

Although one can see some differences in the fiscal treatment of foreign-source interest and domestic interest income, these differences do not appear to be significant in the light of the objective of the corporation tax system, i.e., taxing profits.

In view of the above, one can come to the conclusion that undertakings, which receive interest income from abroad and which are established in the Member State that has introduced the measure, are in a comparable legal and factual situation with undertakings receiving interest income from domestic sources.

Generally speaking, one can consider that the only possible ground for a tax measure aiming at the prevention of double taxation to be regarded as a non-selective measure is to be found in the "justification test," which will now be examined.

[c] Justification Test

As already mentioned in the above, according to the jurisprudence of the Court, a measure found to be selective on the basis of the "comparability test" can still be found to fall outside the scope of the State aid rules if it is justified by the nature or general scheme of the system. It is for the Member State concerned to show that tax differentiations among comparable operators/activities are justified by the nature and general scheme of their own tax system in that they derive directly from the basic or guiding principles of that system.

In other words, the concept of State aid does not apply to State support measures, which differentiate between undertakings where that differentiation arises from the "*nature or overall structure of the system*" of which they form part.

As explained in the Commission Fiscal Notice, each firm is supposed to pay tax once only [46]. It is therefore inherent in the logic of the tax system that taxes paid in the State in which a firm is resident for tax purpose should be taken into account by another tax jurisdiction. It would therefore be in line with the logic of a tax system to prevent double taxation of the same incomes.

With regard to the present case on the reduced tax regime for interest income from foreign source, justifying this measure by the logic of the tax system may raise certain difficulties. At first, one should note that, in the Member State concerned, any type of foreign income -except for interest income- is subject to the credit method based on the imputation of a tax credit. As a result, it might be difficult to consider the introduction of the 80% tax exemption for foreign interest income to be inherent in the "*nature or logic*" in the corporation tax system[47].

46. Commission Notice on the Application of the State Aid Rules to Measures relating to Direct Business Taxation, OJ C 384, Dec. 10, 1998, 26.
47. However, one should not consider this argument as a conclusive one. It may indeed be excessive to conclude that Member States are in the obligation of choosing the same method to prevent double taxation for all types of foreign income.

In addition, special attention should be given to the fact that the tax exemption scheme is unilateral and applies irrespective of whether the interest income concerned is effectively subject to taxation abroad. Hence, if the tax exemption applies although the interest income is not taxed abroad, the measure would not be justified. Therefore, introducing a general tax exemption which applies systematically may be viewed as disproportionate with regard to the few cases where there would be an actual risk of double taxation.

In that respect, the notion of proportionality with regard to the justification by the logic of the system has recently been developed by the Court of Justice in the *Italian Cooperatives* case[48]. The Court assessed that the logic of the tax system implies that the measure should be consistent with the principle of proportionality. The reference made by the Court to the principle of proportionality for the application of the justification test is not a surprise as this principle has already been enshrined in the case-law of the Court regarding the application of the justification test in cases related to fundamental freedoms[49].

This jurisprudence involves that the measure should not to go beyond what is necessary in order to achieve the objective that it pursues. In other words, the objective pursued cannot be attained by less far-reaching measures.

In the present case, the application of the proportionality principle to the justification by the logic of the system appears to be disproportionate, since the tax measure goes further what is necessary to achieve the objective of preventing double taxation in a limited number of cases. This objective could have been attained by less far-reaching measures, such as the application of the credit method based on the imputation of a tax credit corresponding to the foreign withholding tax. One could have also considered accompanying this credit method with measures specific to the tax situation of the State involved (e.g. prevention of double taxation in case of the application of thin cap rules in the source country).

§10.04 CONCLUSION

In line with the foregoing considerations, it emerges that the application of the selectivity criterion in State aid can be subtle in execution in taxation. The assessment of the *Patent Box* with regard to Article 107 TFEU shows that different approaches could have been considered. The Commission however focused on the application of the measure to all economic operators and came to the conclusion that the measure was general. Hence, the measure was not deemed to be State aid. With regard to the hypothetical case of the reduced taxation of foreign-sourced interest, the 80% interest deduction rule seems to constitute a selective advantage for undertakings receiving

48. Joined case ECJ, *Paint Graphos and others,* Cases No. C-78/08 to C-80/08 not yet reported para. 75.
49. ECJ, *Centros Ltd v. Erhvervs-og Selskabsstyrelsen,* Case No. C-212/97 [1999] ECR I-1459 para. 34; ECJ, *Kraus v. Land Baden-Württemberg,* Case No. C-19/92 [1993] ECR I-1663 para. 32; ECJ, *Gebhard v. Consiglio dell'Ordine degli Avvocati e Procuratori di Milano,* Case No. C-55/94 [1995] ECR 1-4165 para. 37.

interest income deriving from foreign source. This measure may therefore be regarded as State aid.

The analysis of these cases is a good answer to the scholarly criticism according to which State aid rules in tax matters would apply excessively[50]. It shows that State aid rules are not designed to be used to vet all legislative proposals of the Member States which could distort competition and affect trade between the Member States. The objective of State aid rules is to focus on distortions of competition, where Member States would grant a particular advantage to certain undertakings by introducing tax measures departing from their overall policy approach. Member States remain free to adopt their own rules, including rules promoting research and development or rules preventing double taxation. By doing so, they should nonetheless comply with the State aid disciplines. Since the recently *Italian Cooperatives* case, this involves also respecting the principle of proportionality for justifying their tax measures: the Member States must refrain from granting advantages if those advantages contradict go beyond what is necessary to attain the objective pursued. It is in the light of these rules that the Member State can exercise their tax powers.

50. A. Bartosch, *Research Handbook on European State Aid Law*, 176 et seq. (E. Szyszczak ed., Edward Elgar 2011).

CHAPTER 11

State Aid and Tax Law: Enter the Taxpayer*

Keith O'Donnell & Anne Muller**

§11.01 INTRODUCTION: WHAT IS THE TAXPAYER'S PERSPECTIVE?

If we had to find common characteristics to all our clients, we would underline that they all are, first and foremost, entrepreneurs who are running businesses. These entrepreneurs can range from individuals with small teams to multinational enterprises employing thousands around the globe. Their key objectives are essentially the same and can be summarized for the purposes of this chapter as follows:

- Maximize revenues and minimize costs, including administrative and tax costs.
- Add value to key stakeholders, generally customers, shareholders, employees and the community in which the business operates. The entrepreneur will seek to focus his time and energy in the ongoing conduct of the business in the areas adding value for stakeholders, often called the "core" areas of the business. This leads the entrepreneur to seek as much stability as possible in "non-core" areas. Generally taxation will be a non-core area so an entrepreneur will expect to deal with a stable tax system to avoid time-consuming monitoring and constant need for adapting plans.
- Take investment decisions for the future. Decisions will be taken based on parameters that the entrepreneur needs to be as predictable as possible.

* This contribution aims to present the taxpayer's perspective on Fiscal State aid, focusing on how the complex procedure implemented by the EU Commission and various judgments of the European Court of Justice create uncertainty. In the last section, we also provide some suggestions regarding areas for improvements.

** The authors wish to thank our colleagues José Luis Buendia Sierra and Maria Muñoz de Juan from Garrigues Brussels' office for sharing their knowledge on the subject and for their assistance in the drafting of this chapter.

Whereas some are inherently unpredictable, such as consumer tastes, or raw material prices, other parameters are expected to be predictable in a developed economy, including the tax and legal system.
- Evolve in a competitive environment. Entrepreneurs are concerned by their competitive position compared to peers. In addition by their nature, they will expect competition between States to offer the most attractive business location for the conduct of their activities.

Literature is abundant when it comes to European State aid, be it the technical developments and analyses on the State aid rules and regulations established by the EU Commission or the numerous articles commenting on the consequences of judgments rendered by the European Court of Justice (ECJ) in the matter. All these papers constitute valuable material to understand the mechanics and, sometimes, very political background of the State aid concept when it is related to the assessment of taxation policies decided upon by Member States. Nevertheless their focus is mainly on the relationships between European Institutions and the Member States and it seems that the position of the ultimate beneficiaries of so-called State aid is often overlooked, or even ignored. In the following sections of this chapter, we will analyze to what extent the very concept of State aid and its current definition by the EU Commission, as well as case law, are contributing to add on a layer of complexity and uncertainty for taxpayers. We will also review some areas for improvements, which would certainly help taxpayers to fulfill their need for more predictability in the matter.

§11.02 THE CONCEPT OF STATE AID: A COMPLEX NOTION AND ASSESSMENT PROCEDURE

[A] What Is State Aid[1]?

[1] General Comments

Within the meaning of the European Law, the concept of State aid encompasses any transfer of public resources from the government to a specific recipient or several recipients. This definition implies (i) a cost or a loss of public funds to the government granting the aid, and (ii) a corresponding accrual of wealth to its recipient(s).

The reason why State aid is a key question and why the EU institutions need to monitor it, is that aids granted by government affect the forces of free competition inherent to open markets. Firms, sectors, or regions benefiting from aids are put in a comparative advantage with respect to those not benefiting from them.

A distinction needs to be made between State aids which distort trade and competition within the EU, but nonetheless have an underlying desirable justification

1. In respect of the definition and legal basis for the State aid concept, reference is made to C. Pinto, *EC State Aid Rules and Tax Incentives: A U-Turn in Commission Policy*, 1 Eur. Taxn. J. 295 et seq. (1999) *as well as* C. Pinto, *EC State Aid Rules and Tax Incentives: A U-Turn in Commission Policy*, 2 Eur. Taxn. J. 343 et seq. (1999).

from an economic and/or social point of view, and those which lack such a characteristic. In this respect, a good example of permissible aid can be for instance, aids granted to firms that invest in a particularly depressed area of the country granting these aids. The harm of the interplay of free competition may be offset by the potential benefits of the aids, namely the likely development of the area concerned.

As far as the EU is concerned, the issue of State aid has increased in importance over the years, along with the increasing liberalization of the Common Market and its transformation into a Single Market.

[2] Legal Basis and EU Legal Rules on State Aid

The founders of the European Economic Community included in the Treaty of Rome specific provisions that were meant to provide both the Community Institutions and the Member States with effective legal tools to safeguard the correct functioning of a common market. One of the fundamental needs to be preserved was to ensure free competition amongst the enterprises engaged in the same business activity and to prevent Member States from distorting the market in any way.

The basic principle, which constitutes the foundation of the Treaty provisions on competition and State aid, is contained in Article 3 paragraph 3 of the Treaty on the EU[2]. This provision is of a very general nature and states that one of the main goals pursued by the EU is the establishment of "*an internal market.*" The Treaty on the Functioning of the EU[3] (hereafter "TFEU") specifically defines in its Article 26, second paragraph, what is expected from the internal market: "The internal market shall comprise an area without internal frontiers in which the free movement of goods, persons, services and capital is ensured in accordance with the provisions of the Treaties."

The rules on competition, elaborated in accordance with these broad principles, may be found in title VII, Chapter 1 of the TFEU, entitled "Rules on Competition". The first section of this chapter defines the fundamental anti-trust provisions applying to private undertakings (i.e., Articles 101 to 105 TFEU) and the second section encompasses the rules on "aids granted by States" (i.e., Articles 107 to 108 TFEU). Article 107 TFEU encompasses the substantive legal principles relating to State aid, whereas Article 108 TFEU is of a more procedural nature. It is worth noting that neither provision is comprehensive: their interpretation and practical application has been clarified over the years through instruments of secondary EU legislation and other EU

2. Consolidated version of the Treaty on the EU (following the amendments introduced by the Lisbon Treaty signed on December 13, 2007, which have entered in force on December,1, 2009),OJ No. C 83, Mar. 30 , 2010, eur-lex.europa.eu/en/treaties/index.htm. Unless explicitly specified, the present article will only refer to the current article numbers as per the current consolidated version of the Treaty on the EU.
3. A Consolidated version of the Treaty on the Functioning of the EU (following the amendments introduced by the Lisbon Treaty signed on December 13, 2007, which have entered in force on December 1, 2009), OJ No. C 83, Mar. 30, 2010, eur-lex.europa.eu/en/treaties/index.htm. Unless explicitly specified, the present article will only refer to the current article numbers as per the current consolidated version of the Treaty on the Functioning of the EU.

Commission documents, as well as through the case law of the ECJ (this aspect will be developed further in the next sections of this chapter).

The first paragraph of Article 107 TFEU reads as follows:

> Save as otherwise provided in the Treaties, any aid granted by a Member State or through State resources in any form whatsoever which distorts or threatens to distort competition by favouring certain undertakings or the production of certain goods shall, in so far as it affects trade between Member States, be incompatible with the internal market.

Article 107 TFEU further goes on by defining aids which are compatible with the internal market or which may be compatible. Hence, on the one hand, Article 107 paragraph 2 TFEU contains a set of automatic exemptions, i.e. aids deemed to be always compatible with the internal market. This is the case for "*aid having a social character,*" "*aid to make good the damage caused by natural disasters*" and "*aid granted to the economy of certain areas of the Federal Republic of Germany affected by the division of Germany.*" On the other hand, Article 107 paragraph 3 TFEU, contains a set of exemptions that do not apply automatically, but are subject to a specific authorization procedure laid down in Article 108 TFEU. Such aids under the scope of Article 107 paragraph 3 are notably the ones referred to as the "*Regional aids*" [4].

In order to ensure full compliance with this set of rules within the EU and their full effectiveness, considering that they are part of the pillar for the good functioning of the Internal Market, far-reaching powers have been conferred to the EU Commission, as the "guardian of the Treaty" (to be further discussed in this chapter in section 11.02[B] below). As a consequence, and based on the provisions of Article 108 TFEU, this Institution is in charge of investigating cases of potential breach of the competition rules and of adopting the necessary measures, among which the imposition of very high fines, as well as of investigating cases relating to State aid. Decisions issued by the EU Commission are binding upon the Member States, for instance, the recovery of illegal aid.

[3] Specific Considerations Relating to Fiscal State Aid

The first official document focusing on the application of the EU State aid rules to the fiscal area was the "Notice on the application of the State aid rules to measures relating to direct business taxation" (referred to as "the Notice") issued by the EU Commission in November 1998[5]. This Notice was adopted within the framework of the process meant to tackle harmful tax competition within the EU, and its basis is contained in the

4. Please note that other exemptions are also available, under the so-called "Horizontal rules" based on EU Commission "Frameworks," "Guidelines" or "General Block Exemptions Regulations" (GBER). In addition, some Aids related to some specific sectors can also be considered as compatible Aids, subject to certain conditions. The latter are referred to as "*Sectoral rules.*" Finally, the last main category of exemptions is related to "Specific Aid instruments" as defined by notices issued by the EU Commission.
5. Commission Notice 98/C on the application of the State aid rules to measures relating to direct business taxation, OJ C 384/3, Dec. 10, 1998 (hereinafter "The Notice").

EU Council's "Package" [6] (which has further on also lead to the creation of the "Code of Conduct" Group, headed by Mrs. Dawn Primarolo).

The Notice forms part of the EU Commission's acts sui generis or "soft law" containing policy statements. Therefore it is not a piece of secondary EU legislation, but nevertheless it is binding on the EU Commission in that it is able to create legitimate expectations[7] for both Member States and interested parties.

The Notice aims at setting uniform principles and standards applicable to fiscal State aid provisions in order to ensure objectivity and equality of treatment between Member States. It also provides an additional tool in the countering of harmful tax competition within the EU. Furthermore, the Notice states as additional objectives the need to ensure "*that Commission decisions are transparent and predictable*" and to guarantee "*consistency and equality of treatment between Member States*[8]."

The Notice explains in detail the application to the fiscal area of the general principles contained in (what has become now) Article 107 TFEU, as developed by the EU Commission and the case law of the ECJ. More specifically, the four cumulative conditions evidencing the presence of State aid within the meaning of Article 107 TFEU are clarified and interpreted with respect to tax measures, i.e., (i) Advantage conferred on a firm (or firms), (ii) Transfer of State-originated resources, (iii) Distortion of competition and impact on intra-Community trade and (iv) Specificity or selectivity.

The following comments can be made with regards to each of the four conditions when it comes to the assessment of fiscal measures.

[a] Advantage Conferred on a Firm (or Firms)

First of all, the advantage conferred upon firms must consist of any alleviation of charges or any relief concerning the tax burden normally imposed on them. In this regard, the Notice makes a reference to the mechanisms used for the granting of the following types of fiscal relief, which may have an impact on a firm's taxable basis, tax liability due or collection of taxes due.

As to the first type of fiscal State aid impacting the calculation of the taxable basis of the taxpayer, any measure having the effect of modifying the standard method of determination of the final taxable amount by affecting the calculation of any of the items taken into account for this purpose belongs to this category. As examples the following can be cited: the granting of special exemptions of certain items of income or the granting of special deductions not normally available under the general tax system,

6. The Package to tackle harmful tax competition, OJ No. C 2, Jan. 6, 1998, sec. 1, para. J (hereinafter The Package).
7. The principle of legitimate expectations forms part of the EU legal order. For a thorough explanation of this principle, please refer to J.A. Usher, *General Principles of EC Law* 55 et seq. (Longman, ed. 1998) and the case law cited therein.
8. See The Notice, para. 4. The Notice also states that these goals are inspired by the incompatibility of State aids with the EU law and the need to interpret as strictly as possible the exemption from it, especially in the light of the increased importance of direct taxation as a consequence of the monetary union and the consolidation of national budgets (The Notice, para. 3).

the possibility to set up special tax-free provisions or to claim special accelerated depreciation, as well as notional methods of calculation of the taxable basis (e.g., cost-plus or resale minus methods). The main problem in all of the above instances is that these measures are very often difficult to be detected, because this type of measures may be granted pursuant to unpublished and/or discretionary administrative practices or may be part of the provisions of a country's general tax system.

The second category of fiscal aid measures encompasses those which work through a modification of the tax liability due by taxpayers. Examples can be special reduced or nil tax rates in favor of income derived from certain activities (e.g., financial services or manufacturing activities) or from operations carried out in special tax-free areas. Also measures such as tax credits, linked, to e.g. investments in business assets, that have the effect of reducing the taxpayer's final liability, can be considered as part of this second category.

The third category deals with the actual collection of taxes due by taxpayers, which is the last stage in the governments' revenue-raising process. In particular, every form of relinquishment by State of its right to recover tax debts not remitted yet by the taxpayer to the Treasury constitutes a fiscal aid measure. For example, lax enforcement of tax rules, leniency in recovery of tax claims and systematic tax debt cancellation or deferment granted by the tax authorities fall into this category. Needless to say, that such practice is extremely hard to discover, because they usually take place on a case-by-case basis and are not disclosed by the tax administration. From the taxpayer's perspective, this can create an interesting situation. In negotiating a reduction in payment or deferral with his local tax authority, whether in view of avoiding litigation or to settle open positions, is a negotiated position truly settled or is there potentially a missing party in the negotiations, namely the EU Commission?

[b] Transfer of State-Originated Resources

The Notice interprets the transfer of State-originated resources as the aid being financed through a so-called "tax expenditure," i.e. a special tax measure deviating from the "benchmark" tax system whose effect is to cause a reduction in the country's tax revenue. Such a special measure may be enacted through laws, regulations or administrative practices of the tax authorities by either central or regional bodies provided with autonomous power. It is worth noting that this condition is closely linked to the specificity condition because it can be argued that the main characteristic of tax expenditures is their special nature as opposed to the standard tax system.

[c] Distortion of Competition and Impact on Intra-Community Trade

The third feature required for a tax measure to qualify as State aid is its potential negative impact on competition and trade with the internal market. In this respect the Notice has not added any particular comment beyond the interpretation that has been given by the ECJ.

It should be noted that the EU Commission has taken the view that small amounts of aid, according to the *de minimis* rule[9] do not have a potential effect on competition and trade between Member States and therefore, such aids fall outside the scope of Article 107 paragraph 1 TFEU.

[d] Specificity or Selectivity

The final condition, regarding "specificity" or "selectivity" is given a particular emphasis by the Notice, which points out that a certain advantage must be granted by way of an "exception to the tax provisions of a legislative, regulatory or administrative nature or from a discretionary practice on the part of the tax authorities"[10]. The Notice goes on to specify that "the selective nature of a measure may be justified by the nature or general scheme of the system"[11], in which case it is not caught by the incompatibility principle laid down in Article 107 TFEU.

In order to clarify what is meant by *"general"* tax system, as opposed to *"specific"* tax measures, the Notice refers to the availability of the latter to all of the firms carrying on a business activity within a Member State on an equal, objective and non-discriminatory basis. Accordingly, *general measures*[12] are those having:

- a "technical nature," such as the ones concerning tax rates, depreciation schedules, period of loss carry-forward, or prevention of double-taxation; and
- an underlying general economic policy objective to be achieved by way of an alleviation of part of the tax burden concerning certain firms' production costs, such as R&D expenses, environment-friendly investments, and training and employment activities.

This criterion raises the most analytical difficulties in the assessment of whether a fiscal measure is to be considered State aid. It will be discussed in more details further on in this chapter in section §11.04[A][2].

9. *De minimis* rule has been introduced in the Commission Regulation (EC) 1998/2006 of December 15, 2006 on the application of Articles 87 and 88 of the Treaty establishing the EU [currently Articles 107 and 108 TFEU] to *de minimis* Aid, OJ No. L 379, Dec. 28, 2006, p. 5. In general, the ceiling for the Aid to be covered by the *de minimis* rule is EUR 200,000 (cash grant equivalent) over any three fiscal-year period.
10. See The Notice, para. 12.
11. See The Notice, para. 12.
12. See The Notice, para. 13.

[B] The State Aid Assessment Process[13]

As mentioned above, the principle of incompatibility of State aids with the internal market requires a careful scrutiny by the EU Commission which has to perform the assessment of such measures. The procedural rules concerning the approval required for this purpose are contained in Article 108 TFEU and related secondary legislation, as well as in the case law of the ECJ.

[1] Basic Methodology Used in State Aid Assessment

Over the last years, a more refined economic approach in the assessment of State aid cases has been introduced. Emphasis has been put on economics both at the stage of the aid qualification (under Article 107 paragraph 1 TFEU) and for the compatibility assessment of aid measures (under Article 107 paragraphs 2 and 3 TFEU).

The assessment of aid compatibility is based on a balancing of the positive effects of aid (in terms of contributing to the achievement of a well-defined objective of common interest) and its negative effects (namely the resulting distortion of competition and trade). In order to be declared compatible, aid must be necessary and proportionate to achieve a particular objective of common interest. The idea behind this is achieving the goal of a "less but better targeted aid."

The "balancing test" is essentially a cost-benefit analysis of the proposed measure, which sets forth the following elements of analysis:

- Aid should be aimed at a well-defined objective of a common interest (such as growth, employment, cohesion, environmental protection, etc.). This can include both efficiency and equity objectives.
- Aid should be well designed to deliver the objective of the common interest identified above. In this respect, answers to the following three questions will be crucial: Is the aid an appropriate policy instrument? Is there an incentive effect? Is the aid measure proportionate to the problem tackled?
- The possible negative effects of the aid and their magnitude should be balanced against its positive effects. In order for the aid to be found compatible, a high magnitude of negative effects (distortive effects on competition and trade) needs to be sufficiently offset by a corresponding high level of positive effects of the aid. The Commission makes an overall assessment of their impact on producers and consumers in the markets concerned by the aid measure.

---

13. In this respect, one can refer to the EU Commission Vademecum of September 30, 2008 on State aid rules (DG for Competition) ec.europa.eu/competition/state_aid/studies_reports/vademecum_on_rules_09_2008_en.pdf.
The *Vademecum* summarizes the main rules applicable to State aid control in a concise manner. It is a first point of reference for Community, national and local stakeholders dealing with State aid control issues, and points to the relevant legal texts.

[2] Notification and Authorization Procedure

Community supervision of State aid is based on a system of *ex ante* authorization. Under this system, Member States are required to inform (*ex ante notification*) the EU Commission of any plan to grant or alter State aid and they are not allowed to put such aid into effect before it has been authorized by the EU Commission (*standstill-principle*).

Under the TFEU, the EU Commission is given the competence to determine whether or not the notified measure constitutes State aid in the sense of Article 107 paragraph 1 TFEU, and if it does, whether or not it qualifies for exemption under Article 107 paragraph 2 or paragraph 3 TFEU. Member States cannot grant any State aid unless it has been notified *and* authorized by the EU Commission. Any aid, which is granted in absence of EU Commission approval, is automatically classified as "*unlawful aid.*"

Under the present procedural rules, the EU Commission is under the obligation to order the recovery from the beneficiaries of any unlawful aid that is found to be incompatible with the common market. Moreover, the ECJ has recognized that national judges are competent to decide whether the notification procedures have been complied with and if not, to order recovery of the aid and recovery of the relevant interest.

In recent years, the EU Commission has started a process of modernization and simplification of State aid procedures. As a result of the modernization process, a distinction needs to be made between aid measures that are exempted from the notification requirement (this is the case for individual aid measures or aid schemes that satisfy all the conditions laid down in the GBER and aid measures falling within *de minimis* Regulation[14]) and aid measures that are subject to the notification requirements.

Regarding the latter, the EU Commission has a two-month period to examine the proposed aid. This examination will normally be concluded either by a "*decision not to raise objections*" or by a "*decision to initiate Article 108 paragraph 2 TFEU proceedings.*"

If the EU Commission decides not to raise any objection, the aid measure concerned can be implemented.

The EU Commission will initiate Article 108 paragraph 2 TFEU proceedings if it has doubts about the compatibility of the notified aid measure with the common market. In such cases, the EU Commission opens a "*formal investigation.*" It publishes a description of the aid in the Official Journal and on its website and invites the Member State concerned and interested parties to comment. At the end of the enquiry, the EU Commission adopts a final decision. This may be either positive (aid can be implemented), negative (aid cannot be implemented) or positive, but subject to stated conditions (aid can be implemented if certain conditions are met). The indicative maximum time-limit foreseen for such an enquiry is 18 months.

14. In this respect, see *supra* notes 4 and 9.

[3] Summary

The previous sections can be summarized through the following process tree. From a taxpayer's perspective in determining whether his tax charge is subject to change under the State aid rules, the process can look decidedly Byzantine.

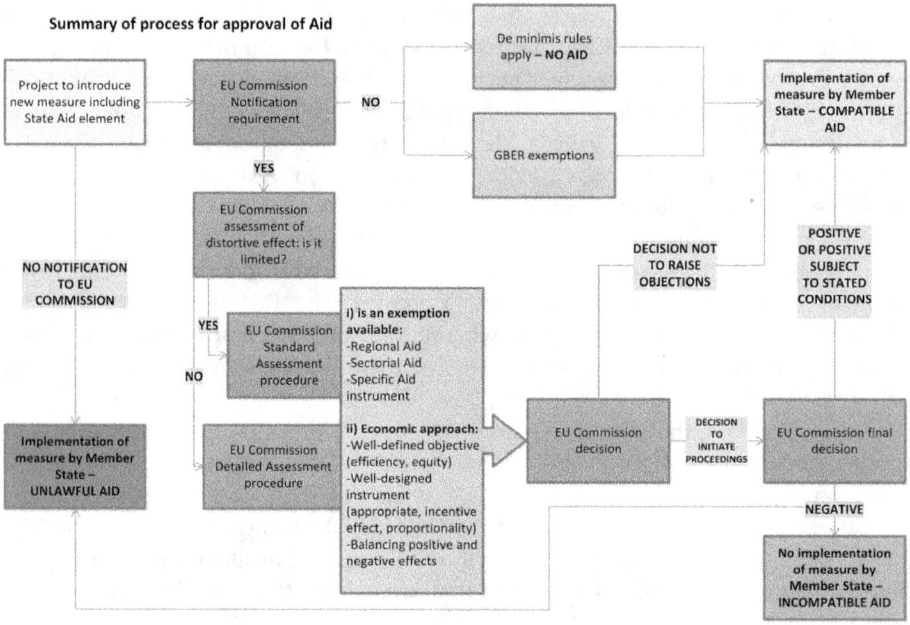

§11.03 REVIEW OF RELEVANT CASE LAW: ABSENCE OF LEGAL CERTAINTY

For a taxpayer having deciphered the complex definition and process described above, the next step will be to consider if the decisions of the ECJ throw further light on the situation. In the following Sections we will review some emblematic case law and analyze whether, based on either the EU Commission's view in the assessment of certain cases or based on jurisprudence and comments provided by the ECJ, a higher degree of comfort has been provided to taxpayers.

[A] Overview of the Luxembourg 1929 Holding Companies Case[15]

[1] Description of the Regime

The Law of July 31, 1929 was introduced with the aim of attracting to Luxembourg specific activities such as the holding the stocks of companies, the management of

15. Aid scheme No. C 3/2006.

collective investments, the financing and licensing intangibles to related entities within a group. The Luxembourg companies benefiting from the regime, i.e., the so-called 1929 Holding Companies were exempt from Luxembourg corporate income tax, municipal business tax and net worth tax. Dividend distributions made by the 1929 Holding Companies were not subject to withholding tax. The 1929 Holding Companies were only subject to the 1% capital duty upon incorporation (such capital duty being now abolished) and to subscription tax of 0.2% on share capital. 1929 Holding Companies were excluded from the benefit of Luxembourg double-tax treaties and provisions of EU Parent-Subsidiaries Directive[16].

[2] Procedure History

In parallel to, and before the launch of the assessment of the 1929 Holding Companies regime under the State aid rules, the same regime has been reviewed within the frame of the Code of Conduct. In June 2003, the Ecofin Council considered that the dividend exemption granted to 1929 Holding Companies constituted a harmful tax measure within the meaning of the Code of Conduct, as the exemption granted was not conditional upon the payment of a sufficient tax by the distributing company. This conclusion lead the Luxembourg legislator, in accordance with the Ecofin Council, to amend the 1929 Holding Companies regime in June 2005, providing that the tax exempt status for 1929 Holding Companies would be lost, if a 1929 Holding Company would receive more than 5% of its annual dividend income from subsidiaries which are not subject to a tax comparable to Luxembourg corporate income tax[17].

Regarding the assessment of the 1929 Holding Companies regime under State aid rules, communications and exchanges of information took place between EU Commission and Luxembourg on the related legislation and regulations over the period from February 1999 to July 2005. By its letter of July 11, 2005, the EU Commission informed Luxembourg that it had come to the conclusion, as part of its preliminary assessment, that the scheme (as amended in June 2005), constituted aid incompatible with the common market.

Luxembourg did not provide the EU Commission with any comment regarding this negative assessment, despite request and, in November 2005, the EU Commission proposed Luxembourg to take appropriate measures to gradually review the scheme. These were rejected by Luxembourg in December 2005.

Early 2006, the EU Commission opened an in-depth investigation based on Article 88 paragraph 2 of the Treaty on the EU (which is now Article 108 paragraph 2 TFEU), which lead to the final decision of the EU Commission taken on July 19, 2006 that the scheme had to be repealed by the end of 2006, with a grandfathering period

16. Council Directive 90/435/EEC of Jul. 23, 1990 on the common system of taxation applicable in the case of parent companies and subsidiaries of different Member States.
17. Regarding this condition, the Luxembourg tax authorities generally consider that it is fulfilled if taxation is mandatory and applied with a rate of half the Luxembourg corporate income tax rate, i.e., currently 10.5%.

granted until December 31, 2010 for existing companies[18]. As the regime constituted Existing aid, no repayment was requested.

Luxembourg accepted the EU Commission's decision and did not bring the case before the ECJ Courts.

[3] State Aid Assessment

Looking at the EU Commission's decision of July 19, 2006, the following comments were made with respect of each of the four criteria regarded for the State aid assessment.

[a] Existence of an Advantage

The advantages provided by the 1929 Holding Companies regime "constitute exceptional measures which are capable of favouring certain undertakings compared with other undertakings, which are, in the light of the objective pursued by the said scheme – namely the prevention of multiple taxation – in a comparable factual situation[19]."

Exempt 1929 Holding Companies "benefit actually and not potentially from a mitigation of the charges which are normally included in their budgets[20]."

[b] State Resource

Although not entailing a transfer of State resources, the regime leads "to a loss of tax revenue and hence constitutes State financing[21]."

[c] Selectivity

The EU Commission's view is that "(...) such exemption scheme is selective since it favours certain undertakings carrying on exclusively certain activities among the various undertakings and activities which are subject to the risk of multiple taxation[22]." The restrictions of activities to be performed by 1929 Holding Companies "(...) confirm the selective nature of the exemption scheme for exempt 1929 Holding Companies[23]."

The EU Commission goes on in its analysis and concludes that "(...) no objective explanation can justify such a tax treatment, specifically reserved for exempt 1929 Holding Companies, seeking as it does, by thus limiting its application to certain undertakings, to place them at an advantage compared with their competitors[24]."

18. Commission Decision 2006/940/EC of Jul. 19, 2006, OJ L 366/2006.
19. *Ibid.*, para. 68.
20. *Ibid.*
21. *Ibid.*, para. 84.
22. *Ibid.*, para. 74.
23. *Ibid.*, para. 81.
24. *Ibid.*, para. 82.

[d] Distortion of Competition and Effect on Trade between Member States

For the EU Commission, such scheme has an impact on competition and trade between Member States, as "(...) 1929 holding companies are active in the financial sector, where they perform specific activities (...) [and] enjoy increased operational flexibility under the 1929 legislation in the pursuit of such financing activities (...)[25]." The complete exemption from the direct taxes normally applicable in Luxembourg to the income from the activities, performed by the 1929 Holding Companies has a considerable impact on the choice of Luxembourg as a preferred financial centre. "(...) [The] Commission considers that there can be no denying how important the scheme is to the financial sector in Luxembourg or how substantial are the resulting distortions of competitions and trade[26]."

[e] Compatibility

No exceptions provided for by Article 87 paragraphs 2 and 3 of the Treaty (now Article 107 paragraphs 2 and 3 TFEU) were applicable.

In addition:

> [the] Commission would observe that the mere fact that the tax advantages in question are exclusively reserved for companies registered in Luxembourg as exempt 1929 Holding Companies seems to contravene the freedom of establishment on business entities established in Luxembourg, as well as being formed in other Member States[27].

[4] Impact for the Taxpayers

Aligning its decision on the decision taken on Belgian Coordination Centres[28], the EU Commission has ordered the repeal of the long-lasting Luxembourg 1929 Holding Companies regime.

The fact that the regime had been amended by Luxembourg to conform to the recommendations of the Code of Conduct Group has not in any manner influenced the State aid assessment performed by the EU Commission. Indeed, based on the EU Commission's decision of July 19, 2006, "(...) Article 87 does not exclude from its scope tax measures of any description (...) [and] neither the Law of 31 July 1929 nor any of its amendments (...) were notified to the Commission (... .). Consequently, the Commission has not had occasion to decide on the compatibility of the scheme in question with the State aid rules[29]." The EU Commission further highlights that the

25. *Ibid.*, para. 87.
26. *Ibid.*, para. 91.
27. *Ibid.*, para. 96, referring to ECJ, *Saint-Gobain*, Case No. C-307/97 [1999] ECR I-6161.
28. Joined cases ECJ, *Kingdom of Belgium and Forum 187 ASBL v. Commission of the European Communities*, Cases No. C-182/03 and C-217/03 [2006] ECR I-05479.
29. Commission Decision 2006/940/EC of Jul. 19, 2006, OJ L 366/2006, 102.

procedure for examining the tax schemes from a State aid point-of-view is legally independent of the work of the Code of Conduct Group.

This decision had a significant impact in Luxembourg, as it was believed that the proofing of the scheme within the frame of the Code of Conduct would be enough to allow the permanence of the regime. In addition to this, taxpayers were also concerned that other measures may fall under the scope of State aid assessment by the EU Commission, such as the Luxembourg SICAR[30] or the Luxembourg Securitization Vehicle[31], for which information had also been requested by the EU Commission from Luxembourg. The 1929 Holding Companies regime is an example of a scheme which was relatively general in nature and was not intended to favor any particular sector of activity. It should be recalled that any person natural or legal, Luxembourgish or foreign, could set up such a company regardless of what business sector the person was involved in. If we consider the first two criteria as relatively non controversial, and examine the second two criteria, the Commissions' decision seems to be based on:

(1) A **selectivity** finding that was "activity" based (i.e., a Holding activity within any enterprise regardless of sector). The Commission phrased it as "*certain undertakings carrying on exclusively certain activities.*" Arguably, the limitation to certain undertakings was a formal one (i.e., requiring a certain legal form to qualify) and should in fact have been dealt with as a restriction to the freedom of establishment, a point raised by the EU Commission in an aside. The remaining selectivity is in relation to certain types of activities carried out by any enterprise. These are generally referred to as functions within an enterprise and can be sales, marketing, R&D, finance etc.

(2) A finding of **competitive distortion** arising from a sectoral advantage, i.e., a benefit to the financial sector "*there can be no denying how important the scheme is to the financial sector in Luxembourg.*" This finding is, in the view of the authors, problematic as this form of indirect benefit to the financial sector seems to be a given when *any* business is encouraged. In effect, virtually all forms of business will be users of the financial services sector, so by the Commission's logic any tax measure that encourages business can become sectoral.

Some voices in the Luxembourg community were of the view that the decision should have been appealed. However, in view of the relatively limited use of 1929 Holding Companies in a business environment—Double-Tax Conventions and EU directives having created more effective means for relieving double taxation—and the perceived need to end the uncertainty that reigned, this view did not prevail and the regime was repealed.

30. SICAR is the abbreviation for "*Société d'Investissement en Capital à Risque,*" i.e. Risk capital Company, which was introduced by the Law of Jun. 15, 2004.
31. The Securitization Vehicle has been introduced by the Law of Mar. 22, 2004.

[B] Overview of the *Gibraltar* Case

[1] History and Description of the Regime

In August 2002, the UK notified the EU Commission of the Government of Gibraltar's proposed reform of corporate tax[32]. That reform included in particular the repeal of the former tax system and the imposition of three taxes applicable to all Gibraltar companies, namely a company's registration fee, a payroll tax and a business property occupation tax (BPOT), with a cap on liability to payroll tax and BPOT of 15% of profits.

The EU Commission decided on March 30, 2004[33] that the new tax regime to be implemented by Gibraltar entailed State aid that is incompatible with the common market and could not be implemented. The General Court annulled the Decision in 2008[34]. The EU Commission appealed[35]. Advocate General Jääskinen proposed in April 2011 that the appeal be dismissed[36]. The ECJ has rendered its judgment on November 15, 2011[37] and overturned the judgment of the General Court, upholding the decision of the EU Commission.

[2] EU Commission Assessment of the Regime

In 2004, the Commission decided that the proposals notified for the reform of the system of corporate taxation in Gibraltar constituted a scheme of State aid that was incompatible with the internal market and, accordingly, that those proposals could not be implemented. The EU Commission found that three aspects of the tax reform were *Materially Selective*:

(i) The requirement that a company must make a profit before it becomes liable to payroll tax and BPOT, since that requirement would favor companies which make no profit[38].

(ii) The cap limiting liability to payroll tax and BPOT to 15% of profits, since that cap would favor companies which, for the tax year in question, have profits

32. However, the reform at issue in the present case did not enter into force.
33. Commission Decision 2005/261/EC, OJ L 85/1, 2005.
34. Joined cases ECJ, *Government of Gibraltar and United Kingdom v. Commission*, Cases No. T-211/04 and T-215/04 [2008] ECR II-03745.
35. Joined cases ECJ, *European Commission and Kingdom of Spain v. Government of Gibraltar and United Kingdom of Great Britain and Northern*, Cases No. C-106/09 P and C-107/09 P not yet reported in ECR.
36. Opinion of AG Jääskinen in Joined cases ECJ, *European Commission and Kingdom of Spain v. Government of Gibraltar and United Kingdom*, Cases No. C-106/09 P and C-107/09 P not yet reported in ECR.
37. Joined cases ECJ, *European Commission and Kingdom of Spain v. Government of Gibraltar and United Kingdom of Great Britain and Northern*, Cases No. C-106/09 P and C-107/09 P not yet reported in ECR.
38. Commission Decision 2005/261/EC, OJ L 85/1, 2005, 128–133.

that are low in relation to their number of employees and their occupation of business property[39].

(iii) The payroll tax and BPOT, since those two taxes would inherently favor offshore companies which have no real physical presence in Gibraltar and which as a consequence do not incur corporate tax[40].

It also found that the proposed reform was *Regionally Selective* since it provided for a system under which companies in Gibraltar would be taxed, in general, at a lower rate than those in the United Kingdom[41].

[3] Importance of the General Court's Position on Material Selectivity

Based on the General Court's judgment, the EU Commission did not demonstrate selectivity (neither material nor regional).

The failure to respect the methodology and identify the selective character of the tax measures results in the EU Commission going beyond its competences:

> Such an approach would (...) enable the Commission to assume the role of the Member State with regard to determination of that State's tax system and of the common or "normal" regime under it, including in relation to the objectives, the tax system's inherent mechanisms for achieving those objectives and its bases of taxation (...)[42].

[4] Importance of the Advocate General Jääskinen's Opinion

Advocate General focused not so much on the material selectivity, but on the identification of an advantage.

Starting point of the analysis of tax measures must be the advantage:

> A measure liable to be regarded as fiscal aid must correspond to a fiscal cost. The Commission must be in a position to identify the value of the tax actually or potentially "lost" which represents the amount of the supposed aid. The only means available to the Commission of estimating the "lost" value is to refer to a general regime applicable in the reference framework being examined[43].

The selectivity analysis comes in a second step:

> It is therefore necessary to start by asking whether a person should have been taxed and, if so, whether the absence of taxation constitutes an advantage. The next issue is whether the other undertakings in a comparable situation enjoy the

39. *Ibid.*, 134–141.
40. *Ibid.*, 142–144.
41. *Ibid.*, 127.
42. ECJ Joined cases, *Government of Gibraltar and United Kingdom v. Commission*, Cases No. T-211/04 and T-215/04 [2008] ECR II-03745 para. 145.
43. Opinion of AG Jääskinen in Joined cases ECJ, *European Commission and Kingdom of Spain v. Government of Gibraltar and United Kingdom*, Cases No. C-106/09 P and C-107/09 P not yet reported in ECR para. 160.

> same advantage. If that is not the case, there is probably a selective advantage. The advantage can therefore be identified only by means of that factual comparison[44].

Advocate General holds that State aid is not the instrument to combat "harmful tax competition":

> It follows that harmful institutional or tax competition between Member States clearly does not fall within the mechanism for controlling State aid established by the Treaty, even though there are cases where measures are liable to amount both to harmful tax competition and to State aid incompatible with the common market. However, the legitimate objective of combating harmful tax competition cannot justify distortion of the EU's legal framework established in the area of competition law applicable to State aid, or even the adoption of ad hoc solutions conflicting with the rule of law as enshrined in Article 2 of the Treaty[45].

The opinion of Advocate General Jääskinen highlights that the Member States' rights over their tax systems has to be respected:

> (...) it is essential to preserve the distinction between tax measures constituting State aid and those corresponding to the normal configuration with which the national legislature wished to endow its tax system, a configuration which may give rise to differential treatment necessary for the pursuit of general public-interest objectives set by the State in the exercise of its sovereign rights[46].

[5] The View of the ECJ: Judgment of November 15, 2011

In its judgment, the Court of Justice held that the General Court erred in law in finding that the proposed tax reform does not confer selective advantages on offshore companies.

The Court considered that a different tax burden resulting from the application of a "general" tax regime was not sufficient on its own to establish the selectivity of taxation[47]. Nonetheless, it held that such selectivity exists where, as in the present case, the criteria for assessment which were adopted by a tax system were such as to characterize the recipient undertakings, by virtue of the properties which are specific to them, as a privileged category of undertakings[48].

In doing so, the Court found that due to the absence of other bases of assessment, combining those two bases of assessment (which are founded on criteria that are in themselves of a general nature) excluded from the outset any taxation of offshore companies, since they had no employees and also did not occupy business property[49]. Those criteria therefore discriminated between companies which are in a comparable

44. *Ibid.*, para. 165.
45. *Ibid.*, para. 134.
46. *Ibid.*, para. 145.
47. Joined cases ECJ, *European Commission and Kingdom of Spain v. Government of Gibraltar and United Kingdom,* Cases No. C-106/09 P and C-107/09 P not yet reported in ECR para. 103.
48. *Ibid.*, para. 104.
49. *Ibid.*, para. 102.

situation with regard to the objective of the proposed tax reform, namely to introduce a general system of taxation for all companies established in Gibraltar[50].

Consequently, the Court concluded that the fact that offshore companies are not taxed in Gibraltar is not a random consequence of the regime at issue, but the inevitable consequence of the fact that both corporate taxes (in particular, their bases of assessment) are specifically designed so that offshore companies, which by their nature have no employees and do not occupy business premises, avoid taxation[51]. Thus, the fact that offshore companies avoid taxation precisely on account of the specific features characteristic of that group of companies gives reason to conclude that they enjoy selective advantages[52].

The Court noted in particular that, contrary to the General Court's reasoning, the classification of a tax system as "*selective*" is not conditional upon that system being designed in such a way that all undertakings are liable to the same tax burden but some benefit from derogating provisions that give them a selective advantage[53]. Such an interpretation of the selectivity criterion would require that, in order for a tax system to be classifiable as "*selective*," it must be designed in accordance with a certain regulatory technique. The consequence of that approach would be that national tax rules would fall, from the outset, outside the scope of control of State aid merely because they were adopted under a different regulatory technique although they produce the same effects[54].

[6] Impact for the Taxpayers

The decision of the ECJ in the *Gibraltar case* was awaited by practitioners and taxpayers, not only because of the long-lasting procedure and the various and, sometimes, contradictory opinions expressed by the EU Commission and other parties, but mainly as there were high expectations for the setting of a clear analytical framework for the analysis of alleged State aid in direct tax measures and, hence, for the definition and limits to the reach of the concept of State aid. This case can actually be seen as the last case in a series of important cases in which EU Courts have tried to identify limits of State aid rules.

As positive merits of the *Gibraltar case*, it can be noted that it has been clearly evidenced that the *selective* nature of a measure is not enough to find State aid. Rather the measure must lead to a *selective advantage*, which must be properly identified. In addition, based on the points 87 to 110 of the judgment[55], the ECJ is actually proposing

50. *Ibid.*, para. 101.
51. *Ibid.*, para. 106.
52. *Ibid.*, para. 107.
53. *Ibid.*, para. 91.
54. *Ibid.*, para. 92.
55. The fiscal measures under examination constitute State aid because de facto (effects) benefit only the offshore companies. In this respect, please refer in particular to judgment in Joined cases ECJ, *European Commission and Kingdom of Spain v. Government of Gibraltar and United Kingdom*, Cases No. C-106/09 P and C-107/09 P not yet reported in ECR para. 87: "First, it is appropriate to recall that the Court has consistently held that Article 87 (1) EC does not

an effect-based legal approach. As an expected consequence of this, the Commission will have to prove the effects of the measures, which is not very common in the Commission's current practice.

The case has also highlighted, without providing definitive answer, the fundamental question of the attribution of competences between EU Commission and Member States and that certain economic policy choices of Member States must be respected.

However, the outcome of the judgment, rather than providing all expected answers, defers the issues and shows that:

- The EU Commission's and ECJ's positions are unpredictable, which creates confusion and a lack of legal certainty.
- The limits of the concept of State aid are still to be defined.
- State aid issue remains a of a high political sensitivity: it is obvious that the EU Commission could not afford to allow the establishment of a tax system designed in such a way that offshore companies avoid taxation within the EU. As a result, even if the opinion of Advocate General was sensible and reasonable, it seems that the ECJ could not follow it without risking the implementation of such a harmful tax system. In the current economic context, this would have proven morally and politically unacceptable.

§11.04 AREAS FOR IMPROVEMENTS: HOW TO ACHIEVE MORE PREDICTABILITY FOR THE TAXPAYER?

As evoked in sections §11.02 and §11.03 of the present chapter, State aid appears to be an all-catching notion, subject to a complex assessment procedure by the EU Commission. Case law and jurisprudence have not yet enabled to provide all answers and have even, sometimes, contributed to the absence of legal certainty for the taxpayer.

This context does raise issues, obviously for the taxpayer, but also for the adviser of the taxpayer, who is required to provide his view on the tax system used by his client, as to whether elements of the system constitute State aid and whether there is a risk of repayment of the alleged aid to the State. Given the uncertainty surrounding this matter, drafting an opinion on the State aid character of a measure is an uncomfortable area for the practitioner: either he will have to exclude qualification from the scope of the opinion or issue "more likely than not" opinions with reservations. Indeed, analyzing the objective legal dimension of the concept is difficult (as some case law have highlighted it) and evaluating the subjective, and sometimes political, dimension of it adds on further complexity. In practice, it proves difficult to advise clients on what actions need to be taken, and ultimately recommendations can only take the form of

distinguish between measures of State intervention by reference to their causes or their aims but defines them in relation to their effects, and thus independently of the techniques used (...)" (95, 101, 102, 103, 104 and 106).

monitoring case law and decide on whether or not the recording of accounting provision is required for the businesses.

Another difficult area for the practitioner is linked to the representation of his client in front of national and/or ECJ Courts during the litigation process. As we will develop it in section §11.04[B] below, the recognition of the taxpayer's right of action in the case that a decision is taken to order recovery of incompatible aid has taken some time to be clearly established[56] and the Member States remain privileged actors in all possible actions before the Community Courts. This may also explain why the inter-relationships between the interested parties, are complex. In particular, one may wonder if eventually, the Member State's and the taxpayer's interests are actually aligned in this context. Indeed, a recovery decision ordered by the EU Commission or the ECJ would finally result in additional and unexpected income for the Member State concerned, which is not necessarily a bad consequence, at least from a Treasury perspective. However, this decision will inevitably mean an additional payment by the undertakings which have benefited from the alleged advantage.

The graph below illustrates the complex relationships between the parties in the litigation process related to State aid cases and the difficult position of the adviser.

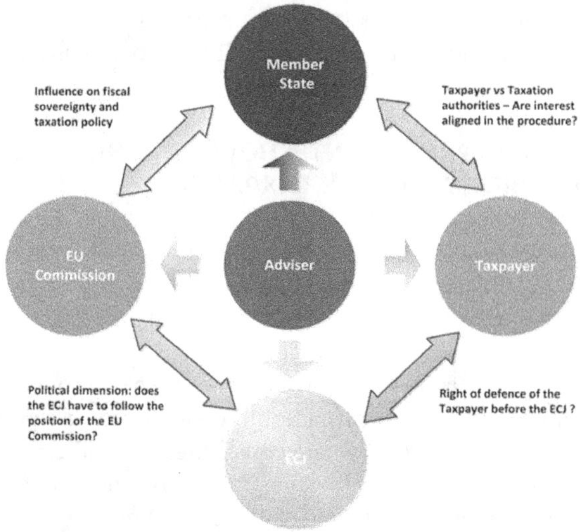

56. Please refer to Joined cases ECJ, *Comitato "Venezia vuole vivere," Hotel Cipriani Srl and Società Italiana per il glas SpA (Italglas) v. Coopservice - Servizi di fiducia Soc. Coop. rl, European Commission and Italian Republic*, Cases No. C-71/09 P, C-73/09 P and C-76/09 P not yet published in ECR (collectively referred to as "*Hotel Cipriani* case law"). After this case law, the discussion on the recognition of the Taxpayer's right of action on the case that a decision is taken to order the recovery of incompatible Aid is closed and thus the beneficiaries of an Aid subject to recovery order have *locus standi*. However, there are other open questions. For instance, what is the Taxpayer's right of action in case an Aid is declared incompatible, but protected by the principle of legitimate expectations? In such a case the *locus standi* of the Taxpayer is not obvious.

This section seeks to identify areas for improvements enabling to achieve more predictability for the taxpayers and also for their advisers.

[A] Establish a Clear Definition and the Limits to the Concept of State Aid

To us, the first step enabling improvement consists in the clarification of the concept of State aid and the way it is assessed. This implies a clarification of the reach of State aid versus "harmful tax measures," a clear framework for the review of the "*Selectivity*" test and finally a more effective use of the possibility to get a "*negative clearance*" within the assessment procedure, i.e., an advance procedure enabling to confirm that a measure does not entail State aid.

[1] State Aid versus Code of Conduct

As mentioned above, the Notice is part of the "Package" to tackle harmful tax competition. Therefore, one may question the relationship between the notion of fiscal State aid and the Code of Conduct.

Generally speaking, the Code of Conduct is broader in scope than the Notice, because it also covers general tax measures implemented by the Member States which are deemed to have harmful effects. By contrast, the Notice applies exclusively to fiscal State aid measures, which must by definition be specific or selective to fall under its scope.

As a matter of principle, the Notice and the Code of Conduct are independent and do not influence one another[57]. The main reason for this lies in their differences, namely:

- In their respective subject areas: the State aid rules have been laid down in the TFEU and are imperative, whereas the provisions of the Code of Conduct are contained in a political resolution lacking legally binding force; and
- In their respective bodies in charge of their supervision and interpretation: the EU Commission for State aid and the EC Council through the Code of Conduct Group for the "harmful tax measures."

Nevertheless, the Notice and the Code of Conduct do not completely ignore one another as to their practical application. For instance, the Notice states that "(...) however the assessment of the compatibility of fiscal aid with the common market will have to be made, taking into account, *inter alia*, the effects of aid that are brought to light in the application of the Code of Conduct[58]." This wording paraphrases what is already stated in the Package: "(...) the Commission (...) commits itself to the rigorous

57. The Notice explicitly confirms this: "the qualification of a tax measure as harmful under the Code of Conduct does not affect the possible qualification as State aid." See The Notice, para. 30.
58. See The Notice, para. 30.

application of the aid rules concerned, taking into account, *inter alia*, the negative effects of aid that are brought to light in the application of this Code[59]."

The EU Commission has in practice far greater power under the State aid rules than it would be expected to have under the general principles of the Code of Conduct.

One can therefore wonder whether at some point the close relationships existing between the Notice, providing guidance for the assessment of fiscal State aid measures, and the Code of Conduct aiming at tackling harmful tax measures implemented by Member States, has not resulted in a confusion. The review of some case law (amongst other, the ones developed in section §11.03 above) may lead to the impression that the concept of State aid has been used extensively over the years by the EU Commission, tending to stretch as far as possible its limits, to make it also a tool to avoid harmful forms of taxation.

As far as taxpayers are concerned, this effectively creates legal uncertainty, as the powers of the EU Commission seem to be very far-reaching, so that tax measures can be considered:

- Both harmful tax measures and State aid: this was the case for instance for Belgian Coordination Centres which have been found incompatible aid without recovery[60].
- Harmful tax measures not being State aid: an example of this is the Maltese International Trading Companies and Companies with Foreign Income for which appropriate measures had to be adopted in order not to be considered as State aid[61].
- State aid not being harmful: in this respect, one can refer to the Luxembourg 1929 Holding Companies regime which has been considered incompatible aid without recovery and subsequently abolished (please refer to section §11.03[A] above).

The question of the inter-relationships between the concept of State aid and the "harmful tax measures" should be clearly established, so as to avoid that some regimes may be approved under the Code of Conduct but still be tackled under the State aid rules. Although some overlap may exist between the two notions, for the sake of clarity and predictability of decisions for the taxpayers, the two concepts should each follow strict and clear guidelines established by the Institutions responsible for their assessment and control. In addition, more cooperation between the EU Commission regarding the State aid control, on the one hand, and the Code of Conduct Group under the control of the Ecofin Council regarding harmful tax measures, on the other hand, would also help drawing a clear framework for the taxpayers and enable more predictability of decisions.

59. See The Package, para. J.
60. Commission Decision C 15/2002 of Nov. 13, 2007, OJ L 90/2008.
61. Commission Decision E 6/2005 of Mar. 22, 2006.

[2] Subjectivity of the Selectivity Criterion[62]

As developed in section §11.02[A] of this chapter, the assessment of whether a tax measure is State aid, relies on the same criteria as for the analysis of any other form of aid. Nevertheless, when it comes to the assessment of tax measures, some criteria are easy to establish for certain types of measures, while others are more problematic.

Common features of tax measures are typically that such measures are imputable to a public authority, they result in a reduction of tax revenues, which is equivalent to the consumption of State resources (as established by case law) and they will affect trade between Member States and be capable of distorting competition.

The analytical difficulties when performing the State aid assessment of a tax measure relate to the requirements that a *selective* advantage must be identified, that is to say the advantage has to apply to some but not all taxpayers, in order for the measure regarded to constitute State aid. The analytical question arising is then whether the advantage identified leads to discrimination between taxpayers. As developed in case law, discrimination exists if *"comparable situations [are] treated differently and (...) different situations [are] treated in the same way unless such treatment is objectively justified*[63]*."*

The steps of the analysis aiming at determining whether the *selective advantage* identified results in discrimination are thus the following:

- identification of the general tax system, i.e., the system of reference;
- determination to which taxpayers the general system applies; and
- determination of whether the tax measure under review applies to only a subset and/or other taxpayers, compared with the general system.

There are two types of discriminations that can be identified which are either based on geography (i.e. referred to as "*Regional Selectivity*") or based on the substantive rules, which limit the scope of application of the measure (i.e., "*Material Selectivity*").

Regional Selectivity will exist if the tax measure leads to an advantage only in a specific part of the territory of a Member State. This issue arises then in particular in countries where taxing and other powers are delegated to regional institutions.

As regards *Material Selectivity*, if only some, but not all of the taxpayers covered by the general system, or taxpayers not covered by the general tax system benefit from the identified advantage, then discrimination based on a Material Selectivity can exist.

The next question is then the one of the burden of proof:

- It is for the "Commission to prove that [a tax measure] created differences between undertakings which, with regard to the objective of the measure in question, are in comparable factual and legal situation[64]." Such "General

62. Reference in this respect is made to T. Müller-Ibold and his contribution to the annual forum on State Aid Law 2011 held in Trier on Oct. 27 and Oct. 28, 2011, entitled "Corporate tax schemes and State aid rules - Material Selectivity in light of the Gibraltar case."
63. ECJ, *Spain v. Commission*, Case No. C-304/01 [2004] ECR I-7655 para. 31.
64. ECJ, *European Commission v. Kingdom of the Netherlands*, Case No. C-279/08 P not yet reported in ECR para. 62.

Measures" must be effectively open to all firms on an equal access basis, regardless of sector, size and company form. Measures may not de facto be reduced in scope through, for example, the discretionary powers of the State or through other factors.

- In addition, "The concept of aid does not encompass measures creating different treatment of undertakings in relation to charges where that difference is attributable to the nature and general scheme of the system of charges in question[65]." Regarding this exception, the burden of proof is on the Member State invoking this exception.

In practice, it is rather difficult to define precisely the criterion of *Material Selectivity* and often it is difficult to apply it concretely. The practice of the EU Commission highlights that some cases where measures of Member States were not limited to certain sectors, regions or types of determined enterprises have nevertheless been considered as selective, only based on the fact that the authority administering the measure had discretionary power. Similarly, the possible justification for the material selectivity of a measure, based on the nature and general scheme of the system also raises some practical difficulties.

From the above, it is quite obvious to hold that State aid is a complex concept, the assessment criteria of which, and in particular the one of "*Selectivity*," entails practical difficulties, as basically over the years, a confusion has started to arise between Selectivity and discrimination.

This raises eventually fundamental questions relating to the sovereignty of the Member States. The constitutional set-up of the EU ensures that that the right of taxation and the decision of what events are taxed remain with the Member States. That right is part of the Member States' right to define and pursue their own economic policies, and thus, their choices as to what they wish to tax and what they do not wish to tax. This results possibly and, often, intentionally, in a difference in treatment between those benefiting from the policy choice and those who do not. Therefore, if more and more the EU Commission tends to consider that differences resulting from a taxation policy choice at State level, entail discrimination and those differences should be abolished, then one could wonder whether State aid tends to be used by the EU Commission as a harmonization tool.

Needless to mention that this situation creates a high level of uncertainty for the taxpayers, as tax measures implemented at State level can be challenged by the EU Commission based on criteria, seemingly applied with a certain degree of subjectivity.

In our view, the key criterion of the assessment of State aid, that is to say *Selectivity*, should also be clarified and based on objective assessment methodology. As regards this element, and this is illustrated by the *Gibraltar* case (referred to in section §11.03[B] above), the practitioners and taxpayers can be left with the impression that the EU Commission is realizing self-fulfilling prophesy: once a scheme is alleged to be "*Selective*," especially "*Materially Selective*," it will be very difficult to have the EU Commission changing its initial view.

65. *Ibid.*, para. 62.

[3] Randomness in the Assessment Procedure

As we have underlined it in section 11.02[B][2] above, the system used by the EU Commission is based on a system of *ex ante* authorization, whereby the Member States have to notify the Commission of any plan to grant or alter State aid.

It seems to us that the system itself is therefore based on the pre-conceived idea that any measure to be introduced by a Member State is de facto entailing State aid elements. The decision of the EU Commission can therefore only:

- either confirm that the measure constitute compatible aid, as a particular exemption is available or as amendments are to be introduced in the measure by the Member State to render such measure compatible State aid; or
- declare the measure incompatible aid or even illegal aid, in the case the measure has already been implemented by the Member State without prior notification to the EU Commission.

Indeed, it seems to us that the importance of a major step is undermined in the frame of the assessment of the tax measures in respect of whether they constitute *or not* State aid: more emphasis should be put on the possibility to obtain a *negative clearance* from the Commission. In other words, the EU Commission should also provide the opportunity for the Member States, and thus the taxpayers, to obtain the confirmation that a particular regime will not be regarded as State aid by the EU Commission. Although not largely known and used, such procedure exists. Indeed the notification form to be filled in by a Member State covers the situation of a "*non aid measure which is notified to the Commission for reason of legal certainty.*" In addition, the Commission can also adopt a decision confirming the absence of aid[66].

The negative clearance process can be illustrated by layering on some additional boxes into our previous process tree.

66. Please refer to Regulation 659/1999, Articles 4.2. (Where the Commission, after a preliminary examination, finds that the notified measure does not constitute Aid, it shall record that finding by way of a decision.) and 7.2. (Where the Commission finds that, where appropriate following modification by the Member State concerned, the notified measure does not constitute aid, it shall record that finding by way of a decision.).

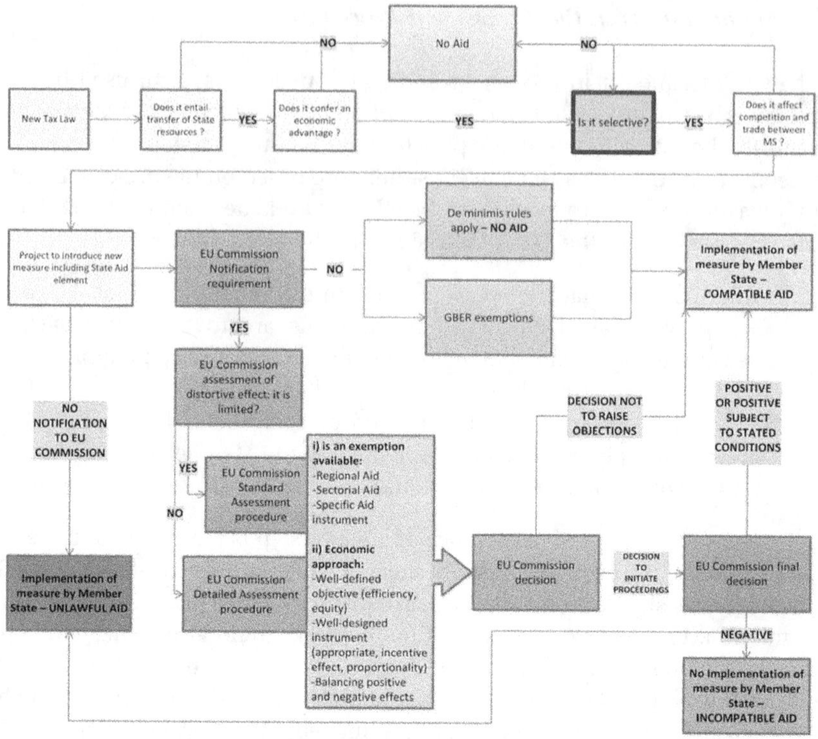

In practice however, very few cases are notified to the Commission by Member States, "just to check." Indeed, in case it is clear that no State aid is entailed by a fiscal measure, then there is no need for a Member State to notify such measure. In case an ambiguous case is at stake, the Member State's natural reaction will be to avoid consulting the Commission and getting into very unpredictable results. One of the barriers to a wider use of this negative clearance may be the perceived or real infringement of the sovereignty of the Member States: after all, why should a Member State have to seek authorization or clearance from the Commission to do something perfectly legal and a normal exercise of its sovereignty? This is of course also the case for existing measures, implemented long before the Member State joined the EU. It is therefore hard for Member States and taxpayers to get a firm confirmation that a tax measure will not be under scrutiny for its State aid character at one point in time and ultimately will need to be amended, if not completely abolished. In or view, the assessment procedure would gain in transparency and predictability if in the cases where measures are notified "*for reason of legal certainty*," the Commission acts diligently and adopts a decision in this respect in relative short delays.

The taxpayer is then left with the overall impression that a certain degree of randomness exists in the way the EU Commission conducts State aid investigations. This is also reinforced by the fact that actually the EU Commission can decide itself which measures it wishes to investigate. All information available can be used by the Commission to become aware of such measures, be it publicly available information (that is to say press articles, published legislation etc.) or information provided by another party (Member State or competitor firm).

[B] *Locus Standi* and the Right of Action for the Taxpayer

Another area for improvement in the field of State aid is ascertaining the right of taxpayers in the frame of a litigation procedure, in particular the right to access the file and the right to bring an action before the ECJ.

[1] The Right of Taxpayers to Access the File: The Technische Glaswerke Ilmenau GmbH Case Law[67]

In its judgment regarding *Technische Glaswerke Ilmenau GMBH* (TGI)[68], the ECJ reversed the finding of the General Court—at that time Court of First Instance—as regards the annulment of the Commission Decision of May 28, 2002 in procedure C 44/2001.

The substantive question brought before the Court refers to the substantive rules governing access to documents in a State aid Commission file by interested parties other than the Member State concerned in the course of the procedure.

By refusing a general right of access to the entire Commission file to interested parties the Judgment rendered by the ECJ is consistent with the ideal concept of State aid control procedures as a pre-emptive mechanism.

However, by refusing access a priori to individual documents in the Commission's file on State aid cases because this would lead to a "*denaturalization*" of State aid procedures[69], the ECJ is more cryptic.

This appears consistent with the idea of *ex ante* control of national measures. It is true that in those cases, granting access to documents submitted by Member States which outline a measure not yet made public merits such documents remaining confidential. However, it appears more doubtful that this "*denaturalization*" is equally likely to occur in cases—like the one at hand—which refer to investigations opened once the measures have been already implemented and when the beneficiary undertakings—and their competitors —are directly and actually concerned by the outcome of the procedure.

67. Reference is made to M. Muñoz de Juan & J.M.P. Rivas, *Commission v. Technische Glaswerke Ilmenau GmbH – The ECJ's Backlash on Access to Documents in the Commission's File on State Aid Cases by Interested Parties other than Member State Concerned*, 4 EsTAL (2010) .
68. ECJ, *Commission v. Technische Glaswerke Imenau GmbH*, Case No. C-139/07 [2008] ECR I-05883.
69. *Ibid.*, para. 58 "It follows from the above that the interested parties, except for the Member State responsible for granting the aid, do not have a right under the procedure for reviewing State aid to consult the documents on the Commission's administrative file. Account must be taken of that fact for the purposes of interpreting the exception laid down by Article 4(2), third indent, of Regulation No 1049/2001. If those interested parties were able to obtain access, on the basis of Regulation No 1049/2001, to the documents in the Commission's administrative file, the system for the review of State aid would be called into question."

[2] The Right of the Taxpayers to Bring an Action before the ECJ: The Hotel Cipriani Case Law[70]

One has to keep in mind that the EC Treaty State aid rules are about competition between Member States, not just about competition between undertakings. This explains why Member States have always had a privileged role in State aid procedures, while beneficiaries and competitors play second fiddle.

The problem with this is that Member States normally do not fight among themselves. They leave the role of arbiter to the Commission, being normally only prepared to attack negative decisions concerning their own aid plans. Positive decisions are only attacked by (courageous) competitors of beneficiaries and almost never by other Member States. This has become a kind of Constitutional convention in the EU.

There is now an increasing policy emphasis on State aid as affecting competition between undertakings. However competitors/complainants have a rather limited role in State aid procedures: they are often presented as little more than a "source of information" for the Commission. There is therefore an obvious gap between the declared political desire of facilitating action by complainants on the one hand and the rigidity of the current legal framework on the other.

One has to remember that the legislator deliberately chose to give third parties a limited role in State aid administrative procedures. It is worth undertaking a quick review of the different actors that may bring actions against State aid decisions.

First of all, under Article 230(2) EC (which has become now Article 263 paragraph 2 TFEU), Member States are privileged actors in all possible actions before the Community Courts, which includes actions concerning State aid. This means that Members States (like Community institutions) would normally be entitled to bring an action for the annulment of a Commission State aid decision provided that they could show an interest to act. However, the situation is different for regional and infra-State authorities of Member States, which cannot invoke the privileged status of Article 230(2) EC (which has become now Article 263 paragraph 2 TFEU) but instead have to prove their direct and individual concern under Article 230(4) EC (which has become now Article 263 paragraph 4 TFEU). This means that they normally would only have *locus standi* before the Community Courts if they are the actual grantors of the aid[71] and not in other cases[72].

At a lower level of the "pyramid," we find the undertakings that are beneficiaries of the aid and/or their competitors: they would constitute the two most obvious—and biggest—groups of potential applicants.

70. Reference is made to J.L.B. Sierra, "Standing before the Community Courts in the Context of State Aid Litigation," Eur. St. Aid L. Q. (2007).
71. See for example, Joined cases ECJ, *Territorio Histórico de Álava – Diputación Foral de Álava and others v. Commission*, Cases No. T-346/99, T-347/99 and T-348/99 [2002] ECR II-4259 para. 37.
72. See for example Order of June 16, 1998 in ECJ, *Comunidad Autónoma de Cantabria v. Council*, Case No. T-238/9 [1998] ECR II-2271 paras. 42–54.

If individual aid is declared to be incompatible with the EC Treaty and its recovery required, it is normally accepted that the actual beneficiary has the right to bring a legal action challenging such a decision. The *locus standi* of competitors of the beneficiaries to attack a positive State aid decision should logically mirror that of beneficiaries to attack negative decisions. However, the case law is less clear and more restrictive as regards competitors.

The case law on *locus standi* is further complicated by the difference between decisions on individual aid and those concerning aid schemes. The question of *locus standi* is difficult in the case of decisions concerning general aid schemes that have not yet been implemented and easier in the case of unlawful aid schemes that have already been implemented.

An association of undertakings enjoys *locus standi* if it has a particular interest in bringing the action because its negotiating position concerning the policy of the sector concerned is affected by the national measure at issue and/or if the association acts on behalf of its members and these are themselves individually entitled to bring individual actions for annulment of the contested Commission decision.

Lastly, apart from beneficiaries and their competitors, there are in theory other potentially interested parties that may want to bring an action before the Community Courts, such as taxpayers, trade unions and other interest groups different from the associations of undertakings. These entities may want to block certain projects for reasons that have nothing to do with competition (political reasons, control of public spending, environmental concerns, opposition to privatization, etc ...). Article 230(4) EC (which has become now Article 263 paragraph 4 TFEU) does theoretically allow these interests to be considered. However, the *Hotel Cipriani*[73] case law shows that it is extremely difficult for private entities or persons other than beneficiaries or competitors to demonstrate that they are directly and individually concerned by the Commission decision[74]. So far the only private interest clearly opening the way to *locus standi* is competition. This seems to be in line with the objectives of State aid control. Opening the way to other interests would amount in actual terms to a recognition of an "*actio popularis*" and would probably be excessive.

On this issue, a recent Judgment of the ECJ in joined cases C-71/09 P, C-73/09 P and C-76/09 P, rendered on June 9, 2011[75], provided some positive news for the taxpayers and their right of action. Indeed, this Judgment confirms that the applicant undertakings had the capacity to bring an action in that they were individually concerned by the decision, by reason of the particular negative impact caused to their legal position by the order for recovery of the aid in question. The actual beneficiaries

73. Joined cases ECJ, *Comitato "Venezia vuole vivere," Hotel Cipriani Srl and Società Italiana per il glas SpA (Italglas) v. Coopservice—Servizi di fiducia Soc. Coop. rl, European Commission and Italian Republic,* Cases No. C-71/09 P, C-73/09 P and C-76/09 P not yet published in ECR (collectively referred to as "*Hotel Cipriani* case law").
74. See for example Order of Feb. 18, 1998 in ECJ, *Comité d'Entreprise de la Société Française de Production and others v. Commission,* Case No. T-189/97 [1998] ECR II-335 paras. 41–54.
75. Joined cases ECJ, *Comitato "Venezia vuole vivere'," Hotel Cipriani Srl and Società Italiana per il glas SpA (Italglas) v. Coopservice—Servizi di fiducia Soc. Coop. rl, European Commission and Italian Republic,* Cases No. C-71/09 P, C-73/09 P and C-76/09 P not yet published in ECR (collectively referred to as "*Hotel Cipriani* case law").

of individual aid measures granted under an aid scheme of which the Commission has ordered recovery are, for that reason, individually concerned.

This positive outcome will have to be confirmed by repeated jurisprudence, so that the right of action of the taxpayer be clearly framed.

[C] Introduce a Statute of Limitation: Recovery versus Prescription

An interesting issue arising in the case that a measure is State aid and that recovery is decided, is the one of the statute of limitation.

Indeed, what if the taxpayer has filed its tax returns based on the applicable laws in force at that time, has had its tax liabilities assessed by the tax authorities of its State of residence, has paid its tax charge and no claim is introduced in this respect within the prescription period provided by the domestic law, and afterwards a measure this taxpayer has benefitted from is considered incompatible aid that has to be recovered? Will the taxpayer be forced to repay the amount of aid it has benefitted from, despite the fact that domestic prescription applies?

One could argue that as a general rule, State aid assessment is performed by the EU Commission as an *ex ante* procedure, so that the taxpayers ideally would not end up in a situation where it has to repay any amount. This situation is the theoretical and desired frame created by the EU Commission. In reality, it is not rare that a measure is considered State aid while already implemented and recovery be ordered.

Another approach would consist in objecting that the principle of *legitimate expectation*[76] of the taxpayers is recognized in certain circumstances, so that this may lead to Existing aids being repealed or amended, but without recovery. This was the case for long-lasting schemes, for instance the Luxembourg 1929 Holding Companies regime, which has been repealed without recovery.

Case law has provided answer to the issue of the potential clash between the decision of recovery and the Member States' statutes of limitation, which was more than a theoretical issue. As a direct consequence of the hierarchy of norms, EU Law has a supremacy over domestic legislation, so that national statutes of limitation do not impede recovery of the aid, if so decided by the EU Commission or EU Courts.

This matter constitutes definitely a significant area of uncertainty for the taxpayers, which potentially could not rely on domestic prescription rules. In order to increase the level of legal comfort for the beneficiaries and avoid such situations where eventually domestic prescription rules are put in question, it would be more than welcome that a clear statute of limitation be introduced within the framework of the State aid assessment procedure.

---

76. The principle of legitimate expectation only applies if the EU Commission or other EU institutions have provided clear assurance in advance regarding the compatibility of the Aid or have qualified the measure as no State aid. Assurances provided by national entities do not grant legitimate expectations.

§11.05 CONCLUSIONS: REMEMBER WHO IS THE ULTIMATE CLIENT

From all the previous developments, one can only underline a paradox regarding the current assessment of tax measures entailing State aid: the undertakings and taxpayers, who are primary actors of the process (being the actual beneficiaries of such schemes), are somewhat left aside when it comes to the procedural stage, be it the assessment process by the EU Commission, where only the Member State concerned will provide information, or the litigation process where the right of the taxpayers to access the file and even being party to the litigation action has been established recently, and only in some defined cases.

Based on our analysis, a business and its investors are facing currently a number of uncertainties and challenges when it comes to State aid. An objective analysis is very difficult, if not almost impossible to carry out, as the Commission's and ECJ's positions are difficult to predict.

A number of measures would help the taxpayers (and their advisers) to achieve the level of certainty that is necessary for the conduct of their business under acceptable conditions, i.e., a clearer definition of and limits to the concept of State aid, further clarification of the right of actions for the taxpayers and the introduction of a statute of limitation regarding recovery of incompatible aid. This would demonstrate that the EU Institutions do not forget or ignore the taxpayers and actually have a clear and global picture of all the implications of the decisions made in this respect. State aid is not only a theoretical and controversial debate between EU institutions and Member States, but does have significant practical implications for entrepreneurs and businesses. This is only a matter of political will and desire to achieve more transparency, in line with one of the objectives of the Notice.

Some glimmers of hope on some of the points noted above have been provided by a Special Report of the European Court of Auditors (ECA)[77] on whether the Commission's procedures ensure effective management of State aid control.

This Special Report examines whether the EU Commission has implemented procedures that enable effective management of State aid control: does the system of notifications, complaints and own-initiative enquiries ensure that the Commission handles all relevant State aid cases; does the Commission have adequate management structures and procedures in place for effective handling of the State aid cases within the deadlines; and, does the Commission monitor the impact of its State aid control?

The audit focused on the organization, decision-making and monitoring processes of the EU Commission during the period between 2008 and 2010, but did not assess the validity of the decisions taken by the Commission. The audit covered the areas of State aid control for which Commission's DG Competition is responsible, i.e., all economic sectors except agriculture and fisheries.

77. ECA, *Do the Commission's Procedures Ensure Effective Management of State Aid Control?*, 15 (Luxembourg Publications Office of the European Union 2011).

The main findings of the ECA can be summarized as follows:

- the EU Commission has made efforts to ensure that all relevant State aid cases are handled, but its systems do not guarantee that all aid is captured;
- the notification procedures for State aid take a long time;
- complaints continue to take a long time to resolve and the procedure is not transparent;
- the Commission does not assess the impact of its State aid control in a comprehensive way;
- in the field of State aid the EU Commission reacted promptly to the financial crisis.

The ECA makes a series of recommendations to improve the Commission's procedures and management effectiveness: to review the allocation of resources devoted to State aid control, to increase the transparency of case-handling procedures, to shorten the duration of the procedures, to implement an enhanced system of time recording and management reporting, and to regularly assess the *ex post* impact of State aid control.

Let us hope that the EU Commission will respond positively to these recommendations, in particular to the concerns of the length and transparency of procedures, so that the management and control of State aid will be improved, for the benefit of all parties involved, and especially that of the taxpayer, who while often forgotten, finally foots the bill.

International Tax Conferences of the University of Luxembourg (ITCL)

1. Alexander Rust (ed.), *Double Taxation within the European Union*, 2011 (978-90-411-3525-4).
2. Alexander Rust & Eric Fort (eds), *Exchange of Information and Bank Secrecy*, 2012 (978-90-411-3995-5).
3. Alexander Rust & Claire Micheau (eds), *State Aid and Tax Law*, 2013 (978-90-411-4557-4)

www.ingramcontent.com/pod-product-compliance
Lightning Source LLC
LaVergne TN
LVHW021727021026
849161LV00004BA/756